GLOBAL CHORUS

GLOBAL CHORUS

365 VOICES ON THE
FUTURE OF THE PLANET

Edited by Todd E. MacLean

RMB

Rocky Mountain Books
www.rmbooks.com

Library and Archives Canada Cataloguing in Publication

Global chorus : 365 voices on the future of the planet / edited by Todd E. MacLean.

Issued in print and electronic formats.
ISBN 978-1-77160-033-0 (pbk.).–ISBN 978-1-77160-034-7 (html).–ISBN 978-1-77160-035-4 (pdf)

    1. Human ecology. I. MacLean, Todd E., editor

GF8.G56 2014   304.2   C2014-904008-3
                                        C2014-904009-1

Cover photo: Misty beech forest © aniszewski
Photos on pages ii, viii, 65, 373, 405, 408, 410: © Evan Dickson
Photos on pages vi, 137, 171, 205, 237, 271, 412: © Louise Vessey
Photos on pages 1, 35, 103, 305, 337: © Stefan Davidson
Printed in China

Rocky Mountain Books acknowledges the financial support for its publishing program from the Government of Canada through the Canada Book Fund (CBF) and the Canada Council for the Arts, and from the province of British Columbia through the British Columbia Arts Council and the Book Publishing Tax Credit.

 Canadian Heritage   Patrimoine canadien   Canada Council for the Arts   Conseil des Arts du Canada   BRITISH COLUMBIA ARTS COUNCIL Supported by the Province of British Columbia

This book was produced using FSC®-certified, acid-free paper, processed chlorine free and printed with vegetable-based inks.

This book is dedicated to the Earth
and to all those who work for It
and for the harmony and happiness of those upon It

"LOVE THE EARTH AND ITS BEINGS
AND ACT FROM THIS LOVE:
THEN ALL 'SHOULDS' SHALL UNFOLD INTO REALITY."

Humans today are confronting the greatest challenge ever faced in the four-billion-year history of this planet: in the face of environmental destruction the world over, devastating prevalence and severity of poverty, continually distressing situations of socio-political turmoil, intensifying effects of climate change, and a general earthly equilibrium that we have gravely disrupted, the challenge we come up against today is how to ensure not only the healthy survival of the human race, but also the preservation of the rest of life on Earth as we seek to achieve the planetary balance that is so necessary to sustainably move forward.

Little by little, we have broadened our understanding of humanity's role in determining the fate of the planet and its species. But this awareness hasn't clearly translated into a collective action. We have yet to bring together into one boundary-crossing book the visionaries of our times, our brightest minds and our most influential leaders. And now more than ever we need to hear their counsel on the future of the planet.

Global Chorus: 365 Voices on the Future of the Planet gives us this chance.

You are holding in your hands a groundbreaking collection of over 365 perspectives on our environmental future. A global roundtable for our times, in the format of a daily reader. This book is a trove of insight, guidance, passion and wisdom that has poured in from all over the Earth. Its message is enormously inspiring, and ominous in its warnings. And yet, united in a thread of hope, its contents are capable of helping even the most faithless global citizen to believe that we have the capacity to bring about lasting positive change in our world. Places at this roundtable are occupied by writers, environmentalists, spiritual leaders, politicians, professors, doctors, athletes, businesspeople, farmers, chefs, yogis, painters, actors, architects, musicians, TV personalities, humanitarians, adventurers, concerned youth, senior citizens, civil servants, carpenters, bus drivers, activists, CEOs, scientists and essentially those who have something thoughtful and visionary to say about humanity's place on Earth. Compiled for your reading as a set of 365 pieces, *Global Chorus* presents to you a different person's point of view for each day of your year.

Contributors to *Global Chorus* have provided one-page responses to the following line of questioning:

> *Do you think that humanity can find a way past the current global environmental and social crises? Will we be able to create the conditions necessary for our own survival, as well as that of other species on the planet? What would these conditions look like? In summary, then, and in the plainest of terms, do we have hope, and can we do it?*

In the case of some contributors to *Global Chorus*, applicable material has been sourced from other writings, speeches, interviews, articles etc., in order to include their highly valued perspectives in this anthology. This route has been taken to feature the pages by Nelson Mandela, the Dalai Lama, Mikhail Gorbachev, Lester Brown, Stephen Lewis, Trudie Styler, David Buckland, Barb Stegemann, Farley Mowat, Thomas Berry (posthumously), Pema Chödrön, Sy Safransky, Jamie Oliver and Stephen Hawking, and through their participation in the conversation, the collection's overall base of insight is further enhanced.

It should be noted here as well that all contributors to this fundraising book have generously and graciously donated their time and efforts, as proceeds from the sales of *Global Chorus* will be distributed to a select group of organizations helping to recover, protect and sustain life on Earth. Please see the info at the end of the book for more on these organizations and their work.

What is abundantly clear in our times is that, if anything, *we need to talk* about the ways in which we are living, what kind of impact we're having on our surroundings, how we can live more sustainably and how we can create a better future for our children and countless generations to come – human and non-human alike. We *all* need to talk about it, *regularly*: through the *conversation* comes the *alteration*. Thus, the aim of *Global Chorus* is to help keep this conversation going and help it to be on our minds daily, to be inspired by those who do think about this regularly, and to carry out the wisdom gained from this conversation into our own daily lives. To *live* it as we work together toward being a more sustainable and harmonious planet in the 21st century.

The right words said at the right time can have the force of a mighty river. Moreover, the right words said at the right time *by the visionaries of our time* can wash away mountains of injustice, leaving only the seeds for a better world planted in their path. And through the many, many *right words* spoken herein, we hope you will be guided to help foster this better world. It is here, and ready to grow at your feet.

This is our most pivotal hour. What we need most is to spark imaginations, to ignite our passions. We need to raise our voices in a global chorus.

> *Our divided voices can only do so much; let's see what happens when we sing in chorus.*

We live in a time of infinite possibility. There are *so many* messages of truth and guidance to glean from this book, but if I were to highlight one in particular for this Preface, this would have to be it.

Throughout the work of *Global Chorus* I have had many contributors ask me if I was going to write my own page of words, as part of the 365 assembled perspectives on our global future. I don't feel this would be appropriate; but if I were to briefly sum up my assessment of our global challenges at this time in our human evolution on Earth, it would be that we are doing *far too much thinking about what is not possible* and *not enough believing about what is possible.*

To bring it to my own experience for a moment, to paint the picture clearly for you about how this project came to be, this book has been assembled by a guy with very few prior connections, little experience as an editor, no experience as an anthologist, and no previous experience in coordinating any kind of project anywhere close to something like this. A guy who has long been painfully concerned about environmental issues, and who simply had an idea in the shower one day that it would be amazing to read a book exactly like the one you're now holding. (And a guy who then listened to the wise advice of both his wife and Nolan Bushnell: "Everyone who's ever taken a shower has an idea. It's the person who gets out of the shower, dries off and does something about it who makes a difference.") A guy who did most of his work at home, in an old farmhouse

in the country in Prince Edward Island, Canada, mostly sitting around in his pajamas ...

A guy who originally thought that this project would be *far* from possible. But I guess I'm now a guy who has learned, in my own little way, what can be done when you choose not to follow what you think and instead follow what you believe.

Doing a project of this nature fifty years ago *would* have been next to impossible. Even twenty years ago, something like this would have taken a team of researchers and administrative assistants, a staggering amount of postage (and/or faxing), and many years of meticulous correspondence. I would venture to say that even ten years ago, pulling off a project of this nature would have been extremely difficult. But now, *we are connected.* And the connections are there to be embraced if you have an idea. This is the kind of thing that you – that anyone – can do in today's world.

So please, embrace this notion: if you do have any idea that can help your household, your workplace, your community, your city, your region, your country to be more environmentally sustainable and/or socially harmonious, do not hesitate. Do it. Because the reality is that these kinds of helpful ideas come to us for a reason: to help us evolve. But a helpful idea is wasted if it is not borne by action into this help-hungry world.

I must emphasize, though, that as soon as I thought of this idea for *Global Chorus*, it became very much not my own. I passed it to the hands of others right away, to let them shape it and bring it to fruition as they saw fit. I came up with the concept, yes, and I've been working incredibly hard over these years to invite, recruit, compile and edit – but mainly it has been created with care by several hundred of the world's most passionate and forward-thinking individuals. And what an astounding miracle it has been to watch it unfold and grow into what it now is.

Truly, I have felt like one of the luckiest people on Earth to have been at the helm of this project for the past four years. My days have been spent interacting with, incredibly, the most socially conscious and environmentally dedicated people in the world, to bring them together *for* our world. If you were to think of the group of writers included in *Global Chorus* as an *actual* choir, I would be like the director who would be standing in front of them, completely in awe of how glorious this choir is and how beautiful their voices sound together, and then lose my place in the music because I'm so enthralled and overwhelmed by the power of it all.

This being said, I did have to be driven by what I've affectionately come to call "failure fuel" many times: people telling me that something like this couldn't be possible, having all kinds of doors shut in my face along the way – and then always trying my best to spring out from the energy of that door slam, to find that other door to try (because, let's face it,

there's *always* another door). Moreover, as I initially thought this anthology would be a perfect project for a publishing house to do – or at least someone with a lot of connections – I soon learned that, in fact, if this project was going to get off the ground, *I* was going to have to be the one to do it, and that's all there was to it. In a way, I felt like Frodo accepting the one ring in *The Lord of the Rings*: "I will take the Ring ... though I do not know the way."

The incomparable Paul Hawken was thankfully one of the very first contributors to *Global Chorus*, and in his piece he speaks profoundly appropriate words for our time in history on this planet: "Do what needs to be done, and check to see if it was impossible only when you are finished."

I have followed his advice ever since then, and it has helped me immensely in the completion of this mammoth project. And it is my utmost hope that you too will follow his advice, to take on what's labelled as impossible and then acknowledge that "Impossible" signpost in your rear-view mirror when you've arrived at where you may not have *thought* you'd be, but where you *believed* you could be.

This world *desperately* needs your action-sprung-from-belief. Please believe. Please act.

And, for every day of your year ahead, please enjoy, be enlightened, be guided, be impassioned, be warned, be informed, be filled with hope, be inspired by all that is this *Global Chorus* in your hands.

Welcome to the Chorus.

– Todd E. MacLean, March 2014

To do the work for *Global Chorus*, all I needed was an Internet connection, a reliable laptop (thank you, Apple), a good search engine (thank you, Google), a cuddly kitty to pet now and then to keep me sane, some really good tea, (several sets of pajamas), several years and a brilliant and wonderful wife who inspired me through it all. Thank you, Savannah, and I Love You. And of course, I also needed *a lot of help* in various ways in order to bring together a project of this magnitude. This help came in various forms, and in some cases I know it came from those who now reside in realms beyond our own. Eternal thanks I send out to:

Mom and Dad, the Belshers, Jaclyn Rogerson, Aunt Inez, Lesley-Anne Bourne, David Suzuki, Elois Yaxley, Jane Goodall, Lawson Drake, Bono – for the initial moment of inspiration, Matt Rainnie, Lloyd Theuerkauf, Richard Lemm, Lobie Daughton, Ewan Clark, Christina MacLeod, Aaron Lewis, Justin Simard, Jim Ferguson, Ann Thurlow, members of the band English Words, my students and their parents (who have rolled so graciously with my ever-changing schedules over the past several years), Karen Rawlines, Chef Michael Smith, Bill Hogg, David Weale, Richard Wills, Kent Driscoll, Karen Mair, Anne McDermid, Rick Broadhead, Beth Doane, Mille Clarkes, Céline Cousteau, Reg Ballagh, Gloria Flora, Teresa Doyle, Elizabeth Kapu'uwailani Lindsey, Marco Ng, Carl Honoré, Tim Hamming, Jen Boulden, John Lundin, Ian Skelly, Jian Ghomeshi and the staff at *Q*, Adam Francis, Sobia Ali-Faisal, Guy Dauncey, Moe McTague, Jan Zwicky, Robert Bringhurst, Glenn Rollans, Brenda Victor, Lou Niznik, Michael Dowd, Thomas Berry, Mary Evelyn Tucker, Nicole Bellefleur, Leo Cheverie, Anna Gustafson, Charlie Sark, Alexander Verbeek, Raymond Loo and all of my close family and friends – those who are living and those who have passed on and who I know are still with us.

Shortly after I started out on my own with the work for *Global Chorus*, a small team of wonderful people came about, and I think I would be 95 years old with a walker and still working on this if it weren't for them. Some of these people have unbelievably helped me without pay, and those who have been paid have certainly not been paid enough for the level of assistance they have provided. And so I give a huge shout-out of thanks and Big Love to the *Global Chorus* team: editorial assistants Jayson MacLean (my supremely helpful older brother, who has been a saint from the start) and Cynthia Dennis (our letter-writing queen!); virtual assistant and social media manager Heather Idt of Zen Business Solutions; web designer Sarah Marie Lacy; creative/ coordination assistance/kisses by Savannah Belsher-MacLean; artistic design and consultation by visual artist Laurie MacLean (my abundantly talented older sister); and special thanks to my amazing and lovely literary agent Drea Cohane at The Rights

Factory, and the ever-dedicated publishing vision- ary Don Gorman at Rocky Mountain Books, who has believed so strongly in this project all along.

Big thanks as well to all those who not only sug- gested contributors, but put me in touch with them. This is a long list of people, and *you all know who you are*. I owe you all a debt of gratitude.

For all those who are not a part of *Global Chorus* and should have been, I have to say this: *I am sorry that I could not get to you*. And I look forward to a future that may perhaps entail sequel initiatives with your valuable involvement.

And of course a very special thank you to ev- ery single contributor to *Global Chorus*, as every writer has so generously given their time in sup- port of this fundraiser initiative. This book *would evidently not be in existence* without your gracious willingness to be a part of the Chorus. Massive out- pouring gratitude to all of you for your generosity and your belief in this project, and an especially big thanks to all those contributors who came on board early in the process. You put your faith in this when it was just an idea, and you started the snowball in powerful momentum. I can never thank you all enough for your work, for your wis- dom, for your words.

When I set out, it was my goal to assemble what I could firmly describe as "the best book I've ever read." And since I am not the writer of *Global Chorus*, I can therefore praise the contributors further in saying this honestly without being labelled as being dis- gracefully egotistical: this is unquestionably the best book I've ever read. It is my sincere hope that you will find this to be the case as well.

– Todd E. MacLean,
editor-in-chief of *Global Chorus*

INVOCATION

– look, now –

it is there
in you. within reach.
in some, it is buried deep
and hid fast. in some,
it is denied voice, and
stripped silent. in
some, it is confused with
rhetoric, and hammered
still.

but, it is there in all.
a desire to change, so
that our mother can re-emerge; heal.
grandfathers and grandmothers
watch us, confused and abhorred.
the unborn must be
wondering and scared, mostly.

it is there
in you; you can see,
you can hear, you can taste,

you can smell and you can feel
the shake that precedes
rumble, that precedes quake.

that precedes (an echoic) earthly silence.

yet, it is right here, and precisely now.
our rising global-chorus-will to
make it right. you can hear
me tonight. I know you can.

We must resonate in you.

reach in, and pull us open so
that our desire, so
that our resilience, so
that our ability to colour
this pale blue dot,
resonates at and through to
the surface
once again.

look at me, now.

–Charlie G. Sark,
Lennox Island, Epekwitk (Prince Edward Island), Mi'kma'ki (Atlantic Canada)

JANUARY

JANE GOODALL

Can we save Planet Earth? Of course we CAN. The question is, will we? We have indeed disturbed the balance of Nature everywhere, as environments are destroyed by the desperation of millions living in crippling poverty and the selfish unsustainable lifestyles of the rest of us.

No wonder young people are losing hope. "We have not inherited this planet from our parents, we have borrowed it from our children" is an oft repeated saying. That is a lie – we have not borrowed but stolen. We are told that unlimited economic development is possible. Another lie, for the planet has only finite natural resources.

Fortunately there is a groundswell of those who realize that Mother Nature cannot continue to supply our needs at the current rate and that the time will come when it is too late to heal the scars we have inflicted. That time is close, but there is hope. Already we are coming up with new technologies to enable us to live in greater harmony with Nature. More and more of us are thinking about the consequences of the choices we make each day so as to leave the lightest ecological footprint. Every individual matters, has a role to play and makes a difference – every day. And Mother Nature is amazingly resilient – polluted rivers, devastated landscapes, species on the verge of extinction – can be restored, given another chance.

Above all, I am inspired by today's youth. Once young people are aware of the problems around them and empowered to take action, their energy, determination and commitment are boundless. They are changing the world one problem at a time, encouraging each other, influencing their parents and grandparents. They will be the next doctors, lawyers, politicians and parents, and they know that while we need money to live, we should not live for money. The human spirit is indomitable. We shall not give up.

– Jane Goodall, PhD, DBE,
UN Messenger of Peace, founder of the Jane Goodall Institute
www.janegoodall.ca

PAUL HAWKEN

The dilemmas we face can seduce us into believing there is no future as we journey through darkness. The enormity of what is passing away is unspeakable. It is not merely species or ecosystems. It includes cultures, the seasons, civilization itself. When asked if I am pessimistic or optimistic, my answer is always the same: if you look at the science about what is happening on Earth and aren't pessimistic, you don't understand data. However, if you meet the people who are restoring Earth and the lives of the poor and you aren't optimistic, you haven't got a pulse. I see everywhere ordinary people who are willing to confront despair, power and incalculable odds in order to restore grace, justice and beauty to the world. Humanity is coalescing. It is reconstituting the world, and the action is taking place in schoolrooms, farms, jungles, villages, campuses, companies, refugee camps, deserts, fisheries and slums.

No one knows how many groups and organizations are working on the salient issues of our day: climate change, poverty, deforestation, peace, water, hunger, conservation, human rights and more. It is the largest movement the world has ever seen. Rather than control, it seeks connection. Rather than dominance, it strives to disperse concentrations of power. It provides hope, support and meaning to billions of people in the world. Its clout resides in ideas, not in force. It is made up of teachers, children, peasants, businesspeople, rappers, organic farmers, nuns, artists, government workers, fisher folk, engineers, students, incorrigible writers, weeping Muslims, concerned mothers, poets, doctors without borders, grieving Christians, street musicians and all who love life. Forget that the task of planet-saving is not possible in the time required. Do what needs to be done, and check to see if it was impossible only after you are finished.

– Paul Hawken,
author, innovative entrepreneur, environmentalist

SCOTT KENNEDY

There's no denying it. Things haven't exactly gone according to plan. Climate change, over-commercialization, corruption, the destruction of habitat and the inability of the world to feed itself – yeah, we all could have done better. As a species our latest report card isn't one that Mum would put up on the fridge.

It would be easy to slip into a spiral of cynicism and embrace the overriding notion that we are just rearranging the deck chairs on the *Titanic* as the band plays on. I have to reject that. And the reason I reject the temptation to yank the ejection handle and give up has nothing to do with me. It's all to do with what the future has in store for all of us. It's all about who's in the driver's seat.

I've seen it time and time again – the youth of the world, whether they be affluent or on the ragged edge of survival, believe with all their heart that we can steer this *Spaceship Earth* of ours away from the iceberg dead ahead. They've inherited our problems and aren't content to make do – they want to change course.

What's the secret? Why can they fix this and we can't seem to sort it out? The answer: they want to change the world. It's not about needing to change, needs are banal and boring. Food, shelter, clothing – it's all so 20th century. Smarter farming is cool, eco-houses made of innovative materials are cool, clothes made from recycled soft drink bottles are cool. Cool ideas with sexy outcomes are the salvation, and the practitioners are all around us.

The youth of today are inspired to change the world because they want to, not because we all need to. The sooner we all get on the bandwagon of wanting to change the world, the closer we'll all be to getting there. And that destination is a place we all need to get to. Besides, a little bit more cool and sexy is never a bad thing.

– Scott Kennedy,
Canadian-born, New Zealand-based writer, photographer, filmmaker
www.adventureskope.com

MERRELL-ANN PHARE

The question before us is this: how do we create a sustainable future? Our solution is both simple and maybe the most difficult thing we have ever done. It is this: consume less, share more. If we consumed to meet our needs, not our wants, and remembered that true value is in noticing life rather than being noticed for what we own, we would chart a fully hopeful and sustainable future. Our societies would grow and contract where needed, depending on human and ecosystem needs and limits. If we consumed less we would have more to share. Sharing between people, communities and nations would provide where local ecosystems cannot fully do so. What would we share? Wealth, goods, healing, knowledge, community, tolerance, compassion, forgiveness, restoration and reconciliation.

What do we do to get to a "consume less, share more" mindset? The first step is modest but absolutely critical: you must reconnect to the Earth. So,

go outside. If you live in a city, find a green space. If you frequent green spaces, go farther out, into wilder spaces. Listen to the sounds of the ecosystem. It supports you. Breathe the air. Find water there, bend down to it and notice it. Indigenous elders say to introduce yourself to all the new water you meet. Run your fingers through it. Sustainability of the Earth requires us to remember we are in a relationship of reciprocity with all of Nature. We need to rebuild that relationship.

If this seems like too much, just recall: when we are silent and still in Nature, we feel the grace that resides there, in Nature and within us. That stillness is a wordless knowing of who we are, separate from all the chatter, demands, goals, thoughts, fears, emotions and experiences that are always roiling around in our minds. When we are there, in that calm, still space, one other important thing happens: we know – not we think, we *know* – that there is hope. So stay there. And then keep going.

–Merrell-Ann Phare,
lawyer, writer, artist, environmentalist

JASON ROBINSON

See every day as a sacred experience.

We and the Earth are one – there is no separation.
The Earth and everything on it is a manifestation of divine will and there is a lesson, an
opportunity, in every moment of every day.
Pay attention to the randomness of life, recognize and act on the gifts the Earth provides.
Every interaction, every person you meet, every bird that chirps, every single thing positive or negative is a divine moment that will by your choice and attention be forever changed, altered, shaped and defined.
We are part of the evolutionary process.
Recognize the role you play.
See every moment of your life as an opportunity to serve others, to relieve their suffering, to meet their needs, and by extension have your needs met as well.

Make the future in your mind
Imagine the world as you want to see it, and make it happen.
Recognize that you are co-creating the future with every thought, word, deed and choice you make.
Your actions make the difference – and to create change you must act.

Choose wisely
With every choice you decide what the future will be.
Choose wisely … because it has repercussions.

Thoughts become things
Seek love above all else.

There is no reason to fear but fear itself.
The act of fear creates the thing you don't want.
The act of believing creates the things you do want.

If thoughts become things, then it's easy to see how together we are co-creating the world with every decision we make.
Heaven isn't some far-off dream – it's right here, right now. To save the world all we need to do is to start with loving and caring for the world and each other a lot more.
In essence, see every day as a sacred experience and your life as a divine journey.

Believe.

– Jason Robinson, FMA,
founder and CEO of Sustainability Television Inc.
www.SustainabilityTelevision.com

MOI ENOMENGA

My father was a man who could see the future. He told me that things would not be easy for us, that the strangers would destroy the forest with their machines. So I learned from him and that is why I have been working for so many years to find a way to keep our communities, our Huaorani people, together. Here, we have many problems with oil companies and the pollution they cause, as well as the impacts they have on our traditional way of life here in the Amazon forest.

The Huaorani people have always lived in the forest. We *are* the forest. It has been our home for thousands of years. It still is our home, even though now we know more about the cities and the things they offer. The young people in the community who saw these things were dazzled and wanted to leave, and I wondered what would be left of us and the way we used to live. My father told me that this would happen and I suppose that in some way I was prepared, maybe more prepared than the others. So we started to think of ways to keep people here in the community and not to lose our identity. People call it tourism, but what we see is a way to keep things from falling apart, of letting people see what is happening to us.

People tell me that this is happening all over the planet. The oil that the companies are taking out of the ground here in the Amazon is causing big problems, not just here but all around the world, and changing the climate. People say the forest will dry up and the world will collapse if we don't change the way we live.

Here, we don't have what other people in the world have: we don't have televisions or Internet or cars, and if the cost of having them is that the world – our world – disappears, then we ask ourselves, "What good are they?" We think people can live more simply and peacefully if they want, but we don't know if they want to.

– Moi Enomenga,
Huaorani leader, president of the Quehueri'ono Association (Ecuador)

GLORIA FLORA

We must pass through the eye of a needle with inexorable forces, a cacophony of warning bells and a growing distant roar at our backs. Spiritual leaders from around the globe repeat the voices of the ancients: the time has come, the shift is now. Yesterday we didn't have to remember or listen or even think about it. But today it's driving us – to action on good days, to madness on others. Ready or not.

My home lies at the intersection of primeval glaciers and ice-age floods. When the ice dams broke, releasing torrents measured in cubic miles, I wonder if the people living in its path knew what was coming. What were the signs, the sounds? Did their stories tell them to run for their lives to higher ground?

Or was it just luck that some survived along with enough plants and animals to rebuild their known world?

Refuge now isn't simply reaching higher ground. Our refuge lies in co-operation with neighbours: human, animal, trees and microbes. Our hearts, our heads, our hands must work together to create shelter in place. And our reliance on place – the power of Nature – must be honoured and recognized as the source of solutions. Permaculture tells us to care for the Earth, care for people and fair-share the surplus; we would be wise to listen.

So let us rise up, enfold our loved ones of all species, define, refine, love and shape ourselves into the future ... right through the eye of a needle.

– Gloria Flora,
Sustainability Leader Reconnecting People to Their Landscapes

BRUCE COCKBURN

There is *always* hope.

Humans are wired to hope even in the most impossible circumstances. Sometimes it seems forlorn and foolish. Sometimes it is what gives us the energy to confront and survive the things which threaten us. I find myself wondering which kind I hold for the future.

I go around with a heart full of hope which, much of the time, seems to defy logic. Look at the things we are doing to ourselves, to each other, to the planetary systems which sustain us! We are digging ourselves into a pretty big hole. I feel time speeding up. Everywhere there appears to be more collapse, more chaos. Brilliant people are trying to address the problems of environmental degradation and economic injustice. Some of them I've been blessed to know. Whenever I look around me, though, I see the world's decision makers guided by, and steering their constituencies using, short-term self-interest, fear and greed. I see yet another piece of the Nature that is our inheritance squandered on "development." I see rage, overt or subliminal, ruling our relations with one another. Even so, there are grace and dignity to be found in unexpected places. There are inspirational human beings. There is love! Can we fix things? Not sure. Much is already beyond repair. Can we slow the rush toward becoming part of the Great Extinction that seems to be occurring? I think so. Long enough to allow the brilliant among us to discover a remedy? Maybe.

We think of survivalism as being all about stockpiling canned goods and guns. It's not my idea, but it seems right to me that true survivalism has to be about building community ... creating strategies which if necessary can bypass the hierarchies of power.

The universe will continue on its course. The planet will carry on. With us? Without us? I hope *with*. Which sort of hope is that?

– Bruce Cockburn, OC,
singer/songwriter, guitarist, social activist

ALEXANDRA COUSTEAU

As a child, I spent countless afternoons on the ocean shore examining tide pools. Populated by many strange, mysterious – and exquisitely beautiful – creatures, the tide pools were like my own personal aquariums. Watching these miniature ecosystems thrive, I marvelled at how even a brackish puddle can serve as a cradle of life.

A few years ago, I returned to the tide pools of my childhood, and I found them covered in algae and missing the diversity of life I once admired. My aquariums had transformed into dead zones in less than a generation.

Our planet is changing rapidly. From overpopulation and threats to global food security, to the water crisis, deforestation, pollution and climate change – the world we will leave to our children is fundamentally different from the one we inherited from our parents. It will require new thinking, new expectations, new collaborations and, above all, ingenuity.

This is the moment in history when the choices we make as individuals and as a generation will shape the future we inhabit. I believe there is no greater aspiration than the one to protect our children and the quality of life they can expect from this uniquely beautiful place called Earth. We must never give up hope in our individual ability to find a way to change – and to leave this world a better place than we found it.

– Alexandra Cousteau,
explorer, filmmaker, water advocate, founder of Blue Legacy
www.alexandracousteau.org

MORGAN SPURLOCK

I'm an optimist and I will always trust in the goodness of people above all else.

While governments or politicians may jockey and shift their values to get re-elected or to serve a corporate bottom line, I believe the power and influence of the common man will remain a constant. The collective wisdom and bravery of a society can stand the test of time and topple any tyranny.

We just need to continue to muster the courage to stand together for what's right, versus what is easy.

We need to be willing to make sacrifices. We need to be willing to do more with less. We need to shake complacency and apathy. But most of all, we need to embrace the idea and reality of the living Earth as a member of our own family. We must treat her with the same respect and love we would our own grandmother, and we have to bear the burden when we fail to do so.

When I was a child growing up in West Virginia, I looked at the mountains and trees and rivers that surrounded my house as part of my "home." This … all of this … was where I lived. But as I grew older, I became blind to my surroundings and ignorant of my impact. It takes a wake-up call for us to understand a world bigger than ourselves. For me, that was the birth of my son.

And because of him, I believe we can take these blinders off and collectively make the changes we need to build and grow our home. To give him, and all of our children, the planet they deserve. At least, in my heart, that is my hope.

–Morgan Spurlock,
humorist, television producer, screenwriter, political activist,
documentary filmmaker, including *Supersize Me* and *Where in the World Is Osama Bin Laden?*

MARK BOYLE

We are living through an age of ecological, social and personal crises, and the hour seems dark indeed. The issues involved are complex and run deep, all the way down to the cultural narratives that we've built our civilization and politico-economic models on. We have walked this path for so long now that we no longer recognize the stories that have woven themselves into the very fabric of our lives. But that is all they are – stories – and as we know, stories can change.

Is there hope of us changing course before we join the rapidly growing list of species gone extinct? That I do not know, if I am honest. At this hour of the night, it is hard to see the dawn, inevitable as she is. What I do know is this: any hope we do have lies in our willingness to stand up to the challenges we face and the forces driving them, with skilfulness, intelligence, dignity, honour and great heart. Now is not the time for half-measures or cowardice. Now is the time for effective action.

This will involve billions of people doing billions of different things. We need everyone courageously following their calling, and sharing their unique gift with the world as passionately as they dare. There is no one right way to act, no prescription. Simply do what you love and be of service to life.

What is certain, however, is that we will need to localize our lives if we are to create healthy ecological systems, and we are going to have to radically alter the spirit in which we meet our needs if we want to create a world worth sustaining. Therefore, I believe that Permaculture values and gift culture principles must be at the heart of whatever comes next.

We need a revolution – a revolution in consciousness, in the cultural myths we live our lives by, and in our politic and economic systems. Anything less than that will be an absolute disservice to the community of life we share Earth with and, ultimately, to ourselves.

– Mark Boyle,
author of *The Moneyless Manifesto*
www.moneylessmanifesto.org

DEBORAH HARFORD

Humans are the most adaptable species on Earth, barring cockroaches. In our blink of historical time we have explored every inch of our globe. We have warded off hunger and cold and learned how to stave off illness. We are feeding seven billion people and leaving footprints on nearby planets. We can also predict the future through visualizing our effect on the planet. I call this the adaptive advantage, because it means we can forecast changes we need to make if we are to survive.

Climate models are telling us that our success has a downside, a fact that is already evident in widespread extreme weather events. The ecosystems on which we depend are struggling as we encroach upon them to extract resources. As we look forward we can also remember the past; human populations have expanded before, those societies often failed, and we know why. They overstretched the capacity of the land to support their needs, and we are falling into the same pattern.

Happily, the answers lie within and around us. We are treating the Earth as though civilization is a body that consumes goods and emits waste. But no body exists in a vacuum; waste has to go somewhere. Nature recycles waste to fuel the bodies within it. Our brilliant minds – all seven billion of them – have to collectively start thinking like the bodies within ecosystems that we are. All that is required is for us to recognize that we live in a circular system, not a linear one. This truth must percolate through all our realities, from economics to eating to energy production.

If we can unite globally and meet this ultimatum, we stand a chance of adapting to climate change. If we instead give in to greed and conformity, Nature will choose against us. It's up to us and our adaptive advantage to create a new paradigm that closes the loop, that feeds our future as an extraordinary species with unprecedented capabilities which, combined with the wisdom of our ancestors, can do anything it imagines.

–Deborah Harford,
executive director of ACT (the Adaptation to Climate Change Team)
at Simon Fraser University (Vancouver, Canada)

ARCHBISHOP DESMOND TUTU

I am a prisoner of hope. And I think that most of us would be that. Why? Well, simply because we have faced many other crises in the history of the world and have almost always, ultimately, survived and succeeded.

For instance, look at the whole question of slavery. There must have been a time when people believed firmly that this was a social system that was totally unchangeable. But we've massively diminished slavery. We in South Africa have been able to overcome apartheid and racism. All the wars, conflict, gender/equality issues and even genocide of the past century, we have endured and overcome. So, it is clear that we have the capacity. What we often lack is the political will.

Take our incapacity to feed everyone on Earth, for example. We have got the means. We *can* feed every single person on Earth. But we do not have the appropriate political will to do so. With regards to the whole question of the environment, people are campaigning very, very powerfully for us to adopt ways of life that are sustainable. But even though politicians buckle to certain pressures, they are beginning more and more to realize that it is far better to be looking for renewable ways of producing energy. And many people are beginning to see that it is not just healthier, it is the one way in which our Earth home is going to be preserved. If we don't wake up to our responsibility, we won't have a second chance. This is the only home we have. If we destroy it, we're done for.

A person is a person through other persons. None of us can survive just as solitary individuals. We are made for togetherness, we are made for co-operation, and we ultimately exist in a delicate network of interdependence. None of us comes fully formed into the world. In the same way, even the most powerful nation in the world depends ultimately on interconnectedness. You can't just live within yourself; no country can do it, no community can do it, no person can do it. Our world must heed this truth to harmoniously move forward.

– Archbishop Desmond Tutu,
South African human rights activist,
archbishop emeritus of Cape Town,
1984 Nobel Peace Prize laureate

DR. RAJIV SHAH

We live at an incredible moment in history. Around the world, human ingenuity and entrepreneurship have made tremendous progress against some of the greatest challenges in development, as child mortality rates have fallen by 42 per cent and poverty rates by 48 per cent over the last twenty years. At the same time, new technologies – perhaps most notably the mobile phone – have changed what's possible, transforming how farmers compare market prices, citizens report corruption and nurses monitor the health of mothers and newborns in rural communities.

For the first time, we have the tools and knowledge to achieve goals that were simply unimaginable in the past: the eradication of extreme poverty and its most devastating consequences, including child hunger and preventable child death.

But the truth is that many people believe the opposite. They simply don't realize that the solutions to great global challenges are within our reach. Every day, I find myself making this case, battling the perception that politics today cannot support great moral aspirations, or that the world cannot come together to achieve these goals.

But in the last four years as administrator of the U.S. Agency for International Development, I have seen just the opposite. Around the world, we are mobilizing the energy of a new generation of students, inventors and entrepreneurs to deliver results on a greater scale than ever before. From a church in inner-city Detroit that looks after an orphanage in Ghana to the nationwide response after super typhoon Haiyan, I have seen the depth of passion and support that communities everywhere have for global development. And from St. Louis to Dakar to Delhi, I have seen people from all walks of life stand together as champions for this global task.

– Dr. Rajiv Shah,
administrator of the U.S. Agency for International Development

RACHEL PARENT

The corporate mentality of profit and growth at all costs is having a devastating impact on our planet, from the dying off of our marine life, bee colony collapse, the melting of our glaciers, the deforestation of our rainforests and dislocation of natives, the contamination of our water and soil, and even the loss of control of our seeds and safe food supply. The magnitude of the destruction can be overwhelming! But I believe we're living in a time of historical change, a time of transformation where people finally realize they have the power to make change and bring about positive solutions for our planet and for our very survival.

It's a time where people, especially our youth, are waking up, rising up and standing up together, regardless of race, colour or religion, to heal our planet. I feel empowered knowing that I am part of a massive global shift in thinking for a better tomorrow.

In order to fix the old problems, we need to find new solutions. As Albert Einstein once said, "We can't solve problems by using the same kind of thinking we used when we created them." We not only need to change the way we think, but also how we measure success.

Corporations' short-sighted focus on greed and profit at any cost has to change. It's time for them to become "socially responsible." Fortunately, we can influence that change by boycotting their products and telling others through social media to do the same. General Mills's recent agreement to remove GMOs from Cheerios after being swamped with emails and social media postings is a perfect example of that. We, as consumers, have the power!

As one of the youth, I can only allow myself to have hope for our future. To lose hope would mean giving up on the beauty of Nature and the miracle of life. Our goal must be to leave the Earth better than we found it. We owe this to ourselves and to the many generations that are yet to come.

–Rachel Parent,
14-year-old environmental global activist,
founder of Kids Right to Know
www.kidsrighttoknow.com

WILLIAM MCDONOUGH

As a designer of things from the scale of a molecule to a region, I have great hope for our future. A designer's purpose is to make life better – hopefully. Design is the first signal of human intention. We must ask if our species, by design, intends to destroy the quality of our home, because, if so, we are strategically and intentionally tragic.

To have a strategy of hope, we have a new design framework to adopt, one that celebrates the abundance of Earth and human creativity rather than bemoans limits. The chemist Michael Braungart and I have dedicated ourselves to articulating the Cradle to Cradle framework, in which everything is designed for continuous reuse in biological or technical cycles; everything is renewably powered, clean water is available to all, and we celebrate diversity. This allows us to joyfully become infinitely resourceful, physically and intellectually, led by profitable businesses that use currency on a mission to create intergenerational capital.

With commerce as the engine of change – looking to be more good, not just less bad – big ideas can be realized now. We know how to convert sewage plants to nutrient management systems, allowing us to grow safe, healthy food in, under and around our cities. Such strategies portend magnificent productivity and quality delivered both efficiently and effectively while we allow our ecosystems to heal. Our designs can focus on globally shared innovations and still reinforce and enhance local cultures, benefiting all scales of economic activity.

I find hope for the future in wisdom from the past. The 12th-century philosopher Hildegard of Bingen wrote, "Glance at the sun. See the moon and the stars. Gaze at the beauty of Earth's greenings. Now, think." In the 20th century, Albert Einstein wrote, "Our task must be to free ourselves ... by widening our circle of compassion to embrace all living creatures and the whole of Nature and its beauty." In the 21st century, our design assignment is simple: how do we love all the children of all the species for all time? It is time to plant an orchard of Cradle to Cradle opportunity to honour present and future generations. We can move forward together – fiercely – with hope, not fear.

– William McDonough,
designer, architect,
co-author of *Cradle to Cradle: Remaking the Way We Make Things*
www.mcdonough.com

IAN SKELLY

Nature is an astonishingly complex, dynamic system that seeks balance at every level. She is harmonic.

The word "harmony" comes from the ancient Greek for "joining things up" and it is an active state. Nature is endlessly in motion, endlessly transforming; the dynamic is alive.

Every minute of the day, Nature is transforming herself, imperceptibly changing from one season into the next. This reveals that it is in life's nature to transform, and thus it is in our nature too to transform – transform our thinking, behaviour and our approach towards Nature's precious resources. Why? Because of what we are.

Shift your perception. Move from seeing yourself "apart" from Nature, but also away from the notion that we are "part" of Nature. The truth is, we *are* Nature. Nature is not a machine made up of parts, but a harmonic, dynamic whole.

As for hope, well, consider whether it is in Nature's character to fail, and observe that you too share that reluctance. We are born with life's innate sense of hope. Humanity is not wired to fail, so consider what can be done if you harness that hope and set it on course to transform.

Observe Nature. Notice that "virtuous" circles, not vicious ones, keep her cyclical economy intact, so be mindful that Nature is necessarily self-limiting in order that she endures without failure. Behave and choose according to this. Slow down, abandon multi-tasking; do one thing with full attention and do it well with care. Seek the deep connection with the marvels of Nature around you. Look up, not down; look from within with reverence, not from without. See life for what it truly is: not just whole, but Holy. Then you will transform yourself and thus the world around you every moment of the day.

– Ian Skelly,
writer, filmmaker, broadcaster,
co-author, with HRH The Prince of Wales, of *Harmony*
www.ianskelly.co.uk

ARAM HUR

At every moment, tears are falling.

It is because of the joie de vivre. Although the ground of life is somewhere dry and barren, I have a strong belief that the seed of hope would grow and finally bear good fruits.

If we think we can do it, we have to do it. It is a humbling principle of my life and perhaps of the hope. Where there is strong belief and good heart, we would be able to build the community of hope, where people don't lose their dream for a better world, keep working to make our societies a little more humane, and carving out spaces of gentleness.

To meet people with this warm feeling of hope is to plant a seed of hope.

The obligations in our life might be challenging, probably most of the time, but we can still be hopeful when ordinary people bring out the best of human nature: courage, solidarity, altruism, generosity and love. And it must be the task of the living to keep hope alive.

Amidst the dark night of indifference, tragedy and disaster, it is possible for our extraordinary species to shine so magnificently.

And this is what I believe.

– Aram Hur,
South Korean educator, publisher, lecturer, social activist,
founder of Indigo Sowon

FRED PENNER

My heritage is Mennonite. My grandparents came from Russia/Prussia in the late 19th century and I have often tried to imagine what it was like on the harsh Canadian Prairie back then and how they were able to survive. The same question can be applied to cultures in every corner of the world. We are all trying to find a way to make this life work. It is complex and challenging to say the least. Basic rights must be fulfilled and beyond that we have a fundamental need to communicate with one another on an emotional and spiritual plane.

We are resilient and adaptable human beings, there is no doubt, and we have proven this time and time again over the centuries. That doesn't make the challenges we face now any easier, but it should give us some sense of optimism. Trust and belief in one another is where it starts. My perspective is blessed and specific to the generation raised with my music. Through recordings, concerts and a television series my creative life journey has allowed me to connect with that generation. The affirmation of my optimism comes from almost daily responses, both personal and through social media, from the children who are now the young adults making their own way through the insanity.

Finding a way to face our global challenges seems too vast and incomprehensible at times.

When I was taping *Fred Penner's Place*, there were times when I felt overwhelmed by all the aspects I was juggling as I attempted to communicate through this medium. My eyes would glaze over for a moment and that was when my director sent The Message to the floor director: "One Child." This was my reminder that the camera was really a portal to a single child who was watching and listening. This allowed me to communicate on a much more personal level with the viewer. We, the parents and leaders of this world, must do the same. We are in this together. If ever you doubt your ability to make this difference, look into the face of One Child.

– Fred Penner,
family entertainer for children of all ages,
former host of *Fred Penner's Place* on CBC television

LEILANI MÜNTER

I have hope for humanity because people are evolving and becoming a better species. We will adopt new technologies and ways of life so we can have a more harmonious relationship with this beautiful little blue-green planet of ours. It's been a bumpy ride and there are certainly more bumps in our future, but it is time for us to adapt or die. Unfortunately if we don't, we will take an incredible number of other species with us. I still have hope we will do the right thing.

Today is an exciting time to be alive, because we are the generation that must push the human race forward to solve our environmental crisis. Because we are witnessing the direct consequences of climate change, the urgency of changing is becoming clear. With every season that passes, this truth is more obvious. Charles Darwin once said, "It is not the strongest of the species that survives, nor the most intelligent that survives. It is the one that is the most adaptable to change." This generation has been called upon to answer to the most noble of duties: to ensure the survival of future generations with the most basic of survival mechanisms – adaptation.

Abandoning fossil fuels for renewable energy, greening buildings, becoming more energy efficient, passing environmental legislation that punishes polluters, adopting a plant-based diet and driving electric cars will all be key players in this adaptation. In addition, overpopulation is an issue many environmentalists often don't talk about, but we need to. With seven billion people on the planet and a growth rate of over 200,000 per day, our demand on finite natural resources is unsustainable. We need to focus on education because it has been shown to play a key role in reducing population growth.

The rise in development of renewable energy projects and the success of electric car companies are a positive sign that the tides are changing, and this gives me hope. Be part of the solution – go vegan, buy an electric car, support companies with sustainable practices and vote people into office who support renewable energy!

– Leilani Münter,
race car driver, environmental activist
carbonfreegirl.com

MIKE HOLMES

Most people think my job is dealing with hopeless situations. But after being a contractor for over 30 years, I've learned no situation is hopeless.

Everyone has a home. And housing has a huge impact on the global environment – from the materials used in building to the energy used in living in them.

As builders, we have a responsibility to construct homes that are sustainable, safe and with nothing but clean air inside to breathe. Homes that will keep you warm not only at night but also during the winter – using very little energy. Homes that improve the quality of life – inside and outside.

Every home should work with its environment.

It just makes sense. Use the rainwater, the sunlight, the temperature in the ground. I've built these homes. Why? Because when you work with Mother Nature, she works for you. You live healthier. You live happier.

I have hope because we know how to build a healthy home. We know how to build a house that respects the environment and uses it to its advantage. And the more homes we build this way, the more we will be building and sustaining our environment. It's all connected.

How we live today will impact how we will live tomorrow. And I'm seeing more and more people realize this and do something about it.

– Mike Holmes,
"North America's most trusted contractor,"
co-creator and television host of *Holmes on Homes*® and *Holmes Makes It Right*

SEBASTIAN COPELAND

Life evolves and so should we. Our planet has seen constant flux from its inception 4.5 billion years ago. Over the last 450 million years alone, the Earth has seen five mass extinction events. And today biologists believe that our period, the Holocene, is at the onset of the sixth mass extinction event, which could see upwards of 75 per cent of today's species gone by the end of the century.

Only this time, floods and asteroids aren't the culprits. Explosive demographic growth tied to a persistent disregard for sustainable development has placed exponential stress on the environment. Is it short-sighted? To put things in perspective, we have not been in existence for very long. In fact, it's a miracle we are here in the first place. And the notion that we will be here forever is, from a paleontological perspective, almost absurd. Flowers appeared only 135 million years ago; anatomically modern humans, merely 175,000 years ago. This should serve to help us understand that the Earth is not here to see us through. That responsibility falls on us.

By 2050, 6.5 billion people will live in cities. A treacherous by-product of urban convenience is a false sense of security and the utter disconnect from our individual footprint. What is the actual cost of the resources we consume? How much trash do we generate? What is the environmental impact of the food we eat, and how far does it travel to reach us? We have conveniently removed ourselves from connecting with those issues by squeezing them all into a little envelope we call a bill. But paying for problems to go away does not make them disappear.

Ours is less an environmental problem than it is sociological and perceptual. More than ever our chances for survival, here in this biosphere, require an emotional bond with the ecosystem that sustains us. We need to reconnect with Nature and commit urgently to the principles of sustainability. That is the next logical phase of our adaptation cycle in evolutionary terms. Short of that, and if we're lucky, we will end up exiting starship Earth in search of another planet to populate. And wouldn't that be a shame: this one has been so good to us.

– Sebastian Copeland,
explorer, photographer, environmental advocate,
IPA Photographer of the Year (2007) for
the book *Antarctica: The Global Warning*,
filmmaker of *Into The Cold: A Journey of the Soul*
www.sebastiancopelandadventures.com

Iceberg IX, by Sebastian Copeland

CHERYL CHARLES

We face an urgent need on a worldwide basis to reconnect people of all ages with Nature, beginning with children. That connection with Nature is at the heart of what I call "the ecology of hope." By reconnecting people with Nature in their everyday lives, we will have helped to create the necessary nutrients for the health and well-being of children, families, communities and the whole of the Earth.

Worldwide efforts to bring peace, prosperity, health and well-being to all of the Earth's people, wildlife and habitats are interconnected. Just as in Nature's ecosystems, all parts are connected. They form an ecology of hope.

Among humans, hope derives in part from the exercise of will. Success in exercising will, on whatever scale, helps to develop a sense of efficacy – that is, a perceived belief that you or I can make a difference. Combine the exercise of will with the experience of efficacy and hope is the result.

Ecologies don't talk about hope; they demonstrate it. So can we humans. Our actions will inspire and support others. We can exercise the will, we can make conscious choices, we can cultivate a sense of efficacy in ourselves and others – especially in children and youth – and we can create a positive, healthy and life-sustaining future.

If you are already among those helping to reconnect children with Nature, I thank you. If you are not yet doing so, please join the cause. Connecting with Nature is good for all of us and is a vital key to a healthy, peaceful and life-rich future. We can be the generation that left a legacy of leadership and an ecology of hope.

–Cheryl Charles, PhD,
co-founder, president and CEO emerita of Children & Nature Network
www.childrenandnature.org

CARL HONORÉ

There is always hope. If we work together and channel our better angels, we can fix this mess.

The first step is to forge a radically new definition of success. Consuming more should cease to be the measure of a good life. Instead, we must build a culture that prizes meaning and connection, that places on a pedestal those who make the world a better place.

The most powerful way to bring about this cultural revolution is to slow down. When we live in fast forward, we struggle to look beyond our own selfish, short-term desires. Decelerating can help us see the big picture. When we take time to live each moment fully, we start to notice and cherish other people and everything else around us.

Bottom line: the only way to save this fast world is to slow down.

— Carl Honoré,
advocate of the Slow Movement,
author of *In Praise of Slow*, *Under Pressure* and *The Slow Fix*

MARK REYNOLDS

We can restore the climate of the 1980s by 2070. It won't require a miracle or big sacrifices, just the will and policies to do it. Top climate scientists confirm this is possible. They haven't proposed it before because it has appeared that we, as a society, would never muster the courage to do it.

Restoring the climate requires that we switch to carbon-free energy by 2030–2050, as described by Stanford's Mark Z. Jacobson, and let the ocean continue absorbing the carbon dioxide we've emitted.

In 1961, President Kennedy declared: "We will send a man to the moon and bring him back safely by the end of the decade." At the time, we had just sent a man into space for 15 minutes. We did not have the rockets, the navigation or the life support systems for a moon trip and most people, including my parents, thought it was complete folly. Seven years later we had developed and demonstrated the technology – ahead of schedule. We had a clear, ambitious goal and a deadline, and we rose to the occasion.

Twenty years is plenty of time to develop the missing links such as batteries, smart grids and domestic manufacturing capability. Compare that to the five years we spent building the 300,000 aircraft that helped us win the Second World War using 1940s technology, or the seven years developing the technology for the moon program with 1960s technology. We now have Google, computers, 3D printers and millions of highly educated engineers connected by the Internet.

Tell your children, your nation's leaders and your representatives which legacy you want to give to our grandkids: restore the climate by 2070. That is our moon shot. Let's commit to it.

– Mark Reynolds,
executive director of the Citizens Climate Lobby

JAMIE OLIVER

True, sustainable, radical transformation of individuals, families or communities doesn't come from one action – everything has to change, everyone has to contribute and everyone needs to be open-minded to change, which makes it tough. But that doesn't mean people can't lead the way, set examples and give people hope. Of course governments should step up and big, responsible organizations should set an example, but there's no reason why change and making better choices can't start with individuals and be fun.

I believe that even the best governments can only think short-term – as far as the next election or, at best, the one after. Big problems that will take decades to solve are overwhelming, and the likelihood is that by the time things get REALLY bad, the other guy will be in power. So I'm pretty sure a lot of them think that big solutions can wait. They can't.

It's not too late to make a difference. As a campaigner and a food lover, but most importantly as a father (and hopefully one day a grandfather), I cannot stand by and watch this global health disaster unfold. That's why I believe passionately in food education and the power of people and communities all across the world to get together to make positive changes.

And that's why I've started Food Revolution Day – one day each year where people all over the world who care about food education can stand up and raise awareness. It's the ultimate expression of people power. It started in 2012 and it's not specifically designed to send a message to governments – most don't listen anyway – but to be the start of a grassroots movement. With not much time to pull it all together, the first Food Revolution Day had 1,000 events, big and small, in 664 cities around the world, all hosted by passionate, brilliant people who care. The second in 2013 had even more. Big change starts with little changes, on a local and personal level. Before you know it, you're part of something huge.[1]

– Jamie Oliver,
chef and campaigner

LAUREN BUSH LAUREN

When I was a student in college, I had the amazing opportunity to travel the world with the UN. It was a life-changing experience to visit places of extreme poverty and meet people who did not know where their next meal was coming from. I would return from my travels feeling inspired to make a difference, but not knowing where to begin.

I knew others would want to help too, if given an easy way to do so without feeling overwhelmed. It was from this premise that I came up with the idea for FEED, a social business with a mission to create good products that help feed the world. The idea is simple: buy a tote bag and help a child. For every product we sell, we make a donation to give meals to people in need. Using this model, we are able to make a positive impact on the world while empowering consumers to get involved. By harnessing people's will to make the world a better place, I have seen first-hand how FEED and other social ventures can serve as conduits for individuals and businesses to make a difference and get involved in helping solve big world issues.

Ultimately, I believe the foundation for real and lasting global change is universal empathy. If our world is connected through a shared Earth, it must also be connected through a shared compassion and common sense of human dignity. It really boils down to the Golden Rule: "treat others as you would like to be treated." If the world could abide by that simple rule, many of the daunting challenges we face today would go away. But in the meantime, it is up to each of us to come up with our own ideas and solutions.

If a simple burlap tote bag can feed nearly sixty million children, I am excited to see what your ideas will do.

–Lauren Bush Lauren,
co-founder and CEO of FEED Projects

ROBERT BATEMAN

The British economist E.F. Schumacher said, "The real problems facing the planet are not economic or technical, they are philosophical." I completely agree. Where there is a will there is a way – where there is no will there is no way. If the various cultures and powerful entities in the world can modify their philosophies toward solving the global environmental and social crises, it is certainly possible. I have three suggestions:

1. We need a critical mass of people to pay attention to issues. Too many people bury their heads in the sand and don't want to hear about issues. We prefer, as Neil Postman says, to "amuse ourselves to death." To this end we need almost total transparency of the actions of people on top. What forces are behind the scenes? What are the lobbies? Where is the money? Financial transactions should be transparent. Government and corporate scientists should be allowed to be open about their work and their conclusions. No more muzzling of scientists or the media. Lack of transparency is the hallmark of tyranny such as the regimes of Hitler, Stalin or Mugabe.

2. We do not need any more studies or commissions to solve problems. We know what we have to do. All we have to do is expect to pay more for a good future. Nature is not a free lunch. There is no free lunch. We can pay now or pay later, but if we pay later it will cost more. Our society seems to say that we would rather pay later. Some have called this grandchild abuse. We must have true cost accounting of everything we spend money on. A good future likely will mean higher taxes and more expensive goods. Actually, cutting corners is too expensive.

3. Finally, a general philosophy of respect would be very helpful: respect for Nature and respect for other humans. The Golden Rule states, "Do unto others as you would have others do unto you." Not a bad idea.

– Robert Bateman,
Canadian artist, environmentalist, naturalist
www.robertbateman.ca

JONATHAN LEGG

There is no doubt our world is full of environmental and social crises, but there is more hope than realized.

As a travel show host I ramble around the planet turning over stones and looking for good narratives. I find that most people live in the bubble of their communities, largely oblivious to global issues. In Calcutta and Iloilo there are always plenty of fish at the market, so the understanding that ocean stocks are extremely depleted hasn't been realized, and probably won't be until the day the market grinds to a halt. On the other side of the coin you'll meet a few individuals in these towns religiously reading the papers and watching international news who believe the planet is going to hell in a handbasket.

The truth is somewhere in between.

Harvard psychologist Stephen Pinker reminds us that the world is safer than ever before, and part of the reason is because of expanded awareness. We believe it's worse because of the flood of stories on the nightly news, but this light shining in the corners and cracks has actually made it better. I believe the same effect will galvanize the world's communities into combating other issues, but don't count on standard media to do the job. Violence may be contrary to everyone's agenda, but curbing consumption probably isn't a priority for state- and corporate-run news.

This is where the traveller and social media will fill the gap. Through Twitter, blogs, short online videos and other devices, information is being shared like never before. A common person with a concern or a cause can now reach anyone on the planet who has an Internet connection. Cataloguing vacation and life experiences online allows us to savour them more fully, in the same way taking a picture does, but more importantly it adds a little more clarity and a little extra contrast to the collective understanding.

The more voices that join this global chorus, the further we will grasp how interconnected we all are and the closer we will get to grappling with the realities of our modern world.

– Jonathan Legg,
co-producer, writer and host of *The Road Less Traveled*

MARIA FADIMAN

"Lizard!" I shrieked.

Chan, a Mexican Lacandon Maya, watched as my hand whipped to the top of my head.

Carefully he reached up and plucked a small branch from my tangled hair.

"Twig," he said softly.

"Oh."

He nodded, turned and padded silently through the forest.

"Well, it *was* a lizard last time," I said as I followed, crashing behind him to keep up.

Linking myself to the environment, whether through a lizard in my hair or knowing which plants cure, kill or both, connects me not only to the natural world, but to myself and others. However, forest dwellers and urbanites alike can lose this bond.

On one of my first trips to an Amazonian Kichwa village in Ecuador, struggling to get my feet clean in the Napo River, I asked the boy tossing stones in the river pretending not to watch me about useful plants.

He dropped the rock, adjusted his baseball cap and replied, "We don't know that stuff anymore." He paused, "But I can find someone who does, someone old."

He did: an old person who became my teacher. I illustrated plants, wrote his words and made a small book for him and his people, preserving their own knowledge.

During my stay I watched as generational attitudes shifted. My curiosity sparked theirs. A group of teenagers ended up educating me about what they still knew and I taught them how to process their own community's information. One evening by the fire, a little girl walked into the circle, took my hand and led me to a bright green fern growing by the river. She puffed with pride and said, "I know this plant."

"How about you tell them?" I asked, nodding towards the teens.

"They don't care," she replied.

"They do now."

She paused for a minute, then turned and strode towards the teenagers. I watched as she gesticulated in front of them, pointing to where the fern grew.

Whether in the rainforest or the city, awareness of our disconnection and the possibility for reconnection is the first step. We can each take it from there.

– Dr. Maria Fadiman,
National Geographic Emerging Explorer,
associate professor of geosciences at Florida Atlantic University

ALANNA MITCHELL

Here's an idea. Let's reframe this question. Let's acknowledge that what we face is not a lack of science or technology; the recipe for triumph is right here, within grasp.

What we face is a faulty narrative. We've become mired in a story whose end we fear is already written. The science tells us, correctly, that if we keep going down the track we're on, we will impair the planet's ability to support life as we know it. Not all life forever. Just the creatures we know, almost certainly including us. It's incredibly scary. The stakes are as high as they can be.

But what if we quite fiercely choose hope and then zero that hope in on the task of rewriting the story's end? It will take sacrifice, loss. We will have to relinquish some of our fear, a lot of our anger and blame and guilt and despair about the state our species has put the planet in. But those emotions are the stuff of paralysis anyway. They suck up good energy, driving it into a black hole of helplessness.

What if instead we use that power to feed the highest human superpower: forgiveness. What if we forgive ourselves and each other and our species for having really screwed up? What if, instead of a story of disaster for humanity, we write a tale of magnificent redemption?

And then just get on with making something better.

– Alanna Mitchell,
journalist, playwright,
author of *Sea Sick: The Global Ocean in Crisis*

FEBRUARY

CHARLES EISENSTEIN

Let's not delude ourselves: according to what we commonly understand to be realistic, the situation is hopeless. To remedy the afflictions of our planet – climate change, tree die-offs, nuclear waste, marine collapse, violence, intolerance, inequality – would require a miracle. It just isn't realistic to expect change of the necessary magnitude any time soon.

That doesn't mean the situation is hopeless. It just means we cannot be too realistic. You see, what we take to be real, practical and possible is far too narrow. It is based on the world-story that has long carried industrial civilization, and which is quickly unravelling today.

It is a story of separation: individuals separated from each other, humanity separated from Nature, self separated from world. It casts us into an inanimate universe in which the qualities of self – intelligence, purpose, intentionality, consciousness – are the province of human beings alone. In such a world, humanity's destiny is to triumph over the hostile or inanimate Other through the exercise of force, measurement, planning and control.

As multiple crises reveal the bankruptcy of that ambition, we are awakening to a new (and ancient) story: of interconnection, of interbeing. Therein lies a new and expanded realism. Miracles await us in the margins, in the holistic, alternative, radical, ecological, non-violent and, above all, the indigenous. Sometimes we experience the "impossible" personally. Sometimes we glimpse the future in events like Tahrir Square or Gezi Park, when without money or planning, the unthinkable becomes possible overnight.

In the new story, we know that everything in the world mirrors something in ourselves, and that therefore even the smallest actions can have vast consequences. We learn to listen to the intelligence of the world, to recognize what wants to be born, and to orient ourselves toward service to, and not control over, other beings and the planet. In that state of service, it is as if an invisible power orchestrates changes beyond our contrivance, and we find that the unrealistic people were right all along.

– Charles Eisenstein,
author of *The Ascent of Humanity*, *Sacred Economics* and
The More Beautiful World Our Hearts Know Is Possible

LAMA SURYA DAS

In recent years, and especially since 9/11, following the news tends to make me feel unhappy and even slightly depressed, if not entirely despairing. What kind of world are we greysters leaving for the younger generations, I sometimes wonder. How are we gonna solve the large-scale and seemingly intractable problems we face? We are certainly gonna lose plenty of species along the way, flora and fauna both, but this seems inevitable.

Yet whenever I meet and look into the eyes of young people, I feel an irrational surge of hope and gratification. They remind of my own and friends' earthshaking, idealistic Sixties energy and collective efforts, and I see how very capable they are of stepping outside the box for creative ideas and new solutions.

Just look at recent technological innovations which have wrought tremendous social and economic changes! Also, the younger coming generations seem to have realized that it is necessary to be doing things together in order to accomplish much of anything.

Being a realistic optimist, I know that – no matter what the doomsdayers and naysayers may say – it's not over till the Fat Lama sings – and this fat lama ain't done yet!

I too have my own shoulder joined with theirs, pushing on the great wheel of evolutionary consciousness. And I like to recall the ancient rabbinical wisdom from the Talmud: "To save one soul is to save the world." The source of my own inspiration remains undimmed.

– Lama Surya Das,
authorized lama in the Tibetan Buddhist order,
founder of the Dzogchen Center,
author of *Awakening the Buddha Within* and
Buddha Standard Time: Awakening to the Infinite Possibilities of Now,
affectionately called "the American Lama" by the Dalai Lama
www.surya.org and www.askthelama.com

ERVIN LASZLO

A crisis is both a danger and an opportunity. With conscious, purposive people, it is above all an opportunity. It is the opportunity to be the first generation of a new world, and not the last generation of an old world. We can build a new world because a crisis sweeps away the useless remnants of the old and makes space for the new.

The new has to be truly, fundamentally new. We cannot build a new world on an old foundation. The new world calls for new thinking because, as Einstein said, we cannot solve today's problems with the same kind of thinking that gave rise to them. But new thinking is available and it is already here – all around us, at the leading edge of the emerging cultures. It is thinking in terms of relations and processes, of interconnection and evolution, more exactly of co-evolution. For a new world can only be evolved together, by you and by me and by every thinking and responsible woman and man on the planet.

Start thinking in these terms yourself, because you yourself need to be the "shift" that you want to see in the world – the shift that we all want to see – because we all need it, so as to allow the new world to rise, as a phoenix, from the ashes of the old.

– Ervin Laszlo,
chancellor of Giordano Bruno University,
president of the Ervin Laszlo Center for Advanced Study

FRANCES BEINECKE

The future of all humankind is on a collision course with our global dependence on fossil fuels. From the Arctic Ocean to the Niger Delta, from the forests of Alberta to the Gulf of Mexico, we are imperilling the natural systems that support life itself. We are poisoning our land, polluting our skies and putting our oceans, forests and rivers at risk in our rapacious pursuit of oil, gas and coal. And, when we burn these fuels, the carbon pollution that's left behind disrupts our climate and threatens us all.

We can protect our people, safeguard our families and sustain our communities, large and small, by turning away from this crippling addiction to fossil fuels. We can create a future of prosperity, security and health for a widening circle of people everywhere, by ending this cycle of degradation and harm. And we can ensure a more hopeful future for the children of the world, when we reduce our reliance on fossil fuels.

We have seen, in our lifetime, the kind of change that is possible when people rally around a common belief that, together, we can build a more hopeful future. We can build entire new industries borne of human innovation, creativity and vision. We can put our people back to work today in the careers of tomorrow, building the next generation of energy efficient homes, cars and workplaces. And we can lay the groundwork for human progress and change by investing in wind, solar and other sources of clean, sustainable, renewable power. We have it within us to do this, not overnight, but over time. We owe our children that much. And the time to begin is now.

–Frances Beinecke,
president of the Natural Resources Defense Council

CRAIG KIELBURGER

Our world is facing enormous challenges: social injustices, debilitating poverty, environmental degradation and countless armed conflicts on every scale. We can be forgiven for feeling overwhelmed, but we cannot be forgiven for inaction. We know that a single person with courage in their heart is as good as a majority. This might conjure the image of the solitary figure standing up to a parade of tanks in Beijing's Tiananmen Square. But it's also the teen that gets his peers to wear pink clothes to school, effectively eliminating the damaging actions of a bully. Did both of these actions take courage? Of course. Did both make a real difference? You'd better believe it.

Human history is rife with unthinkable atrocities – slavery, genocide, segregation. Yet these always meet an end because individuals stand up and declare, "This is not right and I am responsible for finding a solution." Such courage, responsibility and action gave rise to the Underground Railroad that enabled slaves in the United States to escape to freedom in Canada in the 19th century; helped General Roméo Dallaire thwart even more mass killings in Rwanda in the 1990s; and helped abolish segregation in the U.S. in the 1960s and apartheid in South Africa in 1994. And, right now, courage, responsibility and action are helping on playgrounds and in schoolyards more than you might know.

Young people have always been at the forefront of social change. And today, they are ready to "be" that change. We see it in the faces of the 70,000 young people who attend We Days each year, earning admittance through their volunteer work. Single-day showcases for an entire movement, We Days are a series of signature Free the Children stadium events full of youth who come together to celebrate their volunteer accomplishments, to learn about social issues from the world's leading humanitarians and to formulate a plan. More importantly, we see it in the actions of these young people. "Passive bystander" isn't in their collective vocabulary. Neither are "impossible," "unrealistic," "never" or "hopeless."

Children are our hope. And if generations to come are instilled with the same compassion, those world-beating challenges aren't so overwhelming after all. Suddenly, those problems don't really stand a chance.

– Craig Kielburger,
children's rights activist
co-founder of Free the Children and Me to We
www.freethechildren.com, www.metowe.com

DIEGO PACHECO

According to the Plurinational State of Bolivia, the only way forward to restore the balance of human beings with Earth is through the recognition of the existence of the "rights of Mother Earth" as a collective subject of public interest, and through taking into account that the foremost objective should be the one of Living Well. The concept of Mother Earth is completely different than Nature because Mother Earth is a living being. In turn, Living Well stems from the vision of indigenous peoples that refers to living in balance and harmony with everybody and everything – where the most important thing is not human beings, but life.

The only way to keep humanity's hope is to launch in this century the recognition of the rights of Mother Earth at a universal scale. In other words, this century should be the time for the battle for the rights of Mother Earth.

In this regard, Bolivia has carried out a revolutionary step through enacting the "Law of Mother Earth and Integral Development for Living Well" (October 2012), which is oriented to move Bolivian public planning and financial resources investment toward Living Well in balance and harmony with Mother Earth.

After a tough process of negotiation at the United Nations, "Living Well in balance and harmony with Mother Earth" has been acknowledged as a holistic and integrated approach to sustainable development (UNEP/GC.27/CW/L.2/Add.3).

The next step is to recognize the universal rights of Mother Earth.

– Diego Pacheco, PhD,
Head of Delegation for Bolivia in the Convention on Biological Diversity

HAZEL MCCALLION

Mahatma Gandhi once said, "You must not lose faith in humanity. Humanity is an ocean; if a few drops of the ocean are dirty, the ocean does not become dirty," and I take this sentiment to heart and remain optimistic that humanity will find its way past the issues which plague our global society.

The world has seen tremendous changes during its existence and while it is easy to adopt a pessimistic view of the world today in these times of seeming moral ambiguity, I do believe there is an appetite for a return to more traditional morals and values and that a paradigm shift is taking place with regard to a renewed consciousness which will hopefully lead the citizens of the world to the realization that despite our differences, we as human beings are called upon to assume responsibility for stewardship in terms of the preservation of life as we know it. It is up to each one of us to use our unique talents and gifts to find solutions to societal problems and help elevate the human condition. We also need strong leaders and visionaries to step up to the plate and lead by example, demonstrating that their actions are consistent with their professed principles; and we are fortunate to have many such individuals around the world, whose hard work and efforts in a variety of fields are making a difference every day in the lives of others.

I remain hopeful and have faith in humankind that we will do what is necessary to secure our future – not just for ourselves but for future generations – for after all, as the adage goes, "The true meaning of life is to plant trees under whose shade you do not expect to sit."

–Mayor Hazel McCallion, CM, LLD,
City of Mississauga (Ontario, Canada)

RICHARD A. MULLER

Global warming is real, human-caused and dangerous. Yet I believe that humans will not only survive but thrive. My optimism derives from three paradoxical phenomena: the growth of the world population, our terrible waste of energy and our apparently unlimited resources of natural gas.

Human population: The rate of growth is dramatically slowing, and demographers believe it will likely limit itself to nine billion, for the happiest of reasons: liberation of women, improved standard of living, better education and high childhood survival.

Waste of energy: I'm optimistic because there is so much room for improvement. Energy efficiency has increased at 1 per cent to 6 per cent per year for many decades and can continue at such rates for another 100 years. Combined with the population limit, the math shows that by 2100 the globe (including India and Africa) can share the current European standard of living and do it at lower total energy per year than now.

Huge resources of natural gas: Thanks to these reserves we can drastically slow our use of coal. Natural gas produces one-third to one-half the carbon dioxide for the same electric energy produced. Projections show that most of the feared global warming will come from the coal growth of the developing world; if we can help it shift to cleanly produced natural gas, we can slow the rate by two to three, giving us time to make even cleaner energy sources (solar, wind, nuclear) cheap enough for the poorer nations of the world to afford.

– Richard A. Muller,
professor of physics at University of California, Berkeley,
co-founder of Berkeley Earth

PETER DENTON

Hope is a creative act. It is creative because it generates something new out of the daily chaos of our lives. It is an act because, through hope, the possibility of a different future is created.

We can work and dream toward what is possible, but only if hope leads the way.

❖ ❖ ❖

Every day for me begins with a glimmer of hope, as I look out my window and the sun rises on the oak trees. On the prairies, only the odd tree breaks the horizon, along with the windbreaks that mark the location of lonely barns and farmhouses.

The slow-growing prairie oak, the scrub oak, makes a poor shelter from the wind, however. Decades pass before a difference in size is apparent, while the spruce and pine explode into the sky and the poplars grow, spread and rise again.

The scrub oak has none of the beauty of its foreign cousins, the red and white oaks. It will never be sawn into planks for shipbuilding, turned into beautiful flooring or sturdy furniture. It is gnarled and stunted, never growing more than a few feet before twisting off in a new direction and frustrating any craftsman's intention.

Yet, through centuries of harsh winters and scorching summers, rain and drought, wind and storm, it survives. The trees in my yard are hundreds of years old, predating any European settlers, watching over my children playing as they watched over the buffalo grazing the prairie grass another world away.

I find my hope in that resilience, symbolized for

Photo by Peter Denton

me by the scrub oak but found at all levels of life on Earth, whether we can see them or not.

Hope is just as resilient in the human heart as the impulse to survive is resilient in living systems. That resilience does not excuse us from doing things that deny hope any more than it excuses us from actions that destroy life.

When the spirit that is in us aligns with the spirit found deep within the Earth, green will no longer be just a colour.

– Peter Denton,
writer, teacher, United Church of Canada minister,
author of *Gift Ecology: Reimagining a Sustainable World*

TESSA TENNANT

Have you ever played that team-building game where everyone is invited to write down the meaning of a simple word like "money" or "family" or "life"? The point of the game is to illustrate the diversity of ways in which people think and associate with ideas. Our personal mental maps are all so different, like our thumbprints, and it's a wonder and a puzzle that human beings have achieved so much collectively. Against all the odds of confusion, ignorance, fear and greed we still make mostly good things happen.

This gives me great hope. In my lifetime ecological living has moved from the hippiesphere to the high street and is having ever more sway in the corridors of power. Yes, 9/11 and the credit crunch have been big setbacks but they haven't stopped this march of progress. Apart from an asteroid hitting the Earth or some bonkers tyrant hitting the nuclear button, nothing will.

Somehow we will muddle through. We won't be like the cooking frog: we aren't falling asleep as the water gets warmer; we are scrambling to get out of the pot and turn off the gas. Indeed more of us are scrambling every day and a bunch of us have even got as far as figuring out the gas controls!

We must reject the dead hand of fatalism, which never got humans anywhere. There is hope, as the prophets always say; "live for the moment" and enjoy being part of the green revolution. The best is yet to come.

– Tessa Tennant,
fixer, sustainable finance pioneer

JOEL SALATIN

While civilization has never tried nor thought itself more able to sever its ecological umbilical cord, never before have we had the capacity to re-attach it as quickly. As a beyond-organic farmer, I believe the techno-gadgetry that is available today to massage the ecology into dramatic healing is almost miraculous. From computer microchipped solar-electric fence energizers to shuttle-shift, low-profile diesel tractors with front-end loaders, ecology-enhancing food production infrastructure and techniques would make grandpa speechless with amazement.

The local-food tsunami represents a profound culture shift as people rediscover truly community-based food systems and the delight of cultivating domestic culinary arts. The only way to thwart this movement is to continue taxing people to death so families have difficulty staying home to redirect their creativity toward building a secure home economy. In addition to taxes, the food police are systematically marginalizing, criminalizing and demonizing heritage-based production and processing systems.

When Coca-Cola, Twinkies and Froot Loops are considered safe while raw milk, Aunt Matilda's homemade pickles, and compost-grown tomatoes are labelled unsafe by the government food police, the civilization is on a collision course with its ecological umbilical cord. When the freedom of choice movement extends beyond marriage, sexual orientation and education to include food, we will unleash the entrepreneurial creativity of thousands in their kitchens and on acreages. The impediment to redirecting our U.S. ship of state is not technology, resources, people, money or spirit. The impediment is confiscatory taxes to pay for big government to extend concessions and welfare to the largest corporate players – many with evil agendas – in our world. As each of us refuses to patronize evil systems, we inevitably create healing: of soil, nutrition, finances, emotion. We can do this.

– Joel Salatin,
author, lecturer, owner/operator of Polyface Farms
www.polyfacefarms.com

BRYAN WELCH

The question of our survival is uninteresting and uninspiring. Human survival is, from the human perspective, imperative. That's not an aspiration. That's just instinct. Our instinct for self-preservation may support the exploitation of resources and the deterioration of our habitat. It seems likely we could survive for millennia, but under what conditions?

Future human generations can live in ways that are more satisfying, healthier, more prosperous, fairer, more beautiful and more abundant. We can create a natural environment that's healthier, more diverse and more verdant than the Earth today. To realize that potential, however, we must first visualize our aspirations. We need a concrete collective vision of a better world.

I imagine a world where biological diversity is considered a fundamental asset, where an abundance of species is valued above all other ecological values and where we preserve vast swaths of natural habitat to guarantee the plenitude of life. Commerce can be motivated by social justice and environmental preservation as well as by simple value for money. Universal human tolerance can become a fundamental component of civilization. Violence, slavery and human exploitation may be universally vilified.

We've already made significant progress toward these goals. So far, we've done a pretty good job of realizing our ideals in the world. We are less violent, more tolerant and more conscientious as a species than ever before.

With that in mind, it seems more important than ever before that we have great aspirations and the courage to describe them. That is, I think, the foundation of sustainability – for the planet and its human citizens.

– Bryan Welch,
writer, rancher, author of *Beautiful and Abundant: Building the World We Want*,
publisher and editorial director of Ogden Publications Inc.,
publishers of *Mother Earth News*, *Utne Reader*, *Mother Earth Living* and more

FEBRUARY 13

ROB HOPKINS

I regard myself not as a techno-optimist, but as a cultural optimist. I believe that people can do remarkable things when they choose. I have seen time and time again the extraordinary things people can do when they get together with the people around them and decide that they want to start putting in place the future they desire. Whether it's community currencies, locally owned energy companies, new local food enterprises, neighbours helping neighbours to reduce energy consumption, or communities becoming their own developers, it's the missing piece of the puzzle.

The climate crisis is so grave that the solutions proposed need to involve a deep rethink of the scale on which we do things. A decarbonized future will inherently be more local and focused more on resilience and well-being than on economic growth. While government has a key role to play in this, there is much we can do to model in practice not only that such an approach works but that it meets our needs better than business as usual does. Our task is, through our deliberate and compassionate action, to make the politically impossible become the politically inevitable.

Creating the conditions for our survival requires the creation of a new economy, from the bottom up. All over the world, people are coming together to create the new enterprises that local economies need. They are looking strategically at how the boosting of local economies could be to the benefit of everyone, and at how community resilience is itself a form of economic development – indeed, how it is the most appropriate form of development for today. They are creating the new economies we will need and having the time of their lives in doing so.

Do we have hope? Hope doesn't mean much to me, really. It's about doing what is the right thing to do in these times, with a good heart. We can't do more than that. But Transition feels to me to be the most skilful thing to be doing now, and so that's where I put my energy, with the knowledge that extraordinary things are always possible and are already happening.

– Rob Hopkins,
blogger, author of *The Transition Handbook* and *The Power of Just Doing Stuff*,
co-founder/catalyst and outreach manager for Transition Network
www.transitionnetwork.org

ASHISH RAMGOBIN

Hope, in my opinion, is based on the desire and conviction a person has. My instinctive response to the global situation is, "Where have all the people gone?" We have become so driven by concepts, philosophies, methods and practices that the people quotient of our lives and world has slowly begun to disappear.

I have hope for the world because I believe that at the core of every human being and creature there is the instinct to survive. My approach to such survival is to work with a few people at a time, facilitating spiritual, human and sustainable growth, dealing with issues of greed, abundance and the need for more – and then jointly building a compassionate group, which will grow slowly into a compassionate society, and thereafter, with enough players, into a compassionate world. Dealing with large concepts like sustainable development, global poverty, disease, illiteracy etc., are tasks that depersonalize the issues we face; we learn best from example, and in living our compassion we teach it also. All that the world needs to overcome the current destabilization is compassion and the will of people to change their own lives. The changes we need in industry and in government can only come from the pressure of those they depend on – their market and their electorate. That means each of us.

My philosophy for changing anything that seems to be wrong or bad is to first look within and set an example for change. Our actions resonate with the conscience and heart of people and our words resonate with their minds; it is the heart and conscience that drive true, lasting change from within. I work toward touching the hearts and consciences of all people and toward hopefully creating a group of compassionate people who will over time evolve into a community and a world of compassionate people as they touch others' lives.

– Ashish Ramgobin,
founder and executive director of the Participative Development Initiative
at the International Center of Non-violence (ICON) in South Africa,
great-granddaughter of Mahatma Gandhi

PAUL MARTIN

Despite the plethora of international institutions, incredibly there is no global body responsible for ensuring national co-operation in protecting the health of the high seas, yet they represent over 50 per cent of the Earth's surface.

The costs of this gap to society are inestimable. Collapsed fish stocks are putting food security for an eventual world population of nine billion at risk. The UN's climate change assessment panel has reported that the oceans are absorbing more than 90 per cent of the heat trapped in the climate system by humanity's emissions of greenhouse gases. The ocean is also absorbing a quarter of our carbon dioxide emissions, which is causing seawater to acidify at a rate unprecedented in 300 million years, causing a staggering loss of biodiversity. These are only a few examples of what is happening each day in the waters beyond our national scope.

Four years ago the Financial Stability Board was created to deal with among other things the consequences of the international banking crisis. The crisis that will surely face us all unless we act to deal with the degradation of the oceans demands no less.

A global body ensuring the health of the oceans, if properly structured, would not only do much to ensure the health of our economies, it would also ensure the health of humanity.

–The Right Honourable Paul Martin,
former Prime Minister of Canada

CURT STAGER

I believe that the human race as a whole will survive these environmental crises because people throughout history have overcome severe challenges in every imaginable habitat, from burning deserts to polar ice, even without modern technology. But this also means that our descendants will have to live through whatever changes we set in motion within the next few decades. The latest research puts a minimum recovery time of 50,000 to 100,000 years for our heat-trapping, ocean-acidifying carbon emissions to dissipate, and any delay in switching to clean energy sources could stretch that recovery over half a million years.

In this remarkable Age of Humans, a new chapter of geologic time that many scientists are calling the Anthropocene Epoch, we have become so numerous, our technology so powerful and our interconnectedness so profound that we have quite literally become a force of nature. Because the contents of our minds and hearts influence our actions, we now have awesome power to influence each other and our planet far into the Deep Future. But with that power comes awesome responsibility, too; we live at a critical moment in history when decisions we make now can interfere with future ice ages and determine the climatic setting of life on Earth for millennia to come.

This is no time to give up or give in to despair. Although we wield incredible power to cause harm, we also have the power to make the world a better place, and more so now than ever before.

– Curt Stager,
climate scientist, author of *Deep Future*,
Your Atomic Self and *Field Notes from the Northern Forest*

BILL MOLLISON

Yes, there is always hope. Without hope we might just as well sit at home and prepare for death. Humanity will always find and discover ways past global and social crises. We thrive when challenged.

One answer for continuing to create the conditions necessary for our own survival and that of other species is to adhere to Permaculture principles taught by itinerant teachers who are graduates of our courses. When I travel, I am constantly reassured by the high level of activity of my students. They are teaching the practice of sustainable living and their work with cultures all over the world – from Indians in the Amazon to the Inuit of Canada, peoples from the northern islands of the Arctic to 42° south – is constantly ensuring their enriched survival. And they do this by teaching the basic skills that humanity has always lived by, namely responsibility and pride in the protection of our endemic fauna and flora; environmental awareness; growing nutritious food sustainably; storing,

processing and cooking this food; building shelters and sharing with our neighbours. Teaching basic, common-sense life essentials and re-establishing the importance of community will lead to our future survival and a world where many of us will take part in the production of food. By applying these strategies, our future world will contain many more well-informed and capable people.

We need to promote the good in our communities, praise positive actions and outcomes and stop highlighting the negatives in society. By being mindful of how we speak and act we will build hope and provide peace for our future generations.

Having taught the philosophy of Permaculture for decades, I am constantly surprised and delighted to receive acknowledgement from countless strangers who are reading my books for the first time. New generations always want to learn and develop better life skills, so there will always be hope.

– Bill Mollison,
researcher, author, teacher, biologist,
co-originator of the Permaculture design system,
founder of the global Permaculture movement

AMANDA LINDHOUT

We are living in a time unlike any other in history.

The Internet has connected us globally and reminds us that we have far more in common than we have differences. We can reach out and help one another in ways that we have never been able to do in the past. Students in Canada can now have conversations with students in Somalia. Women around the world can join movements for equality which are organized online. The sharing of struggles and success that is born from this interconnectedness will, over time, unite us.

One day soon we will no longer be able to turn a blind eye to the suffering of nations, when we realize that we are all part of one global community.

— Amanda Lindhout,
originator of the Global Enrichment Foundation

JONATHON PORRITT

Given the state of the global environment, we have to be a little bit suspicious about any excess of optimism!

Personally, I'm hugely skeptical about the latest wave of technovangelism which would have us believe that there is literally no problem that new technology cannot solve. Forget systemic dysfunctionality at the heart of our political systems; forget corruption and the ruthless exercise of power on the part of the world's hyper-rich; and forget all those inconvenient datasets that remind us that we're already living way beyond the carrying capacity of certain natural systems. Technology will solve all.

There's always been a certain optimism bias in the Green Movement. It's actually incredibly difficult to sustain motivation if the prevailing mood music is doom and gloom. Without hope, the passion withers; and without passion, the quality of our advocacy can be seriously undermined.

My own optimism bias has waxed and waned over the last forty years. It's often reflected through the metaphor of "the window of opportunity" – as in "we have just xxx years to make the necessary changes." Worryingly, I can't help but notice that I'm still talking about a window of "no more than ten years" – just as I was back in the 1970s!

However, I find myself more hopeful today than I have been for years – not least because I've been writing a new book about "our sustainable world in 2050." This has required me to drill down much deeper into the innovation pipeline for sustainable technologies than I've ever done before. And that pipeline is absolutely bulging.

Technology isn't the problem. Politics, money and power are the problem. Which is why the technovangelists do us such a disservice, fixated as they are by big technologies like nuclear and GM that leave untouched the bigger systemic problems of which they themselves are such a problematic part.

We can only harness the benign power of potential technology breakthroughs if our systems of governance and accountability are hale and hearty at every level in society. And they're not.

– Jonathon Porritt,
founder and director of Forum for the Future,
author of *The World We Made*
www.forumforthefuture.org/theworldwemade

CHUCK LEAVELL

I have always been an optimist, so yes, I believe we can meet our environmental and social challenges.

What does it take? Obviously it will take awareness first for us to fully comprehend what the challenges are and how to meet them head-on. Then it will require exploring the options and coming to a collective decision on which options are best and make the most sense both for the actions required and for economic reasons. We can solve these problems, but it needs to be good business to do so. And I've always maintained that it is good business to do so. The list of challenges and solutions is too lengthy to address in a simple statement, but good old common sense, in my opinion, is the best guide we have.

I believe people care about the future of our children, grandchildren and later generations. If we use common sense and a willingness to make the right decisions and take the right actions, we'll make it.

One thing is certain: doing nothing is not an option.

—Chuck Leavell,
conservationist, long-time keyboard player and
musical director for the Rolling Stones,
director of environmental affairs for MNN, the Mother Nature Network

ROMÉO DALLAIRE

Humanity is synonymous with hope.

There would be no children if parents did not see a possibility of a better world ahead. So we have children and they struggle to advance the plight that they were left with and they themselves, reaching maturity, express their hope by also having children. But a new wave, a sort of revolution has occurred over the last decade or so. And that is the realization that the youth of the world who are mastering the communications revolution so readily available to them have essentially morphed into a generation that I would call the *generation without borders*.

They are going to move the yardsticks of humanity towards its objective of serenity and communion with the planet by shoving older generations into a web coalesced by social media. The generation without borders grasps the concept of the totality of humanity, it lives with the notion that borders are not limits to their potential to affect the environment, they are comfortable in global concepts such as human rights, and they thrive in seeking more and more information on all things.

Hope is not a method, but optimism is the guarantor of humanity's serenity.

–LGen. (Ret.) Roméo A. Dallaire,
former Force Commander of the United Nations Assistance Mission for Rwanda,
Canadian Senator, author of *Shake Hands with the Devil*,
founder of Roméo Dallaire Child Soldiers Initiative
www.childsoldiers.org

QUINN VANDENBERG

For the past year and a half, our work with Life Out of the Box has focused on the social crises that are currently occurring in Central American countries. My experience of living in poverty here has led me to believe that solutions can be made and change can occur on all levels in humanity through education.

This belief that education can be used to change the world has shaped the mission of Life Out of the Box to what it is today. After months of research, we realized that an issue we kept running into as we worked with schools and NGO programs was that the kids didn't have the tools to be able to educate themselves.

To us, this was easily solvable, which led to the creation of the social venture Life Out of the Box. We sell locally handmade products from Guatemala and Nicaragua overseas and for every product sold, we give school supplies to children in Central America. When we give the kids school supplies, we ask each of them what they want to be when they grow up. Half of the process is giving them the tools to learn and be creative (notebooks, pencils, etc.), but the other essential half is to give these children in some of the worst situations hope for a bright future.

We show the customers overseas the child they impacted so that they can truly connect. Our goal is raise awareness of the issues in the countries we give to as well as show people that they really can make a difference.

What we are doing is a small contribution to the overwhelmingly large issues the world is currently facing. However, if we can give hope to just one child that helps them out of a desperate situation, then we have succeeded. My hope is that through our actions, we can inspire others to get out of their own box and make a difference in the world in their own way. Maybe we can't change the whole world, but there isn't one of us who can't change one person's whole world.

–Quinn Vandenberg,
co-founder of Life Out of the Box
www.lootb.com

CHRISTINE MCENTEE

Scientific research and discovery have brought us monumental achievements, such as improved weather forecasts, tsunami warnings, air and water quality monitoring, human flight, life-saving drugs, abundant food, and telecommunications that continue to revolutionize our exchange of ideas, information and culture. These innovations have protected us from natural and man-made threats, and improved the quality of our lives.

Yet, we face daunting challenges on a global scale as a result of human actions that are rapidly and profoundly influencing the Earth's environment and its ability to support us. In spite of our innate ingenuity, we have yet to fully apply scientific knowledge to inform solutions to these problems – from ensuring people have clean and adequate water; to providing communities with efficient and sustainable sources of energy; to preserving threatened ecosystems and biodiversity. Underlying these issues is the greatest challenge of all – to adapt to the inevitable effects of climate change and at the same time mitigate further damage.

Earth and space scientists and their colleagues in related fields are at the forefront of uncovering and explaining what has happened, and forecasting what is likely to happen based on sound scientific evidence and reasoning. Their insight is critical to informing rational decisions about our path forward.

Our long-term success in solving problems of this global magnitude will hinge on the strength of a joint commitment from the scientific community, business and industry, community leaders and government and NGOs, working together to make a long-term, sustainable impact.

For such a partnership to succeed, we are compelled to set ideology aside, to adopt a mindset characterized by a spirit of inquiry and dedication to continually seeking and implementing solutions. We must recognize that the decisions we make today will shape the world that we hand to our descendants for hundreds of generations. The gravity of that responsibility and the potential consequences of getting it wrong are too dire for us to delay action any further. The time to act is now.

– Christine McEntee,
executive director and CEO of the American Geophysical Union

AMITABHA SADANGI

I strongly believe in hope and in the fact that if we just focus on what "is," then probably we will never be able to think of what "could be." The term "human" (Latin = "wise man") includes in it "wisdom," which is not a lower-rung emotion, but a higher-order capacity to guide action!

Today's reality includes an unstable political environment and therefore a lack of desire for public welfare. This translates into action that probably is further promoting greed and a desire to possess instead of a collective understanding/action. However, I believe that this political environment is of our own making – and it is the most informed decision/action that I as an individual can take that will surely contribute to resolving these seemingly complicated "global issues": there is a need to deconstruct these issues and bring them down to an individual level of awareness and therefore action.

In my life of working for the smallholder farmers, I realized, from the very first day, the importance of connecting with each farmer and making an effort to understand their life (not just their problems).

From these interactions emerged their joys, sufferings, victories and challenges. This helped in identifying them not as mere helpless people out there but as entrepreneurs waiting for the optimum environment for their blossoming. An effort to respond to their challenges helped us develop this repertoire of technologies that best respond to their needs, with a framework for implementation that they could most benefit from and that could help them unleash their tremendous potential. A small start in a small village of one state of India has grown to fifteen states (and globally) today, and its recognition as one of the most important solutions for the global irrigation problem, water conservation, building food security and saving the environment. Who could have thought of this? The thought of over six million people walking with their heads held high is both humbling and heartening.

In my opinion, the need is to have belief in the inherent potential. This, coupled with appropriate direction and guidance, can definitely help resolve even the gravest of problems and situations.

– Amitabha Sadangi,
CEO of International Development Enterprises in India

DAVID ARNOLD

For humanity to find a way past our current global environmental and social crises we need to think and behave much differently than we do today. Our only hope is revolution of thought, moving forward one individual at a time.

This paradigm shift requires widespread communication of a message based on human evolution and moral responsibility as individuals, to change the way we perceive other individuals and the environment, with a keen eye on the spatial (geographic) context of the world in which we now live.

The message is based on empathy and survival. Empathy is not a learned trait, but has a biological basis to ensure survival of the species. Empathy involves a connection with other life forms, both human and animal. Initially that connection is emotional; however, in some cases we actively reach out and provide support. The latter is a requirement for survival of both our species and our planet.

The real question is, what stops us from taking that crucial step from emotional connection to actively reaching out?

While empathy is a natural evolutionary tendency, so is our mistrust of anyone or anything that lies outside the bounds of our own relatively isolated cultures. While distrust has served us well as a species in the distant past, we find ourselves facing a much different world today. Technology has advanced at a rate that dramatically exceeds that of human biological evolution, so that now, the tendency to mistrust or become aggressive against those different from ourselves is working against our survival.

Our only hope is to recognize our own biologically based biases, identify them when they occur, and consciously work to fight against them. Only then will we be able to recognize that any advanced life forms and the environment that sustains them, is a part of all of us. In other words, to ensure our survival, we must ensure the survival of all others.

–David L. Arnold, PhD,
executive director of Northern Alaska Environmental Center

JULES PRETTY

The iron cage of arithmetic is compelling: per capita consumption of natural capital rises, as does the total number of consuming people. Yet we know indefinite growth is impossible in a finite world.

At low levels of consumption, it is clear that a large proportion of the world's population needs to consume more – in order to meet basic needs for food, water, housing and health. But the average global citizen is consuming too much. If those without are to have more, then by definition those with too much must consume less. This is not widely accepted.

There are four options for divergence from current paths:

❖ major disruptive and technological innovation followed by widespread adoption;

❖ making possessions, places and environments meaningful and valued, and thus longer lasting;

❖ fixing pro-environmental and low-carbon behaviours into societies by cultural moulding; and

❖ a penetrating policy focus on the links between consumption and human well-being, and increases in investments in the green economy.

In such a green economy, other forms of consumption will be valued, such as of storytelling, walking and engaging with Nature. It will be co-operative, as it enhances social capital formation and reduces inequity: prosocial behaviours cause others to be prosocial. It will offer four options to citizens: resist consumerism by opting out (e.g., downshifting, voluntary simplicity), retain possessions for longer (before replacement), make different choices (ethical or green consumerism) and substitute non-material consumption activities (e.g., nature consumption). It will encourage spiritual consolation as a substitute for materialism.

A shift to a green economy is inevitable. It is simply a question of whether it occurs before or after the world becomes locked into severe climate change and other harm to Nature. On the assumption that *before* is preferable, then we need commitments by affluent countries to reduce their material consumption by a factor of ten; and commitments by all countries to invest in displacement technologies that improve natural capital whilst providing the necessary services to improve human well-being.

– Jules Pretty,
professor of environment and society at University of Essex (UK),
author of *The Edge of Extinction*, *This Luminous Coast*, *The Earth Only Endures* and *Agri-Culture*
www.julespretty.com

LAURA ELIZABETH CLAYTON PAUL

Should you need to be reminded that anything is possible and that this wonderful big world can be saved, you need nothing more than air in your lungs and a heart that is open.

Take yourself outside, watch the sun peek tentatively over the horizon. Light spilling, slowly at first, dripping, splattering, blazing, engulfing the dark night sky, a sky that questioned whether it would ever see light again. Close your eyes, feel its warmth, embrace the awe. This brilliance cannot be rivalled.

The solutions are already here, presented delicately by the Earth and her natural systems. Should we take the time to listen, we will find the cures whispered to us in her ever-hopeful song.

Buildings that give back: purifying their own water, generating power through energy freely given by the sun, creating thriving new ecosystems rather than destroying them. Transportation that uses our own strength and breath, allowing us to fully appreciate these bodies we are blessed with. Food that is not only nutritious but compassionate, that doesn't take life but, rather, gives it.

Change will accelerate as we widen our circle of compassion, noticing that the Earth's scorching crust is intricately linked to our wrinkling skin, and within the saddening eyes of her creatures we find our own.

There is a global crisis, but equally a mountain of opportunity. Nothing is impossible. There is always hope. We are the solution. It's time to show up ready to work, and push forward one seemingly small change at a time.

–Laura Elizabeth Clayton Paul, BEng,
Earth's pupil, eternally curious, change agent,
sustainable building and community specialist in Ottawa, Canada

STUART PIMM

So much of what we hear about the environment is bad news. I contribute some of the worst of it – it's my science that has documented that we are driving species to extinction 100 to 1,000 times faster than is natural. Extinction is irreversible. At least in theory, we can cool the planet to its normal temperature, restock the oceans' depleted fish and so on. We cannot create a Jurassic Park or even resurrect recent extinctions. I feel a keen sense of loss over the species I have seen but which are now extinct. No more, I promise myself.

To fulfill that, I must use whatever skills it takes to protect what we have left. Science is one such skill, but it requires so much more. And I must inject my science into the public debate, especially now when the media spews so much disinformation.

Something else: the world's tropical, moist forests are where most of the wild things live. They house the most species and the greatest number of species at risk of extinction. They've lost area almost as large as the continental USA in my lifetime. Meanwhile, we've put billions of tons of greenhouse gases into the atmosphere, causing untold economic harm. We should stop doing so, for forests are worth more standing than as the barren grazing land so many of them have become. There's more! It's time to restore these lands, allow them to recover, plant them with native trees, heal the planet and save species.

– Stuart Pimm,
Doris Duke Chair of Conservation in the
Nicholas School at Duke University,
president of SavingSpecies
savingspecies.org

MARCH

ALEXANDER VERBEEK

Do you remember the story of Hans Brinker? He was the Dutch boy who stuck his finger in a leaking dike and stayed there overnight in the freezing cold until adults came to help the next morning. His courage saved many Dutchmen from drowning. I often pass the statute of this fictional character on my bicycle, since it is close to my house in The Hague.

In the decades to come, the world will need many Hans Brinkers. We need his commitment to save others from the forces of nature, and above all we need his innovative approach to adapt to the effects of global climate change. The concentration of greenhouse gases has increased, the atmosphere and oceans have warmed up and the amounts of snow and ice have diminished. Experts predict a rise in sea level in the range of 70 to 120 cm by 2100. This, combined with more extreme weather, will increasingly threaten coastal regions and cities all over the world. It would inundate agricultural land; destroy infrastructure; exacerbate urbanization, international migration and food scarcity; and threaten billions of dollars worth of global economic activity.

Whilst the science and the international negotiations on climate change can seem abstract to many, the impacts on health, poverty and international security are increasingly tangible. We are challenged by the growing power of hurricanes, by increasing water scarcity and by worsening food shortages. This challenge demands action at all levels – including businesses, charities, engineers, scientists and local, national and multilateral government organizations – with increasing coordination. However, adaption alone is not enough. The cause of climate change, the rising emissions of greenhouse gases, urgently asks for stringent mitigation measures.

And let's not forget the individual actions one can take. That could be me on my bicycle, or it could be your personal involvement by installing solar panels on the roof of your house. My hope is for a worldwide generation of Hans Brinkers that work together to stand up to the challenges of climate change, first by being unafraid to point their fingers at causes of the problem, and second by being brave enough to tackle them.

– Alexander Verbeek,
strategic policy adviser for global issues,
Ministry of Foreign Affairs, The Netherlands

Hansje Brinker Figure, by Olga de Kock

FRANCES MOORE LAPPÉ

I believe hope is a natural state of being for our species. It arises in us from our deepest centre – as an expression of life loving life, of life wanting to bring forth more life. If we feel disheartened, discouraged or hopeless, it is unnatural.

What's needed for human beings to be in our natural state of hope is not proof of some future positive outcome; it is only that we see possibility for positive change and see our place in that change.

And that depends on developing new eyes, new ways of seeing. Our culture tells us that the premise of existence is lack: lack of goods – energy, food, water, you name it – and lack of goodness, for humans are innately selfish. From this premise of lack we distrust ourselves and see ourselves in eternal, fearful competition for survival. Not trusting ourselves, we believe we're not capable of coming together in common problem-solving to end hunger or protect the environment or build peace. We turn our fate over to others and to a market that inexorably concentrates wealth – creating the very scarcity we so fear, no matter how much we produce!

Hope arises in us and for our planet when we break free of this premise, when we learn to "think like an ecosystem," characterized by connection and continuous change. We see that, as we align with the laws of nature and with all we now know about human nature, there is more than enough for all to thrive. We see that we can align our societies with Nature so that, as we model ourselves on the ecosystem's genius, every economic process feeds another in a continuous cycle.

With an "eco-mind," we see life and our place in it as full of possibility. We realize that the only power we don't have is whether to change the world.

–Frances Moore Lappé,
lecturer, activist, author of *Diet for a Small Planet* and
EcoMind: Changing the Way We Think to Create the World We Want

STEPHEN LEWIS

In 1988 I was fortunate enough to chair the first major international conference on climate change. We had between three and four hundred scientists and politicians gathered together over several days. The debate was of enormous intensity, and at the end of it a declaration was drafted, the opening words of which read as follows: "Humanity is conducting an unintended, uncontrolled, globally pervasive experiment whose ultimate consequences could be second only to a global nuclear war."

That's why I'm going to speak to you from the heart and as honestly as I can.

In my view, the only answer to this crisis is the most dramatic reduction in the dependency on fossil fuel and the discharge of carbon; everything else is incidental. We're in a tremendous race against time. This isn't some abstraction. In order to avert the crisis that is looming, we have to create global citizens. We have to create citizens with acute environmental sensibilities, with a profound and honest understanding of the issues at stake. The truth of the matter is that we have unleashed forces which are not being curtailed, and everybody recognizes that what is required is political will to reverse the process.

It is absolutely unbearable that young people are going to have to live with the consequences we have created. I've often thought, in my own life, that I should have spent a lot more time working on environmental issues. I feel a kind of insensate guilt and shame that 20 years ago I was part of a conference that forecast what was coming, and I chose to do other things and find other priorities in life.

I have three grandsons, ages 9, 7 and 2, and I can't stand the thought of what they're going to inherit. I'm not sure it's possible to turn around an apocalypse, but if it is, it will come through environmental education, and it will come through collective, skilful, principled and uncompromising leadership.[2]

– Stephen Lewis,
distinguished visiting professor at Ryerson University (Toronto, Canada),
former Canadian Ambassador to the UN

HELENA NORBERG-HODGE

I believe that what stands between us and a more peaceful and sustainable world are the ideas that underpin our economic system. That system – based on endlessly expanding economic growth and global trade – is concentrating wealth in big businesses and banks while impoverishing the majority; it is poisoning the air, soil and water; it is turning our children into insecure, brand-obsessed consumers; and it is leading to increased conflict both within and between nations.

We need a radically different economic architecture, one that goes beyond communism, socialism and corporate-led globalization. We need economic localization. Localization means increased employment, reduced waste and pollution, stronger, healthier communities and more accountable institutions.

The good news is that a shift towards the local is already underway, led by thousands of farmers markets, local business alliances and community banks.

But while the localization movement has been growing exponentially from the grassroots, there is also an urgent need for changes in policy: we need to shift the subsidies, taxes and regulations that currently support global business so that we instead strengthen smaller local and national enterprises.

Localization is not an impossible dream. If the many millions of people working to create a better world – from protecting rainforests to feeding the homeless – also address the economic root causes of these problems, then the movement for economic change will grow rapidly, and a better future will be within reach.

–Helena Norberg-Hodge,
director of the International Society for Ecology and Culture,
producer of the documentary film *The Economics of Happiness*

ANDREW BLACKWELL

It's too late to turn back the clock. Our environmental cataclysm is underway and there's no point in pretending we can undo all its effects. Think of humanity as an asteroid hitting the Earth: like an asteroid, we're transforming the landscape, changing the climate and causing mass extinction. And once an asteroid hits, there's no way to make it un-hit.

Weirdly, I don't think this is a pessimistic view. In fact, I believe passionately that the sooner we admit it, the better we'll be able to fight for a healthy environment in the future. All too often, the idea of "saving the environment" means saving some idea of perfect, unspoiled Nature. But that's little more than a daydream at this point. And I don't think we should spend this moment of crisis daydreaming.

Instead, we have to embrace the fact that we find ourselves in a very imperfect, transformed world. This doesn't mean throwing up our hands or paving over the rainforest – far from it. What it does mean is changing our picture of what "counts" as Nature, and it means fighting for all kinds of environments that don't seem worthy of our love. From an already logged forest in Brazil, to a smog-choked city in China, to an industrial waterway on the other side of town, it means being less sentimental about our visions of wilderness ... and more sentimental about environments we usually write off as polluted and ugly. In an era when human effects reach to every corner of the globe, caring about the environment may mean setting aside Nature-worship as we know it, while we strive to make already transformed environments healthier and more sustainable.

– Andrew Blackwell,
author of *Visit Sunny Chernobyl*

KARL-HENRIK ROBÈRT

It is a fantastic experience to understand worthy goals together – across disciplinary, professional and ideological boundaries – and to realize that we need each other in order to attain those goals. Conversely, it is sobering that so few of our leaders in business and policy know how to build full sustainability into their decision-making, and to shape their action programs, stakeholder alliances, economies and summit meetings accordingly. This results in attempts to deal with one issue at a time, often creating a new sustainability problem while "solving" another. And it leads into very costly dead ends and sub-optimizations.

We are now experiencing increasing costs, lost opportunities and bankruptcies in business organizations and even in cities and countries – bankruptcies that are attributed to inherently unsustainable decisions made in the past. What is needed today are decision-makers who are open to learning the crucial competence of strategic planning and the language that goes with it – a language which makes multi-sectoral collaboration possible at the scale required for success.

Luckily, it has been shown, in a twenty-year-long action research program with over 200 mayors and top business CEOs, that it is possible to apply a robust framework, built around a robustly principled definition of global sustainability following these actions:

❖ Aligning their respective organizations within the context of a sustainable global civilization (very concrete, nothing fuzzy here) and simultaneously stabilizing their respective economies by being more relevant for more sustainability-driven markets, reducing costs and gaining in brand values.

❖ Bringing in actors in their value chains and other stakeholders into joint efforts. Very often mayors and CEOs need to sub-optimize their action plans because other actors in the system do. This is a hurdle that the framework currently helps businesses and cities to overcome.

❖ Making better and more systematic use of existing tools and concepts for sustainable development.

❖ Turning to policy-makers and legislators to propose stricter economic frameworks and other support tools to help make the transitions even faster.

The Natural Step's mission is to disseminate the above framework to any forward-thinking governments, businesses or organizations to help bring themselves within the context of global sustainability, draw the strategic conclusions, and get going.

–Karl-Henrik Robèrt,
founder of The Natural Step,
professor at Blekinge Institute of Technology (Karlskrona, Sweden)

RONALD COLMAN

When we contemplate our world, seized by rampant materialism and reeling under multiple ecological, social and economic crises, it is tempting to despair. *And yet* the very bankruptcy of our present system is yielding a new openness and a profound and heartfelt yearning like never before for a genuinely new and sane way forward.

This yearning is no longer "pie-in-the-sky" wishful thinking. We have never had greater global capacity, understanding, material abundance and opportunities to create the change we need. Our scientific knowledge, communications, technology and productive potential are unsurpassed in human history.

In fact, the more life-threatening climate change, resource depletion and species extinction become, the greater the yawning inequities, the deeper the global economic crisis, the emptier the illusory promises of consumerism and the more ineffectual and corrupt existing political and economic structures are, the clearer and more obvious are the shape and premises of the new system that must emerge. It must clearly be based on:

❖ Fundamental human *sanity*: no need for "sustainable development" jargon; every human being simply wants the world to be safe and secure for their children.

❖ *Humility*: Recognizing the truth that we humans are part of Nature, and must therefore respect other species, live within the bounds of what Nature can provide, and tread lightly on the Earth.

❖ *Joy*: Celebrating community, our diverse cultures and our fundamental humanity.

❖ *Contentment*: Instead of an economy based on endless grasping, consuming, dissatisfaction and poverty mentality, simplify our lives to build an economy based on appreciation, contentment, equity and fair distribution.

❖ *Good governance*: The above are not abstract concepts. They can be translated into wise policy: from investing in sustainable infrastructure (like public transit, renewable energy and organic agriculture), to sharply reducing greenhouse gas emissions, to elimination of poverty and tax havens, to ecological tax reform and high luxury taxes, to instituting systems of fair trade, co-operative ownership, and payments for ecosystem services, to full-cost accounting and holistic measurement mechanisms, and more.

We *know* what to do. But the window of opportunity to save humanity and other species has never been smaller – we literally have not a second to waste. *And* the opportunity itself has never been greater. Yes, we can do it! *Now* is the moment! There will be no other!

– Ronald Colman, PhD,
executive director of GPI Atlantic

HAWA ABDI

It is only with hope that we were able to survive through the 23 years of civil war in Somalia.

There were so many dark days, days when we had to bury 50 children in one day, or when I awoke at four a.m. to treat a mother who had nowhere else to turn to. Sometimes at these moments, I didn't know whether I could go on. But I would go out and see the faces of mothers and children who are depending on my strength to carry on. These were women who were incredibly resilient, who had trekked miles with their children to escape violence. It is their strength that fills me still and inspires me with the courage needed to continue to help my community through the most difficult hours.

Hope requires that a community come together with respect and love for one another. It is difficult to survive by oneself. At the Hawa Abdi Village we were able to overcome the divisions that threw our country in disarray. For those who sought refuge at my village, I told them of only two rules: first, there will be no talk of clan division; second, no man is allowed to beat his wife. The strength of a community, bonded through respect for one another, can be powerful to overcome even the most persistent violations of humanity. From the heart of our hospital, we were able to deliver and bring up a generation of children with values of equality.

If we want to find a way past current global crises, we need to teach love, respect and equality amongst all. I believe that the world is one. If one corner of the world feels pain, the pain will travel to other parts of the world as well. The same goes for happiness. Throughout the civil war, the patients I treated all felt the same hunger and thirst. We need to be attentive to our brothers and sisters from different corners of the globe.

I believe that education is key towards this achievement. With education, each global citizen can understand and critically analyze what is going on around us. At the Hawa Abdi Village, we continue to keep the doors open to education, healthcare, clean water and food security. Today we are already seeing a brighter future in Somalia, and we will continue to keep hope alive in all corners of the globe.

– Hawa Abdi Diblawe, MD, LLB,
founder of the Dr. Hawa Abdi Foundation
www.dhaf.org

KEIBO OIWA

The age of crisis is a great opportunity for the downward shift from "excess" to "just enough." This shift, characterized by three "S" words – slow, small and simple – is necessary because of the enormous mess we're currently in, created by our own civilization with its race to get faster, bigger and more.

The motto of our new era is "less is more." In our slow descent, we stop overdoing and find ourselves having more and more time to enjoy life. We'll do less and be more. We will rediscover ourselves as human beings, not "human doings." It is a homecoming to our own nature. And this is a good reason to be hopeful.

Avoiding excess and knowing where to stop is required for every sustainable culture. That is another reason to be hopeful, as we are all essentially cultural beings. Do we need a miracle for our survival? Maybe, but the most profound truth could be found not in some remote place but just around yourself.

An 18th-century Japanese philosopher, Miura Baien, said, "What is really amazing is not flowers on a dead tree, but flowers on a living tree." Life is a miracle. And that is always the hope.

Finally, like that story of a hummingbird that keeps carrying a drop of water in her beak to the burning forest, there is something that drives one to act as if there were hope even in a desperate situation. So, there is hope.

–Keibo Oiwa,
cultural anthropologist, environmental activist,
founder of the Sloth Club and leader of the Slow Movement in Japan

TERRY TAMMINEN

There is a tide in the affairs of men,
Which, taken at the flood, leads on to fortune;
Omitted, all the voyage of their life
Is bound in shallows and in miseries.
On such a full sea are we now afloat ...
— JULIUS CAESAR, 4.3.218–222

We are on such a sea at this moment. We are on the brink and quite frankly the planet doesn't care whether we destroy ourselves ... it will keep spinning. The question is, do we have the collective will to materialize a better world when we continue to drive a living room on wheels and power our homes with flaming chunks of coal?

To materialize this better world I believe we must see all things as connected, unlike science, which takes things apart and studies them in isolation. That's how we are taught in school: to see animals, ecosystems, water, air, food, oceans and even the Earth itself as oddities to be understood as separate things – at best a fractured mosaic – without the perspective of standing back far enough to see how it all works together.

The Hopi people say that one finger cannot lift a pebble. The connected co-operation that we will need to thrive on Earth for generations to come will need many fingers acting in concert. This will be the successful path forward – finding some greater good to put before our individual need and doing something in service to that common value. If we are to move past our current crises we cannot, in the words of Shakespeare, allow ourselves to be in the shallows and in miseries because we didn't have the courage and commitment to take advantage of this moment in time when we still have the opportunity to change the course of history.

– Terry Tamminen,
former secretary of the California Environmental Protection Agency,
founder of Seventh Generation Advisors,
strategic advisor for R20 Regions of Climate Action,
author of *Lives Per Gallon: The True Cost of Our Oil Addiction* and
Cracking the Carbon Code: The Key to Sustainable Profits in the New Economy

TIM SMIT

The writers of the 1950s saw in their imaginations the technological world that we now consider normal. Then it was called science fiction. However, hardly a single one foresaw the social changes that were on the horizon: progress in human rights, gay rights, gender equality, single households and the dawn of an aging population that would remain healthy into very mature years. For me, the future is brighter than it has ever been because we now know many of the problems that confront us – communications makes it impossible to hide them – and 99 per cent of people in the world would like to be able to do the "right thing."

If we fry ourselves or create a world of such dysfunction that aspiration dies to be replaced by fetid survivalism, we deserve it. After all it us, we humans, that called ourselves *Homo sapiens*: the wise hominid. What hubris if we are wrong, but what a triumph if we can live up to it. I delight at living in an age that represents a new enlightenment, where the challenges we face are worthy of being met and the cost of failure is so great it will concentrate the mind. People still do beastly and stupid things, they always will; however what we have now, for the first time ever, is the mechanism that allows the good to get organized. This is, to me, the real spiritual power of the Internet, and why I feel hope burning in me like an unquenchable fire.

– Sir Tim Smit,
co-founder and chief executive for development of the Eden Project
www.edenproject.com

DAN PALLOTTA

Humanity can absolutely win, and the "non-profit," sector, or "humanitarian sector" as I like to call it, will be a major player in that contest, but only if we liberate it from the puritan constraints of deprivation that have held it back for so long.

We have to stop preaching to the sector to act more like business and start giving it the big-league permissions we really give to business. We have to stop being so prudish in our refusal to allow the sector to lure great talent with great pay packages. We have to stop being squeamish about introducing financial incentive into changing the world. We have to allow the sector to fail upward, so it can innovate. We have to allow it to market on the scale we allow Budweiser.

If we do these things, the sector can achieve progress on a scale we never previously imagined.

That will give hope to humanity in and of itself.

–Dan Pallotta,
author of *Uncharitable* and *Charity Case*,
founder of Advertising for Humanity and the Charity Defense Council

SHEILA WATT-CLOUTIER

I am confident the world can come together as one if we could come to know just how connected we all are. The world needs to realize that our environment, our economies and our communities are not siloed or separate, but are all connected by our shared atmosphere and oceans – not to mention through our human spirit.

I truly feel it is important to change the dialogue about effectively addressing climate change and the environmental degradation of our planet solely in terms of the loss of economies to one of *opportunities for a better world*. Moving citizens into action requires us to move this issue from the head to the heart – where all change happens – and reassure civil society that change will not be economically punitive.

The melting ice is trying to show us is that the service the frozen Arctic provided to the rest of the planet is now on the brink of destruction. In other words, the loss of these "ecosystem services" – whether from the white ice reflecting the sun's rays back into space, or our frozen land locking away methane gas, or our glaciers keeping water on the land, which as a whole serves as the "cooling system," the world's air conditioner if you will – already adds up to hundreds of billions of dollars. Therefore this connection works both ways: we can think not only about our economies in human or environmental terms but our environment in economic terms.

If people come to understand the Arctic as an important bridge rather than an inhospitable wasteland that has little to do with anyone else, it will help us to become more open to listening to the wisdom of what the melting ice is telling us.

Politics and economics tend to keep these issues in a "fearful" place where civil society feels it has no power over how the issues are being dealt with. However, I feel real power lies in individuals, families and communities as they become more aware that this issue is just as much about humanity as it is about industry. It is time to allow ourselves to see that our planet and its people are one, and to move beyond the rhetoric of politics and economics to one of the human dimension. Once we start to really "see" one another and better understand our interconnectedness, we will be able to feel more compassion. This compassion will translate into clarity, focus and action as to how else we could be addressing these common challenges of environmental degradation of our planet.

– Sheila Watt-Cloutier,
environmental, cultural and human rights advocate

TARA MCFATRIDGE

We have seen time and time again that the human race as a whole is extremely resourceful. My grandparents lived during a time when recycling, conservation and growing your own food were just normal parts of life. Even when I was young, gasoline was being rationed due to the oil crisis. Back then you didn't just hop in your car anytime you wanted to drive down to the local supermarket. Walking, biking and using public transportation were just what people did back in the day. They also hung up clothes to dry, had leftovers for dinner and made good use of everything they purchased. Nothing went to waste unnecessarily. You see the same sort of thing in many Third World countries. They know their resources are limited and they work together to survive within those limits. They do not waste what they have been given. Many people in First World countries have gotten so used to having certain amenities and resources at their disposal that they probably couldn't even think about living without them, or wouldn't want to think about it at least. If they pay for it, they have a right to use it or waste it as they see fit, right? That's part of the problem. It isn't a matter of not being able to do the things you need or want to do, it's a matter of figuring out a more sustainable way to do them. We have to think sustainably, e.g., renewable resources versus finite resources, conservation versus waste etc.

Now I know some may argue that the Earth goes through this cyclic stage and so there is nothing we can do about its natural progression. While that may be true, there are steps we can take to contribute to the Earth's longevity rather than its demise. How, and how quickly, we utilize Earth's finite resources will determine the quality of life we will have both now and in years to come. There are a number of renewable resources that need to become mainstream energy sources. Future inventions and ideas should be about getting things done without either using up the remaining resources we have or tainting them with harmful chemicals and toxins. It's our world. If we work together as a whole, then we can make the changes we want to see for the future: our own, our children's and their children's.

– Tara McFatridge,
author of *Biofriendly Blog*
biofriendly.com/blog

VELCROW RIPPER

Imagine a world where each and every one of us was committed to discovering who we are truly here to be, committed to unwrapping our gifts, to living from our deepest Being. Imagine a world where we support each other in that quest. Imagine a world where we are seen for our potential to Become – Buddha to be, Gandhi to be, Einstein to be. Imagine a world where we greet each other with compassion and an open heart – Dalai Lama to be, Amma to be, White Buffalo Calf Woman to be. Imagine a world where we thirst for justice and respect – Mandela to be, Joan of Arc to be, Aung San Suu Kyi to be. Imagine a world where we dare to be ecstatically different – Rumi to be, Mary Magdalene to be, Wonder Woman to be. Imagine a world where we stand up for the planet as part of who we are – ancient forest to be, rushing river to be, soaring eagle to be.

Imagine a world where each person reached just a little bit further, towards compassion, sustainability, harmony and creativity. Imagine a world that stretched even further, to the place where ecstasy lives. Imagine a world of celebration for life in all its joy and all its pain. A world where nothing stands in the way but fear itself. Where fear is just a passing fancy, replaced by unyielding hope, undying trust, indestructible vulnerability. A world where everyone and everything that happens to you is part of an extraordinary opportunity to learn and grow and evolve. Imagine a world that reflected back all the love in your heart, beaming right back at you, blinding you with its brilliance. Imagine a world where the extraordinary life you are here to live is here. Imagine if you could start living that life, right now. Your fierce love shining bright.

Another world is possible, this very moment, when we choose to live it. It begins with your very next breath.

– Velcrow Ripper,
speaker and award-winning filmmaker of *Scared Sacred*, *Fierce Light* and *Occupy Love*
www.velcrowripper.com

MICHAEL REYNOLDS

Trains gather people and take them to specific destinations.
They have opened up continents and developed countries ...
but they can only go where there is track.
If there is no track, the train does not go there.

The evolution of humanity on this planet has developed its own track.
Belief systems, religions, economies, political regimes, laws, codes, regulations ...
all have become "tracks" to our future.
These tracks have opened up continents and developed countries ...
but there is a problem ...
a changing planet and a growing population have created the need to go to places
that these tracks do not go.

There is a new frontier now ...
evolution beyond the tracks.

This evolution will require that every decision made on this planet,
by any jurisdiction, anywhere,
be made with the sustenance of all the peoples and all the animals and all the plants
in mind.

The economy, the corporations and other institutions will be placed in their rightful
positions behind the needs of the people and the planet. At this time, an
insignificant economy will emerge. This economy will be a result of the sustenance of
the people. Human equity will be found to be far more valuable than monetary equity.

Life will no longer float on an economy. Life will have its own wings.

– Michael Reynolds,
architect turned biotect, inventor/founder of Earthship

JEAN KILBOURNE

I'm looking at a photograph of my 24-year-old daughter, Claudia, that was taken in Thailand in November. She is playing with a baby tiger and she looks ecstatic. She went to Thailand on behalf of Daughters Rising, a non-profit organization that she and two other young women run. Its mission is to help girls in Thailand and Cambodia who are at risk of being trafficked. It's hard to think of anything that fills me with greater horror and despair than girls being sexually exploited and trafficked. But this photograph gives me hope. Because here is my lovely young daughter, volunteering to do such important and risky work, willing to see the darkest side of human nature – and yet here she is with a baby tiger on her shoulders and a broad smile lighting up her face.

And there are so many young people like her. Young people who teach school in dangerous neighbourhoods, who pitch their tents at Occupy sites, who put their bodies between the bulldozers and the trees, who put down their drugs and stay clean and sober a day at a time, who create dazzling art, who fight for gay rights and women's rights and social justice all around the world. I meet many of these young people as I travel around the country and the world giving lectures. And I hear from them in emails or Facebook messages they send after seeing one of my films or reading one of my books. They tell me what they are doing to bring about change. And they give me hope. Because they are doing this work with joy. Most of them are not succumbing to bitterness, hopelessness and despair.

These young people will find new solutions to old problems. They will create a new vocabulary (such as "the 99 per cent" and "LGBTQ"). In one of her most famous poems, Emily Dickinson described hope as "the thing with feathers that perches in the soul." I believe we can count on our young people to protect this precious feathered thing from extinction.

– Jean Kilbourne, EdD,
author, educator, feminist activist,
creator of the film series *Killing Us Softly: Advertising's Image of Women*

ODEY OYAMA

Protecting the environment does not seem to be a common goal that has been accepted globally. This position is evident in the fact that some of the major powers in the world have still not signed the Kyoto Protocol. Many people, institutions and agencies are still working under the impression that they have the right to continue destroying the environment. In order to cover up for their destructive practices, they offer to pay money or grants to people and communities in other parts of the world for the purpose of ameliorating the destructions caused by them.

It is difficult to believe that those who have contributed most to the pollution of the world's environment over the last one hundred and fifty years can ever come together to agree to reverse the trend. The Kyoto Protocol has been the test case. If all the industrialized nations had agreed to jointly sign the Kyoto Protocol, there perhaps would have been some hope. At the moment there doesn't seem to be much hope of any consensus.

In my view, therefore, humanity can only move beyond the present state of the environment if people develop the consciousness to reduce and control their large footprints rather than continue to depend on other people in other regions of the world to ameliorate the damage they themselves are causing in the environment through their selfish actions in industrialization and energy production.

– Odey Oyama,
architect, politician, environmental and human rights activist,
executive director of Rainforest Resource and Development Centre,
an NGO for environment and development
based in Cross River State, Nigeria

HELEN CALDICOTT

We are at a critical point in the Earth's evolution as the human species wreaks havoc upon Nature and upon itself. I sometimes wonder whether we are an evolutionary aberrant not meant to survive long because of our overdeveloped neocortex and underdeveloped sense of morality and responsibility.

In truth, to use a medical analogy, the Earth is in the intensive care unit, almost terminally ill, and we – you and me – are all physicians to a dying planet. Unless we can muster the same sort of dedication, knowledge and intuitive wisdom that we physicians demonstrate at three a.m. when trying to save our dying patients, it is clear that most earthly species will become extinct.

Education is the key, as Jefferson said: "An informed democracy will behave in a responsible fashion."

The trouble is that most western people and others are addicted to television, which, instead of accepting responsibility for scientific and political education, has been captured by corporations with intent to sell their unnecessary items to a supplicant public, supported by trivia and unctuous programs.

The Earth is now threatened with three major crises:

❖ the ever-present threat of nuclear war, with thousands of U.S. and Russian hydrogen bombs on hair-trigger alert to be launched with a three-minute decision time, which would initiate nuclear winter, a ten-year-long ice age and the death of most earthly species;

❖ global warming which gets worse by the year: by 2100 temperatures will be 6°C hotter, conditions antithetical to human existence;

❖ over 400 nuclear power plants scattered throughout the world, each awaiting possible meltdowns like Fukushima, each accruing thousands of tons of radioactive waste which must be isolated from the ecosphere for one million years, a physical impossibility.

Most politicians are scientifically and medically ignorant. In our democracies it is our responsibility to educate them and insist they legislate for life and not for short-term or long-term death.

They are our representatives and we are their leaders. It is time we roused ourselves from our couches and computer-styled indolence, to thoroughly educate ourselves on these issues and put our souls and bodies on the line to use our wonderful democracies to save the earthly magic of possibly the only life in the universe.

– Dr. Helen Caldicott,
pediatrician, founding president of Physicians for Social Responsibility, a part of
International Physicians for the Prevention of Nuclear War, which received the 1985 Nobel Peace Prize

GUY DAUNCEY

Hope is an extraordinary source of energy. It comes from the heart, and once running, it motivates us to dream new dreams. Let it slip away and everything feels – yes, hopeless.

We don't know enough to give up hope. That would be an extraordinarily weak-minded indulgence. As long as we are alive, we can imagine new ways to tackle our problems, and put them into action.

We know how to farm organically with good yields, how to flourish on a vegetarian diet and how grow our own food. We can feed the world, even at ten billion people. We know how to reduce our energy use and generate energy from renewables; there's a growing list of communities that operate on 100 per cent renewable energy. We know how to conserve water, how to build composting toilets that use no water, how to graze cattle so that carbon returns to the soil and how to save the world's fish by establishing marine sanctuaries. We know how to limit our population growth, how to preserve the world's forests and how to end war and violence.

There are no major technical hurdles that block the path to a peaceful, green sustainable world where we live in harmony with Nature. The barriers are primarily political and economic, so it is here that we must create a global chorus of new dreams.

Our ancestors built a global economy based on "ME," with private property, private wealth and private tax evasion. Around the world, communities are building new co-operative economies based on "WE," with new ways of banking and new ways of doing business in socially responsible ways that are often more successful than their counterparts in the "ME" economy. We can upgrade our democracies to make them more proportional, removing corruption and corporate cronyism. We can upgrade the global economy, eliminating tax havens and turning foul trade into fair.

All these things are possible. We just need to believe, and commit our lives to being part of a green, sustainable future. We have the intelligence. We have the skills. We just need the hope – and the determination.

– Guy Dauncey,
author, eco-futurist
www.earthfuture.com

LESTER R. BROWN

The challenge is, how do we get from here to there?

Oystein Dahle said, "Socialism collapsed because it did not allow the market to tell the economic truth. Capitalism may collapse because it does not allow the market to tell the environmental truth."

Our failure to incorporate the price of fossil fuels into the cost of climate change has led us to create an enormously costly situation for ourselves and certainly for the next generation. The trick is to get the market to tell the environmental truth. And the way to do it is to lower income taxes and offset that with a rising carbon tax. *No change in the amount of tax we pay*; but initiate this reduction and offsetting over the next dozen years, and in stages, so that everyone can adjust and plan accordingly.

We used to talk about saving the planet. The challenge now is to save civilization. Because if the number of failing states in the world keeps increasing, civilization itself will, at some point, begin to unravel. This is *our* challenge: saving civilization is not a spectator sport. It's going to require the participation of every one of us. And we're in a situation now where every day counts. We're in a race between tipping points – natural tipping points and political tipping points. Each of us must get involved politically, work on important issues and help to restructure the economy. Whether it's the energy economy, or the materials economy or the comprehensive re-use/recycle economy – the old economic model, the fossil-fuel-based/automobile-centric/throwaway economy simply cannot take us where we want to go. It will not continue much longer, because it is self-destructing. The challenge is to replace it with a renewable-energy-powered economy, one that has a much more diversified transport system, and one that reuses and recycles everything.

This is our challenge. If you like challenges, this is a great time to be around.[3]

–Lester R. Brown,
president of Earth Policy Institute,
author of *World on the Edge*

KEN PLUMMER

No Other Way

There's no other way.
That's what they say.

Economics must put money before people,
And medicine must put profit before health.
Education must put management before wisdom,
And religion must put war before love.
Technology must put machines before environments,
And politicians must put power before care.
We must follow the way things are done.

There's no other way.
That's what they say.

But what if economics valued feelings,
And medicine always pursued dignity.
If education aimed for the flourishing of humanity,
And religion wanted better worlds for all.
If technology looked out for justice,
And politicians put people first.
If we all just tried to be kind to each other?

There surely is a much better way
Than the one they preach to us every day.

– Ken Plummer,
critical humanist, emeritus professor of sociology at the University of Essex (UK),
author of *A Manifesto for Critical Humanism in Sociology*
kenplummer.wordpress.com

ROSHINI THINAKARAN

She lived on a farm on the outskirts of Hillah, an Iraqi city roughly 80 miles from Baghdad. Wrapped around her head was a red and white shemagh, a traditional headscarf worn by men throughout the Middle East. She did not speak a word of English and to this day I do not know her name, but the life in her eyes inspired me to document the lives of women in war zones.

We arrived in Baghdad on December 18, 2003. My official job was working alongside my boyfriend to build a media company. A company with the sole purpose of providing media support for the Department of Defense. Unofficially, I was on a journey of discovery.

The U.S.-led occupation had wiped out the only government Iraqis had known for decades. We

Photo by Roshini Thinakaran

worked and lived outside of the Green Zone, the home of the Coalition Provision Authority. Iraq had not yet spiralled out of control and we travelled freely. I travelled with a camera in the hopes of capturing everyday life images.

On a trip to the city of Hillah is where I first saw the girl in the men's headscarf. She was herding sheep and I wanted to capture that moment in her life. She looked directly at me and smiled. The life in her eyes was magnetic and her half smile peered through the metal fence separating us. It's as if she was as curious about my life as I was about hers.

I never went back to that place in Hillah, but I thought about her frequently. Did she go to school? What were her dreams for the future? It is not easy to explain, but the strength and hope I saw in her reassured me of her survival, even during the darkest times of the Iraq War that followed the U.S.-occupation of the country.

I left Iraq in 2005 and spent the next few years documenting the lives of women in countries torn apart by war, including Beirut, Liberia, Afghanistan and back to Iraq. The women I documented were from different backgrounds but they had two things in common: they had all gone through war and all of them had hope.

I'm not sure if hope is something we are born with or are taught. Sometimes I think it's a choice.

—Roshini Thinakaran,
National Geographic Emerging Explorer,
TED Global Fellow

LAURENCE OVERMIRE

Yes. The world is on fire. We are in the midst of social, political and environmental upheaval. Will humanity survive or will we throw it all away? Everything is on the line. That makes this the most exciting time to be alive – ever!

Is there any hope? Of course there is. Take a look in the mirror. YOU are the hope for the future.

Now, more than ever before, the world needs YOU.

But you're not alone. All of the good people of this Earth are now waking up. Every day more and more are coming to help us put out the fire.

Our children and our grandchildren and all our descendants in times to come are counting on us to do the right thing.

Now is the time when the whole world needs to come together.

It's all about love. It is our love for one another, for Mother Earth, for our fellow creatures that compels us to act on their behalf.

We are One.

We are interconnected and interdependent upon one another for our well-being. This truth has been expressed over and over again by scientists, poets, artists, musicians, philosophers and every great spiritual teacher. It is what Martin Luther King Jr. called "the interrelated structure of reality." It's what the Golden Rule is all about.

This oneness means that every positive action we take, no matter how small, will have an impact. Every act of love sends out ripples of love into the Universe. That's powerful stuff.

Each of us has different gifts and different ways to help. Each of us must do our part. There is always more and more that we can do. Find those who help and inspire you.

Join the Bucket Brigade! Get in line with all of your friends and neighbours. They come from all over the world, from all walks of life and from every religion. With love in our hearts, we will meet these challenges head on, and I think, I truly believe, we can save the world!

– Laurence Overmire,
poet, actor, genealogist, peace activist,
environmentalist, human and animal rights advocate,
author of *The One Idea That Saves The World: A Call to Conscience and A Call to Action*
www.TheOneIdeaThatSavesTheWorld.com

KLAUS BOSSELMANN

Sustainability means living within planetary boundaries. To survive, everything we plan and do has to be mindful of this imperative of natural law. Sustainability must therefore inform all our policies, laws and institutions. If liberty, equality and justice are the pillars of modern civilization, sustainability provides their foundation and roof – picture a Greek temple. Sustainability is missing in our current civilizational model. But for decision-makers to even ignore it now, i.e., amidst dangerous climate change, spells ecocide and is an insult to human intelligence.

Thankfully, history has shown that people will not tolerate ignorance for too long. More and more citizens live the truth now. They will prevail, first for themselves, then amongst their peers and communities and eventually across countries and the entire world.

This is my belief. It is the belief in the human spirit.

–Klaus Bosselmann,
Professor at the New Zealand Centre for Environmental Law, University of Auckland

TED GRAND

If there is one thing I have learned in this path of yoga and meditation, and the Moksha/Modo Yoga community, it is that there is always going to be an amazing friction between creation, sustenance and destruction. This looping, weaving dynamic is always going on, and not only in the human world – it is reflected in the animal kingdom, in Nature and in the unfolding of the cosmos. We humans, however, seem not to know how to control and balance these impulses, and so we create massive imbalance between our basic needs and the hunger of the ego. The status quo right now is definitely leaning towards reckless consumption and ambition, yet it seems like Nature always introduces something to force us to see our imbalance. Climate change, global pandemics and rising depression rates are but a few of the symptoms.

So, do I see humanity finding a way past these crises? Yes, absolutely! We just need to chill out, take care of our nervous systems, cultivate gratitude and reverence for the myriad systems that give us life, and reinforce the idea that if we are oriented towards peace, we will ensure our long-term survival (or at least better our chances!). Yoga and meditation make us more peaceful, so we become prone to making decisions that benefit others, including all of Nature: we buy less crap, we generate empathy and compassion and we see our planet as a gift instead of a commodity.

When we witness other people and communities that reflect this impulse towards calm and attention, it gives us tacit approval to effect behaviour that reinforces this relative peace. Yoga and meditation are but a sliver of a greater solution, but they provide a framework where we can become aware of our hunger and insecurity and transform them. We can then relax a bit and give ourselves permission to slow down and revel in our gratitude for the complex systems and deep wisdom that Nature possesses – *we see that we are not separate from that which gives us life.* Deep gratitude begins to arise. The more people who participate in this deep recognition, the better the chances are for all species to survive on this planet.

In summary, there is hope, but it won't come by just sitting on our butts. Unless we are sitting on meditation cushions ...

– Ted Grand,
co-founder of Moksha Yoga in Canada
and Modo Yoga International

JILL HEINERTH

I am a cave diver. I swim through the veins of Mother Earth, exploring the shadowy recesses inside our planet. The foreboding doorways of underwater caves repel most people, but I am attracted to the constricted corridors, pressing my way through the blackness while relying on sophisticated technology for each sustaining breath. This is my workplace. Within the darkness of my office, survival depends on subsuming both curiosity and fear.

I work with biologists discovering new species,

Photo by Jill Heinerth

physicists tracking climate change and hydrogeologists examining our finite freshwater reserves. Following the course of water wherever it guides me, my exploration has allowed me to witness new life forms inside Antarctic icebergs, skeletal remains of ancient civilizations and geologic formations that tell the story of Earth's past.

Underwater caves are museums of natural history that teach us about evolution and survival. They are portals to the mythic underworld of indigenous cultures and windows to the aquifer from which we drink. As I swim through these caverns measureless to man, it is not my own survival that I dwell on, but the survival of our water planet.

Sometimes I fear we will not rise to meet the challenges of our current global environmental and social crises. Then I meet a young girl who wants to make the world a better place. My optimism expands.

There is plenty of water on our big blue planet, but we are running out of clean freshwater we can afford. We all need to know where our water comes from, how we pollute it and how we can protect it for the future generations. We have to protect it from corporate interests whose success relies on commodifying and selling it to the highest bidder. Clean water is not just our greatest treasure, it is a basic human right. Helping young minds understand and embrace their water planet is key to our survival. We are water.

– Jill Heinerth,
explorer, filmmaker/photographer, author,
founder of the We Are Water Project
www.IntoThePlanet.com

ANDREW REVKIN

I long thought that the best strategy for sustaining a thriving environment was to envision, and then pursue, a future in which humans lived, worked, harvested, moved and played with a light footprint, leaving room for wild things and using a mix of traditions and technologies to limit impacts and regrets.

There's nothing wrong with visualizing success. But that implies that we know today what success 100 years from now should look like. More recently, I've shifted to an approach I think has a better chance, in a world of rapid change and enduring uncertainty, of maintaining a human relationship with natural resources and non-human inhabitants of the Earth that is productive and protective, but also agile and creative.

Rather than envisioning and pursuing some future shaped by my biases and traditions, I'm tending to focus on nurturing a core set of human capacities that give each generation the best chance of leaving the next one a relatively undiminished suite of options, while not relying too heavily on a precautionary frame of mind.

So what are the traits to cultivate in a sustainable society capable of working assertively on the environmental and social challenges with which we are faced? As I've distilled them, they almost make a rhyme: bend, stretch, reach, teach, reveal, reflect, rejoice, repeat.

Bend, of course, is about flexibility and avoiding brittleness in both structures and policies.

Stretch is about testing boundaries, via both exploration and innovation – sustaining curiosity and the courage to fail and fear.

Reach is empathy and maintaining a collaborative, communicative culture that is best able to share and shape ideas that matter.

Teach is nurturing in children the capacity to sustain the human adventure and cherish the home planet.

Reveal means sustaining the capacity for observation and transparency.

Reflect is analysis and follow up. Initiatives are often launched, but outcomes rarely tracked.

Rejoice means relishing the gift of life and humanness, with all its merits and faults.

Repeat is the discipline to avoid resting on laurels, to retest systems, examine conventions, to go back to step one.

In a world focused on numbers – gigatons of gases, gigawatts of power, billions of dollars and people – any work to shift toward a focus on capacities can work wonders.

– Andrew Revkin,
Dot Earth blogger at *The New York Times*,
senior fellow for environmental understanding at Pace University (NYC)

TONY JUNIPER

Five decades of working to resolve the environmental degradation and social tensions prevalent in our modern world have revealed the fundamental nature of the crisis at hand.

Meeting human needs while maintaining the fabric of Nature requires that we look at changing really quite massive forces – namely our economic system and its related consumerist culture.

This can be done. We know this because it has been done before. The world we live in did not emerge by accident; it was shaped by deliberate decisions.

Diverse groups must now work together to shape deep change toward a more co-operative society delivered through a different kind of economics geared toward the improvement of human welfare while keeping Nature intact.

Academics, campaigners, writers, business leaders, politicians, economists, psychologists and others can collaborate in building a new philosophical context based on reconnecting with Nature and fostering harmonious relations between people.

Like previous historic shifts, this one is likely to occur through a combination of bottom-up and top-down forces. It can be assisted with technology and entrepreneurial thinking, and, like other historic changes, will happen more quickly if it is based on positive ideas that are attractive to many people.

Many of the "truths" and assumptions that shaped our world are subject to increasing doubt, but positive change will only happen if there is a philosophical platform to fill the emerging vacuum. Building that platform and getting support for it is the main job at hand.

– Tony Juniper,
campaigner, writer, sustainability adviser,
former director of Friends of the Earth

SARAH HARMER

Like all of Nature, we humans are both vulnerable and resilient. I believe the key to our success and our survival is found in moving away from our individual quests and toward actions that recognize our interdependence and our moral obligations to each other.

I am compelled to hope, and am fortified in my faith in humanity, by the tremendous acts of courage I've witnessed in the face of danger and persecution. I have seen fear faced and overcome. I have watched victimized women stand up to oppression and impunity in the fight for justice and peace in Central America. I have experienced the changes that can happen in my own hometown when citizens understand they have a voice, and use it determinedly and collectively to improve the lot of their community. For generations, acts of selfless courage and commitment to the greater whole have moved societies forward toward racial integration, voting rights for women and legal recognition of rights for our natural environment.

When we shift our focus away from individual and material success and begin to participate in the collective care of our communities, our lives become more meaningful and more potent. It is our sense of responsibility to one another and to the myriad plants and animals that are our kin that must fuel our efforts toward implementing solutions to pressing concerns like the global climate crisis.

– Sarah Harmer,
musician, citizen

THOMAS PAKENHAM

I am an optimist. Today I am planting an oak tree. It's three years old and I grew it myself. Its mother tree was about 300 years old when I collected the acorn. This tree too could live to that remarkable age. Or it could die tomorrow if I fail to water it. What will our world be like if the tree lives to 2300 AD?

By then our two main problems – overpopulation and climate change – will be solved one way or the other. I feel quite hopeful that we shall see an end to runaway growth of the population. The Chinese population, a quarter of the world's, is expected to fall substantially in the coming years – the long-term result of the drastic one-child policy Chairman Deng imposed on his people. But I am not so hopeful that the world's governments will tackle the problem of climate change before it does irreversible damage to our planet. It will be many years before the western democracies, gulled by Big Oil, finally wake up to the reality that extreme weather is here for good. And extreme weather means more droughts, more floods, more hurricanes, rising sea levels. Meanwhile the consumer boom, based on an addiction to fossil fuels, will go on its merry way, and politicians will keep their heads firmly in the sand.

Fortunately my oak tree is naturally adapted to extreme weather. It will jog along, I think, until the world comes to its senses. Provided, of course, I remember to water it this afternoon.

– Thomas Pakenham,
author of *Remarkable Trees of the World*,
Meetings with Remarkable Trees and *The Scramble for Africa*

APRIL

IAN WRIGHT

Don't get me wrong. I'm not a depressing doom and gloom merchant, and I do believe that humans are the most extraordinary animals that have ever lived – especially when I think about all the unbelievable things we have achieved, all the amazing and inspirational people I have been lucky enough to meet. But when I look at what we have done to this Earth within such a minuscule amount time of being here ... we are screwed ...

Apart from breeding like rabbits, the world's population is run by the 1 per cent that mainly seek financial and personal gain and don't give a monkey's __ about any long-term global effect: "as long as the money's rolling in NOW, why care about the future?" And these evil creatures are never going to give up that kind of power to the likes of you and me ...

I feel a fight behind the bike sheds is brewing!

Or come away with me on my homemade space rocket in the backyard ...

– Ian Wright,
travel television host of Lonely Planet's *Pilot Guides* (aka *Globe Trekker*)

ALAN WEISMAN

There's only one indisputable answer as to whether we can escape today's global environmental crisis: nobody really knows.

Think of it this way: every day, some people somewhere decide to do something reckless. They have one more drink. Or try some new pill. Or free-climb mountainsides, or race in cars, or have unprotected sex with someone they can't be absolutely sure isn't lethally infected. Or they simply go somewhere or do something they suspect they shouldn't.

Nevertheless, they do it. Why?

Two reasons: first, there's an instant payoff. Immediately, you're drunker, higher, prouder, moving thrillingly faster, or you're more deliciously aroused, gratified and satisfied. It feels great.

Second, the odds seem on your side. Sure you could get killed, but people do these things all the time and survive. In fact, you've done them before, and you're still here.

So far, anyway.

And so are we. We humans spring from an ongoing process entailing an unfathomably intricate, natural infrastructure – one we've spent the past 250 years disrupting or dismantling by trashing countless of its components. So far, we're still around to relish whatever payoffs we've gained. But it's pretty reckless behaviour.

At some point our luck may run out. Me, I'd prefer we stop taking dumb chances. But I can't stop us alone. Together, we might.

I just looked: it's still beautiful out there. I can hear a thrush. Our damage may not be terminal, and much of it may be reparable.

Seems worth trying. Please spread the word.

– Alan Weisman,
author of *The World Without Us* and *Gaviotas: A Village to Reinvent the World*

BOB MCDONALD

It took more than two thousand years to see our planet. How much longer will it take to understand how it works?

An Ancient Greek mathematician made the first measurement of the Earth 2,200 years ago using shadows from the sun and simple geometry. It was the first realization that the whole planet was much larger than the "Known World." In other words, our ignorance of the Earth was far greater than our knowledge at the time. Today, even though we have seen the planet from afar as a single blue orb floating in the infinite blackness of space, our ignorance of how it behaves is as great as our lack of understanding about geography was 22 centuries ago.

The complexity and interconnectedness of the atmosphere, hydrosphere, biosphere and geosphere, as well as how they respond to human activity, is a new terra incognita. Despite all our sophisticated instruments and satellites, we cannot predict the weather beyond a week. No one knows where or when the next earthquake or volcano will erupt or tsunami will strike. We know that human activity is changing this dynamic of the planet, often in surprising and usually harmful ways, but exactly how this will play out in the future is still a somewhat inexact science.

To seal our survival in that future, we face three challenges: to more fully understand the dynamics of the Earth, to develop alternative technology and to control our population. The first requires science; the second, engineering. The third and probably most difficult challenge involves making intelligent political and social decisions.

For decades the environmental movement has adopted a warlike strategy against big industry, a white hat–black hat approach that pointed fingers at pollution, demanding new laws to keep the planet clean. But now that we have identified the problems it's time to get on with a new, co-operative approach, one that produces immediate tangible results. The business community has discovered that going green makes money. Consumers want clean, efficient technology, so it's a win for the economy and a win for the environment. Now is the time to innovate, to develop more efficient ways to turn wheels, cleaner ways to produce electricity and keep ourselves warm. The challenge is huge but far from impossible, and the economy need not suffer along the way.

Humans are most innovative when faced with a crisis. We have the ability to make tailpipes and smokestacks obsolete. We can control our numbers and reduce our environmental footprint. Ultimately, if we choose correctly, we can turn ourselves into a smoothly turning cog in the superbly complex and ever-changing machinery of our dynamic planet Earth.

—Bob McDonald,
host of *Quirks & Quarks* on CBC Radio (Canada),
science correspondent on CBC Television, author

JODY WILLIAMS

In his masterwork, *Don Quixote*, Cervantes wrote, "Maybe the greatest madness is to see life as it is rather than what it could be." Moving beyond the environmental and socio-economic crossroads where humanity stands today requires shaking this madness and giving birth to a common vision of a world of sustainable peace with justice and equality.

But creating sustainable peace, including environmental protection and sustainability, is not attained by contemplating doves flying over rainbows while singing peace ballads. Some of the most basic elements of creating a common vision rest on new conceptions of security built on a strong foundation of human security, not national security. Human security is based on meeting the needs of people and the planet, not one that focuses primarily on the often aggressive framework of the defence of the apparatus of the state – at huge costs to humanity and the environment.

Tackling that outmoded worldview must be the *collective* action of civil society and governments.

No one changes the world alone. Alone, thinking about all of the challenges in today's world, can be completely overwhelming and, worse, disempowering. But when we choose to work together in coordinated action toward achieving the common goal of sustainable peace on a sustainable planet, there is little we cannot accomplish. Each and every one of us has the power to contribute to lasting change, and when we choose to use that power together in collective action we can make the seemingly impossible possible.

Creating change is hard work; it is not impossible work. It takes all elements of the global community working together in strategic, coordinated action to make a vision reality. Change does not happen simply because we wish it would. It is the result of the hard work of millions of people around the world – every single day.

Building sustainable peace on a sustainable planet is not a utopian dream. It is possible. It is a wondrous adventure that we must all be part of to turn our vision into sustainable reality.

– Jody Williams,
Nobel Peace Prize laureate,
chair of the Nobel Women's Initiative
www.nobelwomensinitiative.org

JEAN VANIER

Since the discovery of nuclear weapons, the growing greed which can cause serious ecological disequilibrium and a possible breakage of global economy, the question of the future of humanity is put in question. Yet the history of humanity shows the capacity for our societies to rise up from horrible catastrophes. Each new generation seems to have new energies to face and confront – with creativity and lucidity – difficult and seemingly impossible situations. Nature seems to possess an amazing power of resilience. The human heart yearns to live: to live in wisdom and in peace.

Over the years, great men and women philosophers, scientists, artists, psychologists, politicians, people of wisdom, of prayer, of a deep spirituality have risen up as prophets of life and peace to show a road to hope. Mahatma Gandhi, Abdul Kfar Khan, Aung San Suu Kyi, Nelson Mandela, John Paul II, Mother Theresa, Etty Hillesum, Martin Luther King – the list is long and impressive. Millions of people are capable of following and discerning real leaders from dangerous dictators, mafia groups and incompetent politicians. Human hearts can be cowed and paralyzed by fear; but the desire for light, trust and freedom, and the need to live humanely, can break through these fears.

I cannot foresee the global future. I do have trust in human wisdom and goodness. Certainly we shall continue to live through times of pain and destruction. Half the world's population today live in pain, need and oppression. But our hearts will grow in new energies of love. There is a hidden power of love in the hearts of so many weak, crushed and impoverished people. A time will come when they will rise up to confront those who have power and money and possessions. They will show a new way. Humanity can change from the need of rivalry to the beauty of togetherness: the "I" transformed into the "we."

– Jean Vanier,
humanitarian, philosopher,
founder of L'Arche International

PATRICK HOLDEN

At this precise moment of our planetary evolution, many millions of mindful citizens are standing in front of a question: what actions, individually and collectively, could bring about the necessary conditions for a fundamental transformation – away from our present resource consuming, exploitative, globalized and materialistic lifestyles, towards a more resilient, sustainable and fulfilling alternative?

In front of a challenge of this magnitude, it is easy for an individual person to doubt their capacity to contribute in any meaningful way to bringing about such a change, especially on the vast scale that will be necessary. In this connection, I have found it hugely strengthening to come to the realization that in life, as in the universe, everything is connected, and the same laws that inform our present state and future possibilities are also operating in the wider world.

This is the philosophy of the microcosm and the macrocosm, with the individual representing the "cell" of the larger organism. Since both are united by the same organizing principle, it follows that their possibilities for future development are connected and informed by exactly the same laws. This idea has enormous potency, because it lawfully follows that if I change, the intelligence and knowledge that is contained within this action not only becomes an external influence on the system as a whole, but also, and as a direct consequence, will enable it to change as well.

We can apply this approach to our food systems. For example, if I make a deep personal commitment to build greater energy self-sufficiency and systems resilience in my hilltop farm in west Wales, or as a consumer I decide to purchase as much sustainable and locally produced food as is practically possible, these simple actions, amplified at community, regional, national and even international levels, can and will bring about the transformation we seek.

This is a message of hope, of empowerment which is always available and has the possibility of enabling positive change. These conditions can often seem hidden from me, but they will always arise when I bring my attention, both metaphorically and literally, into my own body, my own life, and I start from where I am.

– Patrick Holden,
chief executive of Sustainable Food Trust

MARTIN RUTTE

We all long to live in a world that works – a world in which we successfully solve our worst problems and move in a direction that nourishes and satisfies the deepest part of our soul.

By re-envisioning and restructuring our collective intention, what we hunger for is now within our reach. We *can* create a new story that encompasses, inspires and enlivens us.

This new story is the co-creation of Heaven on Earth and it starts, simply, by asking the question, what is Heaven on Earth for you?

Our answers are the basis of our collective and uniquely individual new story. Heaven on Earth already exists within each of us. Recognizing this, acting on it and asking others what it means to them, is how we're co-creating humanity's new story.

Some of us believe that Heaven exists after death. Here's another point of view: co-creating Heaven is something we can act on right here on Earth, today.

As surely as the seasons change and the calendar turns a new page, we are ready for our next chapter. The winds of a new era are being felt in every corner of our world. It is an age in which we discover what it means to be human and what it means to share our humanity.

What is Heaven on Earth for you?

– Martin Rutte,
international speaker and consultant, co-author of the
New York Times business bestseller *Chicken Soup for the Soul at Work*,
founder of Project Heaven on Earth
www.projectheavenonearth.com

HARRIET SHUGARMAN

Each morning for a moment as I gaze intently at my sleeping children resting in blissful peace, I am re-filled with resolve and hope. I remind myself that it's my job to secure a safe and livable future for them and to ensure that they have the opportunity to grow into adults, to fight for their future as I now fight for my own and for theirs.

Yet a game of chance is underway, with my children's future the ultimate prize. The stakes have never been higher, yet humanity is trying to "rig the game" against itself. "The emperor is wearing no clothes," but by not seeing this, we risk losing the game.

To win, we must teach our children and remind ourselves of three simple life lessons:

Tell the truth. Actions speak louder than words. Don't be afraid.

1. There is no longer any room for denial around the climate crisis. We humans are causing our climate to change. The science is clear, the evidence is overwhelming. End of story.

2. We must acknowledge and recognize that there is no bridge to a carbon-free future. We need to step bravely into the abyss, trust in science and the evidence and make the leap to a renewable-energy future, through our actions now – individual and collective. This will put people to work, grow the economy and begin to heal our planet.

3. We must look "truth" squarely in the eye and NOT be afraid. Scientists are telling us and our planet is showing us that we need to act. Together with our children, friends, family and all humanity, we need to move quickly and boldly forward to reclaim a livable future.

I am hopeful that the odds are changing, ever so slightly, in humanity's favour. More and more caring and thoughtful people are seeing the emperor in the full light of day, standing up to him and demanding that others open their eyes and see him clearly too. Together we CAN and must change the collision course we are on; there is no other option.

–Harriet Shugarman,
mom, activist, writer, climate reality leader, mentor
executive director of ClimateMama
www.climatemama.com

WILLIAM RUDDIMAN

Nearly all climate scientists (more than 95 per cent) who study modern trends agree that our planet is warming, largely because of greenhouse gases we have been putting in the atmosphere. Even conservative future projections indicate that staying on our current path will cause very large climate changes, harmful both to much of humankind and to many other life forms.

Scientists who deny this prevailing view are far fewer in number, have lesser reputations and are mostly supported by "think tank" money funded by some (not all) energy extraction industries. Unfortunately, this tiny minority view has misled many people. Historically, most people in the U.S. have trusted scientific opinion. But talk radio and many blogs are now filled with angry voices denying any human role in this warming. Astonishingly, many Republican politicians question or reject overwhelming scientific evidence that humans are responsible.

By now, the U.S. should be having an open national debate about ways to act: by reducing our carbon emissions, encouraging new technologies and planning for adaptation. But the flood of dirty money from a few entrenched energy conglomerates has muted this discussion.

Most climate scientists see this deadlock as a national disgrace. The only way to avoid a much warmer and potentially dangerous future is for more of our elected politicians to rediscover their ethical centers and act out of concern for the future of this country and all of humankind.

– William Ruddiman,
professor emeritus of environmental sciences
at University of Virginia

PETER CROAL

We have all witnessed at some time in our lives the incredible sight of thousands of birds or fish suddenly changing direction and flying or swimming in a new direction. How do they do this so quickly and why? The answer to this question is central to our own planetary destiny.

We are all too aware of the environmental challenges that face humanity today. The Earth has started to tweet messages that we are now paying attention to. These tweets come in the form of increased weather events, health issues and overall quality of life indicators. We are listening and responding.

The Stockholm Resilience Centre has identified nine planetary boundaries that sustain life on Earth. Three of these boundaries have been exceeded, including carbon dioxide in the atmosphere, phosphorus in our soils and water, and loss of biodiversity. Ocean acidification and access to drinking water are two boundaries that will be exceeded next. We know that our species will not survive into the next millennium if we continue on this path.

However, similar to the fish and birds that change direction in response to a threat, people the world over are starting to alter their behaviour. There are over 150,000 organizations in the world devoted to environmental protection; companies are discovering that respecting environmental boundaries is good for community relations and profits; and governments in many countries are shifting to green economy practices.

This incredible blue planet, third from our particular sun, is a perfect crucible to create life, and it has done so for over three billion years. People, in all their wonderful varieties of cultures, lifestyles and practices, are central to the kinds of life that will exist on Earth in the future.

The shift to a more sustainable future is happening. But, to make a more rapid shift in response to the threats we face – similar to the birds and fish we have watched – we need to take to heart an ancient saying from the Hopi tribe of the United States of America: "We are the ones we have been waiting for."

—Peter Croal, PGeol,
international environment and development educator

CAROLYN KRAFT

Today we spend more time looking at our phones than at the natural world around us. Yet the natural world is the very reason we can wake up every day and look at those tiny, glowing screens. Earth provides us with everything we need to live ... fresh water, food and shelter, spiritual and emotional sustenance. Just think of the last time you watched the ocean's waves roll in, witnessed a breathtaking sunset or hiked through the woods and felt at peace.

Despite the fact that our planet provides us with all the necessary ingredients to support life, we go about our daily lives with an air of indifference. We've lost sight of the fact that Earth is a living, breathing system that we fully rely on to survive. Not a day goes by that we don't use Earth's resources to sustain us. The question is, what are we doing to help sustain Earth?

Moving forward, we all must embrace a caretaker mentality. It's the little things we do on a consistent basis that have a positive ripple effect on our planet. Picking up trash in our communities prevents it from being washed into local waterways and the ocean where it harms wildlife. Eating sustainable seafood keeps ocean ecosystems healthy and marine life populations thriving for future generations. Using reusable totes for shopping reduces waste and prevents plastic bags from ending up in the environment.

So let's spend more time being caretakers and less time on our phones! As we take action we'll inspire others to join us leading to bigger changes.

It's easy to feel overwhelmed by the current global environmental and social crises we face, but as caretakers we can never lose hope. Where there's hope, there's fire and a burning desire for circumstances to improve and things to change. Our hope fuels visions of a different and better way of living, which in turn sustains possibilities for a brighter future that wouldn't be achievable otherwise. You hold your vision and I'll hold mine and together we'll create something beautiful.

—Carolyn Kraft,
blogger at oceanwildthings.com

B.K.S. IYENGAR

I am a yoga student and a teacher, and as such it is my duty to guide those who come to me to learn how to keep this God-given body and consciousness in a state of sanctity. This understanding and the method to progress is hidden in the yogika discipline, in which students must keep their external environments clean in order to keep their internal sheaths – namely the physical, physiological and moral – healthily surrounded.

I am also an optimist, and as such I believe that the present fear of global environmental and social crises must evaporate sooner or later.

No doubt the present-day attitudes of money-making people is to amass, and amass with no respect to their fellow beings. But like the spokes of the wheel that go down and come up, so is the life of the universe: that which goes down has to raise up. I believe in this, and that wisdom will dawn on those who exploit Mother Earth – as this exploitation will only come back to affect their own survival – and our collective survival.

– B.K.S. Iyengar,
yogi, author, teacher,
founder of Iyengar Yoga

DEDAN GILLS

They say there ain't no hope for the youth but the truth is there ain't no hope for the future.

— TUPAC SHAKUR, URBAN POET AND
PURVEYOR OF INCONVENIENT TRUTHS

The late Tupac Shakur could not have been more prophetic. There is no hope for the future unless humanity wakes up to its great calling. Never before in the history of our planet has the future of all life been imperilled as it is today. Scientists and various other experts all agree that the way we ravage the environment and each other is the reason we find ourselves in such dire straits. Ironically, therein lies both the opportunity and the challenge. The challenge is clear. The opportunity is that we will wake up in time to reverse our violent and bloody history of war, hatred and environmental degradation.

I see humanity entering into a period of conscious and intentional withdrawal from the hypnotic influence of modern, consumer-based culture. I see this new awakening led and inspired by the marginalized and disenfranchised people of the Earth. Many of them are already teaching us how to live like the forest that recycles itself and lives forever.

I see humanity declaring peace and ending our ancient war with ourselves, our beloved biosphere, and each other. I see us planting millions of trees across the Earth and having ceremonies and rituals that honour the spirit and memory of the dead and vanquished we have left in our bloody and tragic wake. I see us building new and qualitative relationships with each other and the planet as we lower the level of deadly carbon and raise the levels of love, compassion and community.

As we stand in silence amongst the trees in these tree-planting ceremonies, I see our tears of sadness and joy moistening the soil of our common humanity and germinating seeds of compassion, mercy and forgiveness that will blossom in a way that heals our collective suffering.

We are children of the stars and the Earth is our home! Yes, there is hope and it has already been born.

–Dedan Gills,
"soulutionary" and co-founder of Growing a Global Heart

PAM COOLEY

Humanity is dependent on the Earth and its resources. On this planet "we grow it, mine it, fish it, drink it and breathe it" – that's all we have to work with! How we do those things are indicators of humanity's collective intelligence and our values. I believe we can do better.

I think the survival of humanity depends directly on humans learning "collaboration" instead of the old paradigm of "power over" Nature or other humans. My friend Maggie, who grew up on a farm, has the best definition of collaboration. It is "people coming together to achieve for the benefit of themselves and others." I believe collaboration is the new "survival of the fittest."

True collaboration requires us to recognize "interdependence," meaning we are part of this massive system of interconnectedness where everything that exists is dependent on something or someone else. Collaboration requires us to recognize that our existence is an intricately woven tapestry of everything in our lives. Interdependence means that everything we do affects others and they affect us. Our understanding and scope of interdependence has grown with the evolution of technologies. We now live in a global interdependence because of technology.

All of us have our legitimate experiences, knowledge, perspectives, desires and fears. If this is true, then no person, group or country has the whole picture of anything. No person, group or country has the answer. We all have a piece of the answer. That's why we need to collaborate!

Our existence has always depended on collaboration and innovation; the difference now is that the effects we have are now global. We have a choice. We can collaborate with the resources the Earth provides or we can fight each other for them. If we fight, it will be our demise.

What do we need to become "collaboration ready"? I think it always comes down to personal daily choices.

Whether humanity survives is not the question for me. We don't know the future. What matters is, how am I "being with" myself, with others and with the Earth? Am I being kind? How am I making decisions? Am I ready to collaborate or am I ready to fight? Do I work well with others?

Hope implies that one has a combination of information and faith that leads to a positive outcome. Every day, I witness these human qualities. I am sure you do too.

—Pam Cooley,
social entrepreneur, practical visionary,
founder of the Continuum of Collaboration and CarShare Atlantic

SVEIN TVEITDAL

Whenever danger threatens, we tend to quickly pull down the blinds and settle for comfortable, short-term "business as usual" solutions. This represents a dire risk of failure. Serious climate changes are no doubt the greatest threat that humanity faces.

Global warming will most likely exceed 2°C above pre-industrial times. This represents the very threshold world leaders have decided that we should not cross. Regrettably, they have not proved able to produce a climate policy that makes 2°C a likely limit. And yet, even at this level of global warming, as much as 30 per cent of the world's species may disappear. Judging from today's rate of emissions, a 4°C increase during this century is *not* inconceivable. This scenario is truly a formula for a climate disaster that no doubt will threaten the very existence of humankind.

If we want to protect future generations from catastrophic climate changes, 80 per cent of all known resources of coal, oil and gas must remain in the ground. Today's societies have at their disposal *five times* the amount of fossil energy that is safe to burn. Although these reserves, technically speaking, still remain in the ground, they are, economically speaking, already in use. They are embedded in stock prices, and companies borrow money on their value. We can have companies in healthy balance, or we can have a comparatively healthy planet. But we cannot have both.

Of course there is hope, and we are able! But we must ensure that renewable energy gets cheaper than fossil energy, thereby making the market the very engine of the green shift. Today, fossil energy receives subsidies of more than 500 billion dollars annually, or more than six times the allocations to renewable energy. World leaders should agree on cutting subsidies from fossil energy and increase the support of renewable energy accordingly, thus truly boosting a rapid green shift. When we succeed in establishing a truly global grassroots movement, we will have the necessary power to combat the fossil industries' pollution before it is too late. But time is running out fast. With today's rapid rate of emissions, we – humanity – will have spent within the next 25–30 years the carbon budget that limits global warming to 2°C.

– Svein Tveitdal,
director of Klima2020, founder of GRID-Arendal,
former UN director

CARLOS MANUEL RODRIGUEZ

Definitely humanity can overcome the current global socio-environmental challenges. We need to recognize that poverty eradication, changing unsustainable and promoting sustainable patterns of consumption and production, and protecting and managing our global natural capital as the resource base of economic and social development are the overarching objectives of – and essential requirements for – sustainable development. To achieve the above we need to:

1. promote sustained, inclusive and equitable economic growth, creating greater opportunities for all, reducing inequalities and raising basic standards of living;

2. foster equitable social development and inclusion; and

3. promote integrated and sustainable management of natural resources and ecosystems that supports, *inter alia*, economic, social and human development while facilitating ecosystem conservation, regeneration and restoration and resilience in the face of new and emerging challenges.

My country, Costa Rica, is a good example of a nation that has committed to a new development path where all development policies must rely on a healthy natural capital. In the last 25 years, Costa Rica has tripled its income per capita and doubled its population while halting deforestation and doubling the forested area – proving that growth and social development can go hand in hand with ambitious conservation and restoration targets. This effort in protecting our natural capital has generated economic and business opportunities based on our condition as a global biodiversity hotspot. In Costa Rica, ecotourism and nature-based tourism are the main drivers of economic growth, generating $2.2-billion annually to the local economy. Locally, farmers and indigenous communities are being paid for the various environmental services provided by their forest in terms of carbon, water and biodiversity. This innovative financial mechanism known as *payments for environmental services* addresses market failures where environmental contributions are overlooked, and recognizes the value and contribution of Nature to human well-being and economic growth. Lessons coming from Costa Rica in terms of innovative sustainable development policies and tools can indeed contribute to abate global challenges related to climate change and loss of biodiversity and freshwater stocks.

The shift towards a new development model must rely on respect for all human rights – including the right to development, the right to an adequate standard of living and the right to food – and must also hinge upon the importance of freedom, peace and security, the rule of law, gender equality and women's empowerment and the overall commitment to just and democratic societies for development.

–Carlos Manuel Rodriguez,
vice-president of Conservation International,
former Minister of Environment and Energy for Costa Rica

VIVIENNE WESTWOOD

If we don't stop climate change now, we will have runaway climate change which will accelerate beyond our control. It will eventually stop at a temperature so hot that if you were to draw a line level with Paris, the land below that line will be too hot to live in. There will be mass extinction of all life, including us.

The first thing we need to know is what's going on, how it all fits together and how we fit in. Then we will know what to do. Climate change is caused by our rotten financial system. This system is designed to create mass poverty and to siphon off any profits for a few, namely big business.

This system is backed up by politics and by war. Everything is connected – the power structure needs its victims to prove its power and maintain it. Culture is especially important. We live in a global consumer society – no matter how poor you are, this is the ethic. Consumers just suck things up, whereas true culture is acquired by investing in the world, by learning all the best that has ever been shown, thought and said. From this you review and criticize all the received opinions and stock notions (propaganda) of the present age. Armed with knowledge, you think. *You get out what you put in.* Go to art galleries, find out the names of trees, read, etc. You will get off the consumer treadmill and change your values and aspirations.

Two things that are practical to do: support Greenpeace in its campaign to save the Arctic, and support Cool Earth in its campaign to save the rainforest.

We need to get out on the streets and campaign, therefore, because it's all connected – demonstrate whenever you can with specific NGOs in the hope that we can all group together in global demonstrations where everything is connected.

Climate Revolution! "Get a Life."

– Vivienne Westwood,
fashion designer, human and environmental rights activist
www.climaterevolution.co.uk

THE DALAI LAMA

These days, the environment – the source of life for all beings in the world, including Tibet, the Land of Snows – is undergoing extensive degeneration. At this time it is extremely important that every human being, according to his or her ability, consistently puts effort into ensuring the conservation and protection of this planet's environment and its inhabitants. ...

Peace and the survival of life on Earth as we know it are threatened by human activities which lack a commitment to humanitarian values. Destruction of Nature and Nature resources results from ignorance, greed and lack of respect for the Earth's living things.

This lack of respect extends even to Earth's human descendants, the future generations who will inherit a vastly degraded planet if world peace does not become a reality and if destruction of the natural environment continues at the present rate. ...

I feel it is extremely important that each individual realize their responsibility for preserving the environment, to make it a part of daily life, create the same attitude in their families, and spread it to the community.

Because of the material wealth and resulting environmental problems seen in the West, some people say we need to discard the modern way of life. But I feel this is a bit extreme. We must use wisdom and understanding to tackle this ecological problem. I am very happy there are so many experts from different fields to inform the discussions of these issues. ...

When you say environment, or preservation of environment, it is related with many things. Ultimately the decision must come from the human heart, isn't that right? So I think the key point is a genuine sense of universal responsibility which is based on love, compassion and clear awareness.

If we have a genuine sense of universal responsibility as the central motivation and principle, then from that direction our relations with the environment will be well balanced. Similarly with every aspect of relationships, our relations with our neighbours – our family neighbours or our country neighbours – will be balanced from that direction.[4]

– His Holiness the 14th Dalai Lama of Tibet

KENNY AUSUBEL

In this epoch of moving from breakdown to break-through, we're being called to reimagine civilization in the Age of Nature.

The Mayan people call this epic threshold the "Time of No Time." Ohki Siminé Forest, a Canadian wisdom keeper of Mohawk descent, describes it this way:

> *From here on, we're on Earth time.*
> *Mother Earth is shaking to her core. It's a*
> *time of madness, disconnection and hyper-*
> *individualism. It's also a time when new*
> *energies are coming into the world, when*
> *people are growing a new skin.*

The Mayan vision says that we in the West will find safe harbour only if we can journey past a wall of mirrors. The mirrors will surely drive us mad – unless we have a strong heart. Some mirrors delude us with an infinity of reflections of our vanity and shadows. Others paralyze us with our terror and rage, feeding an empire that manufactures our fear into resignation.

But the empire has no roots and it's toppling all around us. In this time everyone is called to take a stand. Everyone is called to be a leader.

To get beyond the wall of mirrors, the final chal-lenge is to pass through a tiny door. To do this, we must make ourselves very, very small. To be very humble. Then we must burrow down into the Earth, where indigenous consciousness lives. On the other side is a clear pond. There, for the first time, we'll be able to see our true reflection.

In this Time of No Time, we can go in any direc-tion we want – by dreaming it. Our dreaming can shift the course of the world.

That's our deepest well of resilience. The dreams are already within us. One day we may awaken to find ourselves living in our wildest dreams.

– Kenny Ausubel,
co-founder and co-CEO of Bioneers

LIZ HOSKEN

Creating the conditions for a future in which the entire Earth Community is able to thrive demands nothing less than a total U-turn in our thinking. It requires us, the architects of our global crises, to emphatically restore a respectful relationship with the Earth, our source of life.

To paraphrase the great Albert Einstein, we cannot solve our problems with the same thinking that created them in the first place.

Ecological and social crises will not be ameliorated by the detached, objective logic born of industrial governance and the reductive sciences. It is imperative that we change the way we see our world and our behaviour. But how do we rekindle a mutually enhancing relationship with our Earth?

Earth Jurisprudence, the philosophy of law, recognizes that Nature is our primary source of law and learning, and encourages us to align our actions with the awe-inspiring order of the universe. It nurtures in us a more expansive and generous human consciousness in which the Earth is experienced as a community of subjects who enrich our lives, rather than as a collection of objects to be exploited.

Such a transformation of our psyche will bring us back into alignment with our inner moral imperative which yearns to protect, respect and cherish Gaia, the Mother of all life, thereby ensuring the health and well-being of future generations of all species.

The great work of our time is thus the widening our circle of compassion to embrace the totality of life on Earth. Everything we require to thrive in communion once more already exists within ourselves if we are willing to be open to it.

—Liz Hosken,
director of The Gaia Foundation
www.gaiafoundation.org

LAWSON DRAKE

Do we have hope? We must have hope! Hope is the first response to the auguries of disaster that confront us daily. Not blind, uncomprehending hope, but hope that is grounded in a clear understanding of our present situation, hope that confronts reality.[5]

What is the current reality? Other contributors to this book have described it far better than I could do, and from a more vast perspective of knowledge and experience. My abbreviated concept of reality is that we have given "economic growth" priority over all else and that we regard our Earth and its resident species as source and servant of economic growth. We have lost the ethic of living with respect in Creation; we are no longer in awe of the intricate web relating ourselves to our fellow species and all species to the environment – the web we call "ecology."

Hope without action is futile. By what actions may we seek to realize our hope? A starting point is a concern for our fellow humans, for the myriad species with whom we share the Earth and for the Earth itself. We must recognize and seek to alleviate poverty, inequity and want. We must show kindness and respect for our fellow species: we must not over-exploit; we must replace, when possible, where we have taken away; we must seek to ameliorate and heal where we have done damage and caused hurt.

We begin at the personal level. We encourage others by our example until, together, we come to understand that what we call the "ecology" ranks higher than what we call the "economy" – indeed, that without the former, the latter is doomed. Then we must convince our governments of this simple truth so that they will be moved to create local, national and global policies that put the brotherhood of humankind, respect for creation and the assurance of our future at the heart of all their dealings.

Am I naive in my hope? Will I, in my lifetime, or you, dear readers, in yours, see any of my hopes fulfilled? Maybe not, but we shall have passed on in the knowledge that we sought the good, and that hope yet remains.

–Lawson Drake, PhD,
former dean of science at University of Prince Edward Island (Canada)

SYLVIA MCADAM (SAYSEWAHUM)

The spirit of resistance instilled within Idle No More has spanned generations since Europeans arrived on the shores of our people's lands. Idle No More is an indigenous-led resistance to ongoing colonization of indigenous peoples on Turtle Island (Canada), a resistance steeped in a sacred hope and dream for justice, freedom and liberation for all.

One of our most sacred and peaceful laws has been invoked as part of the resistance: nâtamâwasowin is a law carried by Nēhiyaw (Cree) people in times of great threat and crisis. Nâtamâwasowin means to defend for all human children of the world as well as future generations. Also nâtamâwasowin directs us to defend for the children of all animals, plants, water and the winged ones – every thing in creation that has a spirit. Part of defending is recognizing that we all want freedom, liberation and justice for our children. In my people's language, children are called "awâsisak" which similarly means "glowing sacred flames"; in this we must view future generations as sacred flames that must be protected, loved and nurtured.

The vibration of the Earth is out of balance. Our human actions and activities have taken us to a situation of crisis and threat to our humanity and creation. Now is the time for the world to reach into that place of a collective profound love and peace for all awâsisak and invoke nâtamâwasowin. The highest accomplishment for any person in the spirit of warriors is achieving peace for their nation, but an even greater achievement is to create a world of peace for future generations in a manner that sustains a vibration of love that is healing. It is not enough to say "I love children"; we are now called upon to take meaningful peaceful action in times of conflict and destruction to remember that our defending be layered with collective sacred love of all children. Let our actions unfold the future. Let us be Idle No More.

– Sylvia McAdam (Saysewahum),
Nēhiyaw indigenous knowledge keeper,
co-founder of Idle No More,
Turtle Island, Treaty 6 lands

VAN JONES

The chief problems our world faces today are radical social inequality and radical environmental destruction. But there is a solution. We can solve both problems by creating millions of green jobs to put people to work in industries that will heal both our economic suffering and the Earth.

The two big systems that most need change are in the areas of food and fuel. If we change the way we power our buildings and our machines, that will be the clean energy revolution. If we change the way we power our bodies, that will be the green food revolution. If we change both systems at the same time, we can create billions of new jobs and ensure that the 22nd century will be one worth living in.

It's time to innovate. The next wave of jobs must push the boundaries of technology with wind turbines, solar panels, geothermal systems, hybrid and electric cars, next-generation batteries and biofuels. Let's build energy-efficient homes, buildings and recreational spaces. Let's build the foundations of a fuel-efficient and environmentally sustainable world to leave to our children and grandchildren.

Our other challenge is the green food revolution. Today's big industrial farming model is based on poison and pollution. Thousands of farmers with invaluable wisdom have been displaced. There must be a space for agricultural workers in this economy. We should work for those who work the land to breathe health and life back into our communities. The organic and slow food movements offer not just a surer pathway to physical well-being but also to wealth and work for people in or around cities. If we commit to bringing local and organic food to every table, we can make innovations like vertical farms and hydroponics transform our urban landscapes.

An immense responsibility rests in our hands. It is time to assume our role as not only environmental stewards but stewards of the future – we are creating the world our children will inherit. Let's make it a world where we respect ourselves, our communities and the spaces we inhabit.

– Van Jones,
environmental and civil rights advocate,
founder of Ella Baker Center for Human Rights,
Green for All and Rebuild the Dream
www.rebuildthedream.com

OSVALD BJELLAND

We need to break the link between the pursuit of human ambition and the depletion of the natural environment. To move people and goods without warming the climate. To transform waste into a resource. To redirect consumption away from the accumulation of stuff. To power ourselves – heat our homes, preserve our food and light our lamps – without making our air unbreathable.

In short, we need to reinvent growth.

It is all too easy to dismiss these aims as lofty dreams. Yet they are no loftier than the telephone was during the last days of the telegram, nor any more improbable than the internal combustion engine was when the preferred mode of transport was the horse-drawn carriage. In fact, I would argue that it is those who call change impractical who are the impractical ones.

I believe businesses can and will be at the heart of this change, and that is why I founded the GLTE partnership, which connects global businesses engaged in the pursuit of resource-efficient, low-carbon growth. The partnership has a bias for action – conceiving and conducting projects that aim to enable businesses to grow in a new way, fit for the resource, climate and demographic realities of the 21st century. Through collaboration across industries, sectors and geographies, the GLTE partnership is working to show that the "unthinkable" – stripping carbon and other forms of waste out of growth – is not only a possible alternative, but also a highly desirable imperative, leading to a safer, cleaner world, prosperous economies and competitive, dynamic business.

Now is the time to act: the companies that get into the driving seat and push for a new kind of growth will reap the rewards as their customers increasingly call for ethical and sustainable business practices. And by collaborating, working with other companies across traditional industry divisions, businesses can make the changes that are required more easily, quickly and safely. I believe in human ingenuity, and that by working together, across business sectors, industries and geographies, the balance between our natural and human resources can be restored.

– Osvald Bjelland,
chairman and CEO of Xyntéo,
founder of the Global Leadership and Technology Exchange partnership

MIREYA MAYOR

At a time when we are we are losing species at an alarming rate, destroying our incredible planet and in the midst of an economic crisis, it is difficult not to feel inundated with thoughts of hopelessness and fear. But in spite of all this, I do have hope. I have spent almost two decades working with some of the most critically endangered animals in the world. Many of these species were on the brink of extinction. And yet, we have managed to ensure their survival. I have lived in remote, impoverished villages with little to no access to water or healthcare, where the local people don't know where their next meal is coming from. And yet, they find ways to survive day to day, smiling all the while.

Human beings are one of the most adaptable species on the planet and what we need to save our planet is adaptability: adaptations in the way we use our limited resources, and in the way we must prioritize the treatment and condition of our planet.

Nature's resilience and human determination should not be undermined. The destruction of our planet is preventable. Although humans are largely responsible for much of this destruction – pollution, deforestation and global climate change – we also are its best hope for survival.

– Mireya Mayor, PhD,
National Geographic Explorer,
author of *Pink Boots and a Machete*
www.mireyamayor.com

DAVID QUILTY

As innovative as humans have proven themselves to be over time, I do believe we can find a path through our environmental issues – but only if we accept the fact that they are actually happening.

With climate deniers prophesying from their comfortable perches and media outlets offering up their opinion as fact, it can be difficult for the average global citizen to hear the truth about what dire straits we are currently in and will be facing in the near future. Once the majority of civilization understands this, it is my opinion that we will be able to mobilize and use our vast scientific abilities to overcome anything.

Whether it means we are somehow able to geo-engineer our way around dramatic changes to the climate or we work to make life habitable on Earth while living with the coming changes, success depends on educating the population with facts and not rhetoric. As a unit, the human race responds to the truth and there is strength in numbers. Above everything else, education is key to our survival; without it, we won't be able to make the collective, worldwide effort to find the solutions we need to adapt and survive.

We can do this, but it's going to take a majority to make it happen. Let's get to work.

– David Quilty,
publisher of *The Good Human*
www.thegoodhuman.com

SARAH TAWAKA

Planet Earth is a treasury depository from which humanity – the most powerful group of beings on Earth – draws most of its raw and natural resource materials, which then drive powerful economies of the world. The human race depends on Earth for its survival and for the survival of other species. For centuries, humankind has been drawing from planet Earth. It is about time humanity realizes the exhaustion of its reserves due to overdrawing capital assets from planet Earth. It is time for us to *invest* in planet Earth to ensure the survival of humanity and all species.

The human race is innovative, creative, dynamic and above all possesses HOPE! And yet, even though we have seen triumph over adversities throughout the centuries, a new crisis is now at hand, environmental and social. In order to properly address this crisis, *humanity needs to invest in planet Earth*.

With a hopeful outlook, interventions at the regional, national and global level are calling for practical actions with the objective of creating a future for every living organism – which will in turn ensure the continued survival of the human species. This future will be enabled by reinventing humanity's wheel of life and shifting from the business as usual attitude. This future includes the equitable reallocation of resources and the benefits arising from the utilization of such resources. This future is encompassing and inclusive, and recognizes the values and natural services provided by natural-based capital. This future is emphasized by collectiveness and connectedness and the realization that no being is an island.

This is the FUTURE WE WANT. Deliberations at international forums are already negotiating this future, which will be cascaded down to national, regional and local communities.

It is a future for all on planet Earth! Collectively, we have hope, and humanity will rise to the crisis at hand.

– Sarah Tawaka,
independent environmentalist advocate,
Banaban Community, Rabi Island, Fiji

TREVOR GREENE

Humanity is already triumphing over today's crises through a combination of anger and wonder: anger at the way we've so fouled our beautiful world that will galvanize us to finally act decisively without dithering, and childlike wonder that sparks miracles like poor African schoolgirls discovering they can power a generator on urine. There is a spirit of activism and hope alive that is personified by a quote, "The activist is not the man who says the river is dirty. The activist is the man who cleans up the river."

Mankind has realized that we are not the only sentient beings on this world. We have proven that great apes, dolphins and whales are self-aware, can plan for the future and recognize themselves in mirrors. Dolphins have saved countless people from drowning. Chimpanzees have lived for years with human families using sign language. These non-human persons have shown altruism in caring for others and have complex social structures. Our new awareness will hopefully make us more compassionate and responsible for the other sentient beings we share our planet with.

Ecuador has enshrined the environment in her constitution so that lawsuits can be brought against destroyers of Nature on behalf of rivers, forests and mountains. The Maldives archipelago is slowly being reclaimed by the sea but Maldivians are committed to carbon neutrality by 2020 and every child is educated in sustainability practices. There is an urgency there that can only be engendered by watching your homeland slowly being eaten away.

We must all be Maldivians. We must all feel the seawater rising inch by inch on our ankles. We must all stand as one and rage against the soulless corporations pillaging our Earth with impunity. We must all rant at the spineless politicos slavishly doing their bidding. We must all roar with one voice at the greedy bastards gang-raping the Earth: not on our watch.

–Captain Trevor Greene,
Afghan War veteran,
author of Canadian bestseller *March Forth*

OLIVIER DE SCHUTTER

We have overcome previous crises by thinking progressively bigger. We have cultivated more acres of land, sought greater economies of scale, ploughed more inputs into the Earth, brought more people to cities, opened more trade routes and engaged more people in globalized exchanges.

These efforts may have sustained today's burgeoning global populations, but only just, only unevenly and only at a huge cost for the planet, its ecosystems and the generations that will succeed ours.

The global economy is not only unsustainable, it is often irrational and perverse. It is a world where the speculative positions of a powerful trader in Chicago or London can trigger the stockpiling of commodities, global price hikes and more hungry mouths in poor countries. Where trade rules encourage developing countries to export raw materials and re-import the final product, paying for the added value. Where products travel thousands of kilometres just to be wasted by end consumers. And where we knowingly overfarm and overfish our land and oceans, foreclosing our future food supply.

We must become rational again. We must do everything we can to support smallholders to produce food for their families and for local markets, in the face of growing pressures to divert this land to intensive, large-scale, export-oriented food and fuel production. There can be hope, but only if we are duly skeptical in regard to those who promise hope in the shape of large-scale solutions. In order to think long-term, we may have to stop thinking big.

–Olivier De Schutter,
UN Special Rapporteur on the right to food

ELIZABETH MAY

The current global crises pose the largest danger to humanity and the planet since the Cold War and the nuclear arms race. The closest the world came to humanity exterminating ourselves occurred in the Cuban missile crisis. Since the end of the Cold War, leadership by Mikhail Gorbachev and Ronald Reagan has resulted in the end of the arms race. We have not eliminated nuclear weapons, however, and we must remain vigilant to do so, though the imminent threat has largely passed.

The most pressing global threat is the climate crisis. As the 1987 climate conference "Our Changing Atmosphere: Implications for Global Security" concluded: "Humanity is conducting an unintended, uncontrolled, globally pervasive experiment whose ultimate consequences are second only to global nuclear war."

We are rapidly running out of time to avoid runaway global warming. Global emissions of GHG must stop rising and begin their decline no later than 2015.

When the world is most in need of global leadership, we have Canada's government pulling in the wrong direction. And the U.S. under President Obama is experiencing the most dysfunctional politics in its history. Where do we find hope? How can we continue to believe a sustainable world is possible?

Choosing to be hopeful is an act of individual courage. The odds are not good, but we have a powerful source of support in the Earth itself. We simply do not know enough to give up, and it is arrogance to think we do.

Turning from the abyss and embracing a green and sustainable future is the challenge of our generation. I believe, because I must, that we will succeed.

–Elizabeth May,
environmentalist, writer, activist, lawyer,
Member of Parliament for Saanich-Gulf Islands (B.C.),
Leader of the Green Party of Canada

TERRY COLLINS

My generation is sleepwalking while sustainability crises are casting cruel shadows over the living world.

To my students I say, don't let oppressive jeopardies forged from our inadequacies crush you. Turn instead to wisdom, vision, courage, justice, ingenuity and self-discipline. These mighty weapons can overcome our indifference, incompetence and greed. Kill our unsustainable legacy at its roots. Our money-first-in-all-things dictum must perish or your world will. Jettison the crippling precept that only humans should count when money and jobs are at stake. In our better moments, we have produced some sustainable technologies for you – sustainable energy is already a significant reality in a few wise countries. Eliminate endocrine-disrupting chemicals that are undermining the nature of life itself, perhaps irreversibly.

Each country is a ship sailing the great ocean of time where sustainability is a direction, not an endpoint. Globalization is grouping countries into an ever-tighter flotilla. Find charismatic admirals who can inspire the whole fleet to cherish the living world. Appoint creative navigators who care not what peers think, but pursue first the welfare of future generations. Choose sober helmsmen to follow over the long haul the compass settings toward sustainability. Commission officers you can trust not to be seduced by money, tribute or political favors. Build for everyone on board full justice and equitable opportunity.

There is no place for pessimism. Human beings are endowed with the ability to hold the welfare of life and the future good as precious beyond compare. So let's reset civilization's compass accordingly.

– Terrence J. Collins,
Teresa Heinz Professor of Green Chemistry,
director of the Institute for Green Science at Carnegie Mellon University

FAHAD BIN MOHAMMED AL-ATTIYA

Science has spoken unequivocally. Unless substantial and sustained changes to our development and environmental models are made, our common legacy to future generations on Earth may well be the ultimate destruction of our planet.

Whether in the field of climate change, renewable energy, water management, food security or conservation, reneging on our commitments has become a tolerated habit and postponing our actions the new norm.

Surely, solutions to the various challenges that we face as a global polity are complex, transversal and difficult to enact. However, we no longer enjoy the luxury of time.

Brazilian legal theorist Roberto Mangabeira Unger once described the fundamental problem inherent to "social change" in the manner of a conundrum, namely that the goals achievable over a lifetime do not appear worth fighting for, while the goals actually deemed worth fighting for are not achievable over a lifetime. How does one, he asked, find the will and indeed the means to alter the status quo, when the "future" is not part of our cost-accounting mechanisms?

Part of the answer to Unger's riddle, I strongly believe, lies in informed, persistent and innovative public policy. Part of the answer to humanity's future rests on our ability to design holistic approaches – both tangible and intangible – to tackle the most pressing realities of our global commons. Part of the answer to the issue of trans-generational reforms ultimately remains in the power of our collective institutions and the unsuspected value that can be unlocked from smart governance.

The Qatar National Food Security Programme is my country's humble contribution in light of this predicament. It is a growth plan that seeks to balance the relationship between economic and population growth, reduce overall risk to the country and foster a diversified economy.

Designed for a country subject to severe resource constraints and unprecedented demographic pressures, the plan's solutions are based on the principles of security, system sustainability and private sector development.

May this kind of policy innovation find 364 additional echoes around the globe and play its rightful part in making our world truly sustainable at last.

–Fahad bin Mohammed Al-Attiya,
executive chairman of the Qatar National Food Security Programme,
Member of the Legislation Council of Qatar and the Board of Governors of the World Water Council,
chairman of the Organizing Subcommittee for the
2012 United Nations Climate Change Conference (COP18/CMP8)

PAMELA MEYER

Anyone who has taken a workshop in improvisational theater has learned the most important lesson necessary for a hopeful future. Improvisers, those courageous and playful souls who create entire evenings of theatre based on a single suggestion from the audience, have learned that in order to create something out of nothing, on the spot, they must say, "yes" to whatever they are given, no matter how outlandish or mundane. This "yes" is not the anemic variety of passive acceptance or disengagement, but an enthusiastic wholehearted embrace of the possibilities that will be uncovered and the adventures that will be had if we accept what we are given and build on it.

Improvisers have full confidence that they have all of the resources they need to create a positive future, because they do not say "yes" in the spirit of resignation or compliance, but with an attitude of inquiry and collaboration. Improvisers are not just saying "yes," they are saying "yes, and …" Before they have even set foot on stage they have made an agreement with their fellow players to accept whatever they are given and then add to it as they co-create a more interesting present and future rich with possibilities.

I do believe there is hope for creating this future on a global scale because I have seen it done hundreds of times in classrooms, community groups and corporations by people from diverse backgrounds and beliefs, who came together with the shared intention to accept what they were given and build on it. "Yes, and …" is a powerful facilitator of progress, even in the midst of significant differences. Improvisers have learned that they deny another player or the audience's idea, or the current reality at their peril along with destroying the trust needed for the players to continue to co-create.

The conditions, then, that are necessary to move through our current reality are to approach it with the same attitude of gift-giving as do improvisers in the theater. When we intentionally practise the principle of saying "yes, and …" we also create the conditions for inclusion, where there is room for all voices and perspectives to be heard and for all to build on the gifts that we bring to the party.

−Pamela Meyer, PhD,
author of *From Workplace to Playspace: Innovating, Learning and Changing Through Dynamic Engagement*,
director of the Center to Advance Education for Adults (CAEA),
president of Meyer Creativity Associates Inc.
www.meyercreativity.com

DAVID TRACEY

We have hope because hope is a strategy too.

We know the alternatives don't work. Extreme responses are no solution for troubled times, although some expect answers from fundamentalist religion or fascist politics. Apathy and cynicism do less harm but still not much good – certainly not what we need to turn the planet away from meltdown.

We also know big change is coming. Many fear it, but why not consider it an opportunity? We can do better than a world where one billion people have

Photo by David Tracey

no clean drinking water and three million children die each year from malnourishment. Lessons we take from this failed experiment can only help with the next.

But can we make it that far?

Hope says we can. And so does logic, if you think of what we can do as a species. We're good in an emergency. It brings out the best in us. It's when we discover how powerful, and how good, we really are.

Heroes are forged out of fire. A crisis is an opportunity for any of us to become something larger than ourselves. Look at the footage of people in yet another climate catastrophe. Volunteers filling sandbags are not gloomy. They're working. Together. In confronting the latest disaster, they're gaining a chance to discover what it means to be human, a social animal, bound to care about each other and our shared home.

It's too bad it has to come to a crisis so big the living Earth itself is at risk. It's also too bad there are still some who believe profit is worth risking the future of everyone. That's their burden. Right now, for the rest of us, we have a new world to create, and so many opportunities to thrive

– David Tracey,
writer, designer, community ecologist
www.davidtracey.ca

JOHN SEED

Of all the species that have ever existed, less than one in a hundred survives today. The rest are extinct. Extinction is the rule. Survival is the exception.

As environment changes, any species unable to adapt, change and evolve is extinguished. All evolution takes place in this fashion. In this way, a fish starved of oxygen, an ancestor of yours and mine, commenced to colonize the land. The threat of extinction is the potter's hand that moulds all the forms of life.

The human species is one of millions threatened by imminent extinction. While it is true that the "human nature" revealed by 12,000 years of written history does not offer much hope that we can change our warlike, greedy, ignorant ways, the vastly longer fossil history assures us that we can change. We are those fish, and the myriad other death-defying feats of flexibility which a study of evolution reveals to us. A certain confidence (in spite of our recent "humanity") is warranted. From this point of view, the threat of extinction appears as the invitation to change, to evolve. After a brief respite from the potter's hand, here we are back on the wheel again. The change that is required is a change in consciousness. Indeed, nothing but a revolution in consciousness can possibly save us.

Surely consciousness emerged and evolved according to the same laws as everything else. Moulded by environmental pressures, the mind of our ancestors must time and again have been forced to transcend itself.

The conditions for evolving a new consciousness must include fully facing up to our impending extinction (the ultimate environmental pressure).

We must now stop shying away from the truth and hiding in intoxication or busyness from the despair of the human, whose four billion year race is run, whose organic life is a mere hair's breadth from finished. Join in community to publicly embrace this despair and allow it to squeeze and pressure new consciousness into existence.

–John Seed,
founder of the Rainforest Information Centre

KENNETTE BENEDICT

With the unleashing of nuclear energy, we have developed a source of energy for economic growth, but we also have created nuclear bombs: a technology that can destroy the Earth and nearly every living thing on it.

Incredibly, and for nearly 70 years, we have survived this existential threat. How have we done it? What are the conditions that have prevented us from blowing ourselves up? Are there lessons to be learned that could be applied to other problems?

After World War II and the atomic bombing of Hiroshima and Nagasaki, scientists foresaw the dangers of a nuclear arms race culminating in a nuclear war between the United States and the Soviet Union. To prevent such a terrible war, these scientists established regular dialogues with their counterparts in other countries – even those hostile to them, and even at the risk of being called traitors. This same group of scientists, along with medical doctors, informed the public about the harmful effects of radiation from nuclear weapons tests in the atmosphere, and supported citizen protests demanding an end to testing. And as advisers and government officials, scientists also influenced and supported leaders who called for an end to the nuclear madness.

Out of these actions by independent scientists, informed citizens and courageous political leaders came the Limited Test Ban Treaty, the Anti-Ballistic Missile Treaty, the Strategic Arms Limitation Treaty, the Nuclear Nonproliferation Treaty and most recently the New Start Treaty. These treaties and their implementing agencies are the institutions of co-operation that have prevented nuclear war so far. And since 1992, working side by side, Russian and U.S. engineers, military officers and government experts have begun to end the nuclear arms race by reducing their combined nuclear arsenals from nearly 80,000 in 1987 to less than 20,000 in 2012.

While the threats to humanity from nuclear weapons are not over, we are beginning to create the conditions for our survival, including telling the truth about the dangers of nuclear technologies; building networks for communication, especially with our adversaries; and co-operating with other countries to dismantle nuclear weapons and relegate them to the dustbin of history.

– Dr. Kennette Benedict,
executive director of *Bulletin of the Atomic Scientists*
thebulletin.org

JOSEPH TAINTER

The collapse of our civilization is too gruesome to contemplate. Millions of people would die. Diseases once conquered would return. The wealthy alone would have access to education. Most of us would be farmers, often hungry, tilling someone else's land and living short lives (about 40 years) in poor health. Most people would die in infancy or childhood. No one wants such a future. Clearly we must find a path to sustainability.

Societies sustain themselves by combining ingenuity and resources to solve problems. Societies grow complex as they solve complex problems. Complexity requires resources, especially energy. Here is our dilemma: we achieve sustainability by using resources to solve problems, yet the rate at which we use resources is precisely our current challenge. Will we have the resources to solve sustainability problems? Can we solve problems using less energy?

Humans did not evolve to think broadly in time or space. We think of little beyond the circumstances of our lives. This is the scale at which we solve problems. Yet the challenges of sustainability are great in size and long in duration. Are humans intellectually able to solve the problems of sustainability? Can we develop ways of thinking that evolution did not equip us for?

Our first challenge is to understand how our limitations and inclinations undermine our chance to become sustainable. A sustainable future requires that we change fundamentally in how we think and act. That step is the most difficult challenge of all.

– Joseph Tainter,
professor at Utah State University (USA),
author of *The Collapse of Complex Societies*

GÖRAN BROMAN

Transformation of society toward sustainability both demands, and brings great opportunity for, innovation. Since there is no attractive alternative to sustainability, organizations that learn to innovate toward sustainability will have great opportunities for economic success while serving a higher purpose. By systematically reducing their contribution to the problem and by early-on becoming part of the solution, they support the transition in a direct way and become more attractive and successful in the increasingly sustainability-driven market. Doing this, they become good examples that also encourage others, both in business and governance, to be proactive and strategic about sustainability.

In this way, we get an accelerating countermovement that will hopefully overcome the current unsustainable development before we reach a tipping point of self-reinforcing degradation. To support this transition, we need new research and education. It is not enough for scientists to acquire more and more evidence of unsustainability-related impacts. Nor does it suffice to make more and better predictions of impacts should civilization fail to put a halt to unsustainable development. Nor does it suffice with psychological or sociological theories aiming at explaining why more is not done to stop unsustainable development. Finally, it is not enough to attempt to develop various solutions, in isolation, to individual sustainability problems. There is now a strong need for making much more and much better use of the great results from the above types of research.

Therefore, the next big challenge is systems science for cross-disciplinary and cross-sector leadership and innovation for sustainability. We need this to develop coordinated solutions so that they support each other and together result in societal change at a scale and pace appropriate for sustainability to become a feasible option for the future. To develop and promote this type of science, we have formed an international alliance for strategic sustainable development (www.alliance-ssd.org), aiming at providing ways of putting any specialist discipline in the context of, and to the service of, strategic sustainable development. We invite all who want to contribute to join this alliance.

– Göran Broman,
professor at Blekinge Institute of Technology (Sweden)

KATE DILLON

When I was eighteen years old my parents and I travelled to Alaska. I remember sitting on the banks of the small creek trickling past our cabin in the forested foothills of Denali, feeling awestruck by the wildness of my surroundings – the trees, bears and moose, the soil, shrubs and mountain peaks. It was an extraordinarily beautiful and formative moment in my life, and I understood then that neither I nor my species – however unique and intelligent – were as central to life on Earth as social conceptions instruct.

I had always observed that humankind was at best the Earth's steward and at worst its master. I believe the environmental and social crisis we now face is a result of this core belief, and decision-makers and thought-leaders must contribute to a new worldview, one of respect for the global ecosystem we inhabit. We can and we must learn to live our lives as a part of the natural world rather than outside or above it.

I have hope because we have come so far. When I was a high school student in the late 1980s, talk of global warming, recycling and eating local was fringe at best, reserved for hippie holdouts and eccentric vegetarian restaurants. Today these ideas are mainstream, and environmental consciousness is actually chic. We have proven our ability to change our most insidious historical practices, and while we cannot reverse all the damage done, there is ample time to be better human beings.

– Kate Dillon,
mommy, fashion model, environmental advocate

ERNESTO ENKERLIN

Today is a beautiful day and it is wonderful to be alive. Such awareness comes from being human and confers a sense of duty for maintaining life and making peace with Nature.

In such a day, and in times ahead, there will also be despair and sadness. This is part reality and part perception. Even in those moments we can find many good reasons to stand strong. "Hope?"

YES, hope based on real possibility to change the world. The future is what we make it. We can help to heal Nature so it continues to nurture us. We are increasingly interdependent and opting for the good. Technology and simple things like protected areas will make all the difference.

What can I do as an individual and influence others to do what is good for Nature and therefore for humans? Every day … every moment …: Inspire: What can I do? Expire: What can we do?

This Decalogue shared with students 20 years ago remains pertinent and practical to living and securing a space for Nature and ALL life in the Anthropocene.

These are just some ideas. I challenge you for even better ones but please … be part of the solution:

TEN THINGS WE CAN DO FOR OUR PLANET, OUR COMMON HOME

1. Seek, envision, apply and enjoy a lifestyle that is light on the planet. Repel materialism.

2. If you exercise your privilege to have descendants these should be at most two and brought up as champions for the planet.

3. Learn, recognize, promote and be willing to pay the real value for Nature's goods and services.

4. Work as a volunteer in your community.

5. Use your purchasing power to demand a better world.

6. Participate actively in restoring and healing Nature.

7. Demand from our leaders or be a leader caring for the planet and be true and congruent.

8. Photograph, paint, write, meditate, touch, observe and in general know, respect and love Nature.

9. Respectfully explain to whoever neglects the environmental crisis, becoming a joyful ambassador for Earth.

10. Live and persevere on the previous nine points (or your own list) and spread the word. Get others to join in!

CARING FOR NATURE AND EARTH IS THE BEST WAY TO LOVE THE REST OF HUMANITY AS WE ALL DEPEND ON IT!

–Ernesto C. Enkerlin-Hoeflich,
conservationist, ecologist, pragmatic dreamer,
professor of sustainability at Tecnológico de Monterrey (Mexico),
president for science at Pronatura (Mexico), chair of the World Commission on Protected Areas-IUCN
www.iucn.org/about/work/programmes/gpap_home

ROB DIETZ

In the early 21st century, humanity sits in a precarious position. Reams of evidence support a conclusion that's hard to comprehend: people are consuming resources at a rate beyond the Earth's regenerative capacity. Like Icarus, humanity is flying too high, ignoring the warning signs and courting disaster. The main question, then, is how to straighten out and fly right – what's the most practical path for achieving the good life on our one and only planet?

The dominant philosophy of nations since the birth of industrialism and capitalism has been *more*. More people, more production, more consumption, more technology, more income. Professors, politicians and pundits commonly tout increasing devotion to *more* as the way to solve our environmental and social problems, but it's a deeply flawed approach. There's no logic in resorting to the very philosophy that has pushed us into planetary overshoot. Instead we need to reconfigure our economic systems to embrace the philosophy of enough – we need to recognize the limits we face and structure the economy so that it meets people's needs within environmental limits.

To build an economy focused on *better* rather than *bigger* requires surprisingly straightforward policy changes. For example, we can limit the flow of materials and energy to sustainable levels, stabilize population by means that are compassionate and non-coercive, achieve a fair distribution of wealth and income, reform monetary and financial systems for stability, change the way we measure progress, secure meaningful jobs and full employment, and reconfigure the way businesses create value. We'll continue to fly, but we won't blindly fly into the sun, soaring beyond planetary means. Hope for achieving an economy that works for people and the planet resides in the simple concept of *enough*.

– Rob Dietz,
co-author *of Enough Is Enough: Building a Sustainable Economy in a World of Finite Resources*

PATRICK CURRY

When I look at the world dominated by human beings, I see (in the words of Max Weber) one of unpunished injustice, undeserved suffering and hopeless stupidity. So far as I can tell, the future consists of humanity sliding further into the abyss and continuing to take much of the natural world with it. Anthropocentrism – the assumption that human beings are the centre of the world and its highest (if not only) source of value – will continue to dominate actions and discussions. The model for how to live will continue to be dominated by corporatism and big business on the one hand and increasingly fundamentalist monotheism on the other. Both are inherently anti-ecological and, insofar as human beings are natural beings, anti-humanity. Both will also continue to undermine the kind of education we most urgently need: not teaching our young to be consumers or believers, but citizens. The attack on civil society will continue but mesmerized by the twin gods (under Mammon) of Convenience and Entertainment, few will notice, and fewer care.

For the same reasons, we will continue to destroy, pollute and desecrate the natural world past the point of our own ability to flourish and possibly even survive. The mass extinction of species for which we are responsible will continue to accelerate as will global climate change, driven by our addiction to industrial-scale energy and "development." Will humanity survive? I think so, although in what numbers and with what ways of life I cannot say. But we seem to be well on our way into a new Dark Age where culture, in the old-fashioned sense of the word, only survives in isolated pockets.

The only thing that prevents despair is that I don't know beyond any doubt that this is the future. By the same token, though, no one else knows for sure that it isn't. In any case, it is only after fully acknowledging how dire is the situation and the outlook, without indulging in any comforting nostrums or pious evasions, that we are entitled to whatever hope remains. And even if none, we can still resist; you don't need hope for that. What you need is courage.

– Patrick Curry,
independent scholar, writer, environmentalist

151

LINDA LEAR

Over the course of the last fifty years, many of us, but not enough of us, have understood the extent of the damage that human hubris has inflicted upon the natural world. Some of us tried to ignore the indisputable fact that global pollution was caused by human actions and activities, and not by some invisible malevolent hand. Others simply denied reality.

In 1962 the nature writer Rachel Carson (1907–1964) awakened us to the horrific consequences of human activity on the Earth's systems in her iconic and still revolutionary book *Silent Spring*. Carson began her tale of the potential death of Nature with a fable based on the real and terrifying disasters suffered by many American communities where chemical pesticides had been used and misused. "No witchcraft, no enemy action had silenced the rebirth of new life in this stricken world. The people had done it themselves." Rachel Carson never knew how prescient her words would be.

Her hope was that the potential silencing of spring would spur us to recognize the terrible consequences of putting anything into the natural world before we understood the impact it might have on human and nonhuman nature: on all life. She trusted, perhaps naively, that the next generation would carry forth an inextinguishable "sense of wonder" that would ensure that life would continue and that humans could and would live co-operatively with Nature. Sadly, we have not heeded Carson's warning well enough, and human destruction of the planet has continued with terrifying speed. But is it really too late to turn around?

Carson's hope, and mine too, is based on a belief in our continuing sense of moral responsibility to the future of human and nonhuman life. It is imperative that we be very clear about what we stand for and what we oppose. The continuation of the life support systems of the living Earth – clean water, fresh air, fertile soil and the biodiversity of the species – is our responsibility to the future. We can do it. We simply must do it. And we must do it NOW.

–Linda Lear, PhD,
environmental biographer/historian,
author of *Rachel Carson: Witness for Nature* and *Beatrix Potter: A Life in Nature*

JOANNA MACY

Prayer to Future Beings

You live inside us, beings of the future.
In the spiral ribbons of our cells, you are here.
In our rage for the burning forests, the poisoned fields,
the oil-drowned seals,
you are here.

You beat in our hearts through late-night meetings.
You accompany us to clear-cuts and toxic dumps
and the halls of the lawmakers.
It is you who drive our dogged labours to save what is left.

O you who will walk this Earth when we are gone,
stir us awake.
Behold through our eyes
the beauty of this world.
Let us feel your breath in our lungs,
your cry in our throat.
Let us see you in the poor, the homeless, the sick.
Haunt us with your hunger, hound us with your claims,
that we may honour the life that links us.

You have as yet no faces we can see,
no names we can say.
But we need only hold you in our mind,
and you teach us patience.
You attune us to measures of time
where healing can happen,
where soil and souls can mend.

You reveal courage within us we had not suspected,
love we had not owned.
O you who come after, help us remember:
we are your ancestors.
Fill us with gladness for the work that must be done.

– Joanna Macy,
root teacher of the Work That Reconnects
www.joannamacy.net

PETER SALE

In 2013 the world is a lot less rich than it was when I landed in Honolulu in August 1964, ready to begin my life as a coral reef ecologist. Since then, our activities in the coastal oceans have reduced, simplified and homogenized the biotic richness that used to be. Our CO_2 emissions are altering the climate and the oceans in fundamental ways. And coral reefs are in global decline. The Great Barrier Reef and most of the Caribbean have lost over 50 per cent of their living coral cover in just the last 30 years. By 2050, on current trends, we will not have anything resembling the reefs I first saw in the sixties. This fact alone should be a wake-up call, but it's not just reefs. We are reshaping our world, creating a new environment outside our collective experience across all of history, civilization and tribal memory. It's a world bringing great hardships for us and extinction for much of Nature.

Evolved to jump out of the way of sabre-tooth cats, but to ignore advancing glaciers, we are slow to respond to the damage we are causing. Cocooned in our civilization, many of us fail to see what we are doing; deluded by our technology, others assume we can invent our way out of this mess. Still others understand the problem and the possible solutions, but we fail to act because the pain is not yet great enough. We need that approaching predator to shock us into action. It might come as a series of extreme weather events, or as a global pandemic, an abrupt rise in sea level as the West Antarctic shelf fails, or continental-scale famine following widespread drought. It might appear as a global economic collapse. If it comes soon, and if it is not too vicious, we can still get to a good future. If it does not, I fear we will simply watch and wonder as our civilization collapses. I hope that cat is coming soon.

– Peter F. Sale,
university professor emeritus at University of Windsor (Canada),
former assistant director of the Institute for Water, Environment and Health at United Nations University,
author of *Our Dying Planet*
www.petersalebooks.com

SATISH KUMAR

I am an optimist: I believe that the human spirit is resilient. Faced with the demise of biodiversity, rise of population, prospects of climate change, world hunger and many other similar global crises, humanity is bound to rise to the occasion and bring about changes towards a more sustainable future.

Once upon a time, colonialism and imperialism were powerful forces, but in the first half of the 20th century that came to an end. Similarly, former Soviet satellite states and Eastern European countries were liberated from the Soviet empire and the Berlin Wall came down through non-violent means. After 27 years in jail, Nelson Mandela became the president of South Africa and the apartheid system was dissolved. More recently, after 16 years of house arrest, Aung San Suu Kyi has been elected as a member of the Myanmar Parliament and there are good signs of freedom in that country. These examples give me hope that another world is possible where sustainability, conservation, an end of hunger and world peace will prevail.

A few years ago the idea of generating power through windmills and solar collectors was considered utopian, but now governments around the world are subsidizing renewable energy. Businesses are investing money in it and scientists and technocrats are busy innovating new ways of harvesting natural energy.

It is my conviction that we can create a world where humanity can be at ease with itself and stride toward an elegant and simple lifestyle which is benevolent to Nature and fulfilling to humanity.

– Satish Kumar,
editor-in-chief of *Resurgence & Ecologist Magazine*,
founder of Schumacher College (UK), author of *No Destination*
www.resurgence.org and
www.schumachercollege.org.uk

ROBERT FERRARI

Renewal

Change is too constant for history,
Which comes, considers and makes a stand,
In clearings, and elsewhere along the road of
Values, questions, necessity and growth;
Constant the change comes, sometimes quietly, as though,
Holding its breath, it is planning a lesson;
Or sometimes unquietly resting, like an animal,
Being tracked, made to camouflage,
Hunted by progress,
Tired and terrified, chased by dreams,
By aspirations, man's fears of being lost,
Beneath the world, beneath leaves,
Hidden forever in the secrets of weather.

Whether time, water, wind or fire invades
With violence upon history,
Or, with even less drama, flatters inhabitants
With long memories, beyond the recollections
Of a millennium, a folk-song, or even this morning,
Whether these strikes breach the walls,
Patina the years, favour the return to leaves
Or not, there is a pressure to place the past
Into smaller spaces, disappearing venues,
Closing circuits and cramped opportunities.
This is the change too constant for history,

The insistent rewriting that wanders into
Our lives and underlines in the dictionary
The word renewal.

There's a murmur in the world theatre:
The curtain is drawing,
And the third act has yet to be written.
In act one, the sun prays for renewal;
In act two, renewal prays for sunlight,
For some truth unvarnished by myths of collapse,
That life is not a last look or sometime space,
But an immersion in change, fibre deep, forest deep,
And willing.

Renewal is yours, your task and work and hope.
Understand it as a name, and call it.
Everything yields. Yesterday's poems are dead,
And the poets have gone off to fish.
The temples of Art and Hope are constantly rebuilt,
Less so by masters and more by neighbours,
Seeking shelter from the rains, finding
That the clouds in their lives speak only grey ideas,
Or rebuilt by those asking for directions to the theatre,
Hearing that the third act has not yet been written,
And feeling that their tongue has the courage to speak the lines,
And recite the monologue of renewal.

— Robert Ferrari,
physician, father, husband

PATTY WEBSTER

It is difficult to be optimistic about the human capacity to survive when, as a whole, we appear so hell-bent on creating the perfect conditions for our demise. Observing the natural world in the Amazon jungle, I have seen thousands of species coexist perfectly with the environment that supports them. Why can't we do that? Is it that other "simple" species actually "think" long-term and we "big-brained" humans only in the short? We are destroying what keeps us and other species alive – the plants that provide the oxygen we breathe, the rivers, oceans and forests that supply the food and medicine that sustains us.

People complain that technology is moving too fast. I disagree. Unless a major global event alters our trajectory, we are never returning to a time when things were "better." In fact, if we are to outrun an approaching crisis, technology is part of the answer and must be propelled to hyperspeed. We need to put extreme effort into technological innovations that have the potential for global impact. Incredible breakthroughs, such as turning plastics and algae into oil, have been developed by people just like you and I, people who saw a negative situation and wanted to change it.

Twenty years ago, I was inspired to bring desperately needed medical care to the neglected people of the Peruvian Amazon. My advice is to discover what motivates YOU and get involved in improving our situation. It's easy to be overwhelmed by the immensity of the issues and adopt a complacent, "get-what-you-can-while-you-can" attitude, but people who take on one problem at a time are overcoming paralysis and having great success all over the world. Their small triumph connects with other small triumphs and together, they become a force. Everyone is part of the solution. Governments are not the change agents. We are.

– Patty Webster,
founder and president of Amazon Promise

JAMES HOWARD KUNSTLER

The master task at hand for the human race is managing the contraction of an industrial economy that has reached its limits.

The human race has no experience with this, and for the moment we are in thrall to wishful thinking in the hope that some techno rescue remedy will allow us to keep that system going – shale oil, hydrogen, electric cars, thorium reactors, methane clathrates, etc. We're wasting our time wishing for these things. We need to downscale and relocalize all the activities of daily life: agriculture, commerce, capital finance, governance, education, healthcare.

It is important to remember that reality has mandates of its own and will compel us to behave differently whether we get with the program, or not – it just depends on how disorderly we want the transition to be.

I attempted to depict such a successful transition in a series of two (soon to be three) recent novels set in the post-petroleum American future: *World Made by Hand* and *The Witch of Hebron*, if anyone is interested in an imagined outcome that is not in the *Mad Max* mould. It's not utopia but it shows people managing to remain civilized under conditions of relative hardship. Farming has come back to the centre of their economy, they work shoulder to shoulder with their neighbours on things that matter, and they make music together. It's a start. It's also still recognizably American culture.

– James Howard Kunstler,
author of *The Long Emergency*, *Too Much Magic*, *The Geography of Nowhere*,
The City in Mind and the *World Made By Hand* series,
weekly blogger and podcaster at www.kunstler.com

OLIVIER OULLIER

We humans entertain the belief that we are rational and intelligent creatures. However, our creative and innovative power endangers our own species on a social, economic and environmental level. Not the best display of intelligence and rationality.

Although (sometimes) unintentional, the negative consequences of our behaviours on our peers and the planet are more and more visible each day. The measures taken by public authorities – i.e., bombarding us with alarming facts and figures together with endless lectures on what to do – are simply not working.

Humans and their behaviours are beautifully complex. So are their perceptions and attitudes toward their physical and social environments. This complexity cannot be captured by the ungrounded rational economic models policy-makers rely upon that consider short-term focus, biases and affective fluctuations as (economic) "anomalies." Big mistake. They are just human nature.

People in charge need to face this reality and use the recent findings in psychology, behavioural economics and neuroscience to inform and improve their social change strategies. The unprecedented insights provided by these fields allow us to better study, learn and understand why real people engage (or not) in certain behaviours, make counter-intuitive decisions and put their lives and environments at risk, in spite of being well aware of the stakes.

Behaviourally evidence-informed policy-making is the only way to better engage citizens in taking care of themselves, their peers and the planet. In order to be successful, such an approach requires a profound systemic change. Designers, together with behavioural and brain scientists, must help policy-makers embrace our emorational nature and therefore ground their strategies. Making it as easy and effortless as possible for people to change their behaviours to improve their health and well-being and stop destroying our ecosystem must be a priority.

Good news: this is possible. But we need to quickly take a vital step by putting the best innovation ever at the core of policy-making: humans themselves.

– Olivier Oullier,
emorational behavioural and brain scientist, strategist and musician
www.oullier.fr

SARAH BACKHOUSE

How do we get humans to care about and take action on climate change? As an environmental journalist and media entrepreneur, I am haunted by this question. The science is in, we know the facts, and yet we're swimming against the tide to engage the public.

To be fair, storytelling around this issue is challenging. Climate change is abstract – it's a difficult concept for people to grasp. The scope of the problem is overwhelming – we've suffered profound ecological damage and species loss, much of it irreversible. Climate change is inaccurately perceived as long-term – it has to compete with more immediate concerns like jobs and mortgages.

To get humans to engage, we need to *humanize* climate change. We need to share powerful stories about the thousands of lives it's affecting everyday. Sobering stories about families in Los Angeles whose children suffer from asthma. Tragic stories about victims of weather events like hurricanes Katrina and Sandy in the U.S. and savage wildfires in Australia and about ecological refugees in Bangladesh and Africa. Inspiring stories about the innovators who are working tirelessly to develop clean-energy solutions, design better products and create new business models that encourage sharing and responsible use of resources.

One of our most compelling video stories is about a sustainably built school in San Francisco, as seen through the eyes of a remarkable teenager. Fourteen-year-old Sonia effortlessly cartwheels through sustainability concepts and possesses a passion for life that touches everyone who watches.

This story became more than one about a green school. It viscerally embodies the imagination and hope of a future generation – one that appears ready to tackle the threat that has paralyzed their parents. Sonia proves that we can change the world, one story at a time.

–Sarah Backhouse,
television host, founder and CEO of future360.tv

JEFF GAILUS

Looking out across the political landscape these days, it is easy, even logical, to conclude there is little hope we will take the necessary actions to overcome what U.S. Secretary of State John Kerry recently called "the greatest challenge of our generation."

For 17 years one Canadian government after another has failed to meet our international commitments to reduce the greenhouse gas emissions that cause climate change, and we are on track to fail again. Recent polls indicate that today, the majority of Canadians want the federal government to protect the planet from the ravages of runaway climate change, and yet the politicians who represent us still refuse to adequately regulate greenhouse gas emissions. They know we *hope* they will do otherwise, but they're betting, as they always have, that we will forgive them for their sins.

So far, they've been right: we are mired in hope.

It's easy to see that hope is not the answer. "Hope," derived from the Germanic word for "wish," is an illusion, a false prophet. Hope is what we cling to as our ship sinks into the cold dark waters of fear.

We did not hope an end to slavery. We did not hope an end to the Second World War. We did not hope an end to discrimination based on the colour of our skin. All of these challenges were overcome by government intervention made strong by the concerted efforts of individuals just like you.

We will not hope climate change away. When we quit hope, we free ourselves from the bondage of our fears and allow ourselves to act, to protect the people and places we love.

I implore you: abandon all hope and commit to action. Only then will we be able to build the clean-energy economy that will provide our children and grandchildren with the prosperous and stable futures they deserve.

– Jeff Gailus,
father, writer, educator, lecturer, environmental advocate,
author of *The Grizzly Manifesto* and *Little Black Lies*

HAZEL HENDERSON

Humanity is already finding many ways past our current global environmental and social crises. 2012 was the inflection point when we began reintegrating our knowledge and transitioning from the fossil fuel Industrial Era to the knowledge-richer, more equitable, cleaner green economies of the Solar Age. From digging into our Earth for energy, we began looking up and seeing the infinite abundant flow of free photons showering our planet. Just one hour of this flow could meet all our energy needs for a year! We began in earnest to harness these photons, just as green plants do with photosynthesis – providing all humans with our food and fibre today.

We do not need much more research – only to accelerate our investments in energy efficiency, renewable solar, wind, ocean, hydro and geothermal sources – while ending our wasteful subsidies, 95 per cent of which go to fossil fuels and nuclear power. With this level playing field, even the 5 per cent of subsidies to solar and efficient use of renewable energy will be cheaper than polluting dangerous fossil and nuclear power. This crossover has already made solar and wind power cheaper than nuclear.

When the social and environmental costs are finally counted and included in prices, renewables will out compete all earlier energy. If the current $1-trillion in annual private investments continue ($4.1-trillion by 2013), by 2020 humanity will have exited the fossil fuel Industrial Era and entered the sustainable Solar Age and the promise of an equitable, abundant future for all life forms on our planet.

– Hazel Henderson,
president of Ethical Markets Media LLC (USA and Brazil),
author of *The Politics of the Solar Age*, *Ethical Markets* and *Building A Win Win World*,
co-author of *Planetary Citizenship*
www.EthicalMarkets.com and
www.GreenTransitionScoreboard.com

RICKEN PATEL

Even more than hope, we have good sense, and I believe that a clear-eyed look at our past and present tells us not only that we have a very strong probability of surviving, but that many signs point to a tremendous awakening and acceleration of our wisdom as we meet the real challenges we face.

Look at our recent past – in just the last generation, we have massively reduced global poverty and deaths in war, massively expanded the number of people living under democratic governance, rapidly increased public health and life expectancy, profoundly elevated the status of women in our societies and governance, and achieved historic progress in a host of other ways.

We do face profound challenges that threaten our survival. Humanity's interdependence, vulnerability and power is escalating, and with it our capacity to destroy ourselves. Nuclear weapons were our first "doomsday power," and we're quickly acquiring more.

But as our power to destroy ourselves is escalating, so is our wisdom to manage this power. Disciplines like psychology, management and leadership are quite new, but are accelerating in their capacity to help us understand and manage ourselves. The empowerment of women to greater political and social leadership is profoundly impacting the emotional intelligence and wisdom of our societies. And while we may not be able to change human nature with all our flaws and fears, we know that with attention to children and families, education, and the culture of our institutions, workplaces, democracies and art, we can get better and better at bringing out the best in each other collectively. It's not a utopia, it's the difference between Somalia and Sweden, Congo and Costa Rica.

So I believe that not only can we make it, we can come together to make it big. And far more than just a basis for hope, we have every reason to dream.

—Ricken Patel,
executive director of Avaaz
www.avaaz.org

JIM BARTON

Every good chorus has a director – but how do we create a global, democratic chorus?

All too often, people speak of "global citizenship," but fail to talk of citizenship structures for:

1. Common welfare

2. Common biosphere stewardship

3. Common security

4. Common decision-making

Many peace and ecology advocates look at the UN and see only its failings. They don't realize that earlier peace advocates, like Jane Addams, worked long and hard to create global democratic structures to enhance the lives of all people on Earth.

Many people think the UN and global co-operation have achieved nothing. They are wrong. We have created treaties that have eliminated atmospheric nuclear testing, and have just about done away with any nuclear tests since 1996. The nations of the world agreed in 1968 to negotiate seriously for nuclear disarmament. We need a renewed global chorus of voices to call for disarmament and a conversion to a global peace economy.

One crucial element of a global peace economy is the elimination of the extreme poverty affecting the poorest one billion people – one seventh – of the planet.

Through the UN Millennium Development goals process of 2000–2015, we have continued to substantially reduce illiteracy, deaths of children under 5 and deaths from hunger and malnutrition. Smallpox has been eliminated, and polio has been reduced by 99 per cent since 1988, with entire continents polio-free.

In 2015 we need to renew and extend these objectives into the Sustainable Development Goals. We need to complete the previous goals and add new ones to deal with the looming ecological and resource crisis, as well as include goals on nuclear weapons and reducing arms and conflict.

But we should go beyond this, and talk of stronger global law, openly arrived at, and a global parliament, directly elected.

Let's take a pause from singing so that we can get on the same page with a common song. And when we get there, let's sing as loudly as we can – a song by, of and for all of us on our planet.

– Jim Barton,
director of Smith Mill Creek Institute,
board member of Citizens for Global Solutions

PIERS GUY

A recent discussion with an eminent climate scientist gave me hope. He said that extreme climate change scenarios predicted a few years ago are now less likely in the short to medium term. Phew! The problem is still enormous but maybe our climate system is more resilient than first feared. So let's take this undeserved reprieve and have a new culture to reflect a new era; where the majority of our (reduced) consumption is sustainable with any environmental impacts either avoided or properly mitigated. This is the approach I try and work with in my own industry of wind farming.

Generating electricity from the wind is sustainable, but there are impacts, real and perceived, and addressing them provides wonderful opportunities for all kinds of creativity: like the creation and enhancement of large-scale wildlife habitats around the wind farm that otherwise would not have happened and community and educational initiatives which build upon what the local community really values long-term.

Applying a sustainable approach to business does mean less financial profit and a consumer base that begins to pay the real cost for goods. It is not likely without multilateral regulation. But to get to this point, we need to start as individuals who make good choices and understand that happiness and well-being are not inextricably linked to material wealth. We must recognize that our population is excessive, and know that biodiversity is essential for our survival and our happiness.

We could socialize, shop, travel, have babies and even do Christmas differently! This is activism in our own homes. By communicating, demonstrating, lobbying and voting we can change things. I have hope that there is a majority of people out there who would be quite prepared to rid themselves of a lot of their consumerist paraphernalia in exchange for a more balanced, happy and healthier life and planet.

−Piers Guy,
wind farm developer

ERIN SCHRODE

I am an eternal optimist – and I have hope for humanity and the planet. My whole-hearted belief in the goodness of people propels me to use my words and deeds to activate the spark that lies within every individual, to catalyze the inner change-maker around necessary action in all walks of life.

Education is the crux of change. I view information as a liberating force, rather than a paralyzing one. The more one knows, the more global and comprehensive a frame of reference one possesses, and the more diverse experiences one can draw upon, the more capable that individual becomes to innovate, develop ideas and realize solutions to pressing global challenges. A person can never be "aware enough" or "active enough" – there is no plateau at which one arrives where the journey of learning or doing ends. Inaction is the largest issue plaguing society today, so we must collectively vow to change that state of mind and lead a collaborative, purpose driven, positive movement.

The opportunities for discovery and impact are limitless – and the need for action by individuals, corporations, government, all actors on both local and global scales is critical. When a person makes the conscious choice to *not* stand apathetically in the face of injustice or wrongdoing, he or she changes the future of our world.

Through cross-sector communication, global leadership and the sharing of tools and resources, humanity can transform the revolutionary into routine and bring about a paradigm shift that prioritizes peace, health, justice and sustainability for this generation and beyond.

I passionately believe this to be true.

–Erin Schrode,
eco-expert, co-founder of Teens Turning Green

EDWARD O. WILSON

Humanity is in a strange period at the present time (2013), which I hope will prove to be only a brief interval. We've awakened to the critical state of Earth's environment in general, but by for the larger part of public and scientific attention is focused on the physical part, for example, on climate change, pollution and resource shortage, as opposed to biodiversity – Earth's variety of ecosystems, species and genes. In a phrase we are destroying much of the rest of life, a unique and precious part of our natural heritage. Forever.

How much biodiversity is there, and how fast is it disappearing? A lot, and tragically fast, although exact measures are hard to come by. In 2009, when a careful count was made of the species of plants, animals, fungi and microbes known to science, the number worldwide was found to be about 1.9 million. But the true number, including small invertebrates and (especially) microorganisms, could be somewhere between five and 100 million. In short, we live on a little-known planet.

The human agents of destruction – in descending order of impact: habitat destruction, spread of invasive species, pollution and overharvesting – have lifted the rate of species extinction by 100–1,000 times the basal rate before humanity began its expansion from Africa over the remainder of the world. Sadly, because of underfunding of the science and the overall inadequacy of conservation efforts, we are destroying many million-year-old species before we even know they existed.

In speaking for the rest of life, conservation biologists are not asking for anything close to the amount of funds and effort being devoted to the nonliving environment. We are in agreement that an expansion, say a doubling, of funding for research on biodiversity and widening of protected areas around the world would yield an immense improvement in the quality of the environment, for ourselves and for future generations.

– Edward O. Wilson,
university research professor emeritus and
honorary curator in entomology at Harvard

JOEL BAKAN

Humanity is in crisis. Over the course of modern history we have failed, miserably, to create just and sustainable societies. Moreover, much of what we have created – petroleum-fuelled engines, synthetic chemicals, nuclear weapons, to take just a few examples – now threatens our very existence. Climate change, social inequalities and dysfunctions, deteriorating ecosystems, war – these kinds of problems have to be solved. And the only way we can solve them is through coordinated, collective action, at all levels of society: local, national and international. But here's the rub – our very ability to act collectively, in the public interest, has been profoundly weakened and diminished by growing corporate power and influence over governments and public institutions.

Finding a way past current global crises, and creating conditions necessary for good, just and sustainable societies, requires, at a minimum, restoring the authority, integrity and legitimacy of public democratic institutions. We need to actively resist the creeping logic of private ordering and collapsing public spheres; to understand, for example, that corporate social responsibility and sustainability programs cannot replace mandatory public regulations; that privatized public services cannot replace public delivery; that consumer preferences in markets cannot replace citizen participation in democratic institutions.

At the moment, our governments and public institutions, unduly influenced by the needs and perspectives of big business, are justifiably mistrusted as protectors and promoters of public interests. That needs to change. We need to reoccupy government and the public sphere, push back the current occupation by big business, and then begin work to solve the world's problems, collectively. That is, after all, what democracy has always envisioned and required of us.

– Joel Bakan,
professor of law at University of British Columbia (Canada),
author/filmmaker of *The Corporation: The Pathological Pursuit of Profit and Power*,
author of *Childhood Under Siege: How Big Business Targets Your Children*
www.joelbakan.com

MELANIE FITZPATRICK

Tell me a story. Because story is how we make sense of our world. The journey we are on as a planetary community is surely a heroic epic, one that involves all of us as protagonists.

Our current narrative, though, is the distressing tale of the demise of our ecological home. Of the terrible destruction wrought on island communities by super typhoons, where thousands lose their lives and millions become homeless. Of the failure of international climate negotiations to agree on reducing our heat-trapping emissions, the very emissions that make the weather more extreme around the world.

However, the outcome of this story is still being written. The invitation for you and me is to become its authors. Our path ahead, as in every hero's journey, will be replete with challenges and obstacles. And along the way we will experience loss, we will

grieve and we will learn to accept that the world we used to know has changed irrevocably – the climate my parents grew up with is no longer here.

So, tell me a story. Discover what the planet needs from us in this time of emergency.

Physics reveals that all things are interconnected, from the galactic level to the sub-atomic. And psychology shows connection is the essential ingredient for a sense of belonging and a sense of purpose. We know connection to the Earth inspires wonder and awe. It is this connection that drives many of us to do the work we do. In the words of Rachel Carson, "Those who contemplate the beauty of the Earth find reserves of strength that will endure as long as life lasts." As more and more people feel a deep sense of connection to this planet, solutions to the ecological crisis will become limitless.

So connect. And let's write a different story.

– Melanie Fitzpatrick, PhD,
climate scientist, wilderness educator,
currently with the Union of Concerned Scientists
www.ucsusa.org

CAROLYN HERRIOT

Dear Brothers & Sisters,

Have you forgotten who you are?
That you are a multidimensional spiritual being in-
habiting a highly
evolved human body?
The unborn babies, the sick children and the de-
mented elderly are
calling you to remember.

Have you forgotten why you are here?
That you are here to learn Love.
To learn how to Respect and live in Harmony with
other sentient
beings.
Mother Earth, the polluted air and dying oceans are
calling you to
remember.

Have you forgotten what to do?
Simply go back to the garden
Reconnect to Nature.
Learn to Love yourself.
Nurture your miraculous body.
Put LOVE into action.
Shift from "Me" to "We."
Participate in the transformation of Human
Consciousness
And together sow seeds of Hope to create a world of
Peace & Plenty
for future generations.

*We are stardust, we are golden, we are
billion year old carbon,
And we've got to get ourselves back to the
garden.*
— JONI MITCHELL

Bless Us All!

– Carolyn Herriot,
author of *A Year on the Garden Path: A 52-Week Organic Gardening Guide*,
The Zero Mile Diet and *The Zero-Mile Diet Cookbook*,
founder/operator of The Garden Path Centre

JUNE

CHEF MICHAEL SMITH

Food is the way forward. Our relationship to our food is our best chance to catalyze systems evolution and generate ongoing hope for humanity. Current food systems contribute mightily to our global paradigm largely because of western ignorance. The environmental atrocities perpetrated on our wasteful behalf dwarf our awareness of them. Thus any solution must begin with engagement with our food. Easily done when you're friends with a farmer!

There are more great reasons to integrate local food into your lifestyle than there are local ants a picnic but perhaps the most compelling is the opportunity to forge a personal connection with a food producer. In fact, much of what ails the global food system is a direct result of its dehumanization. As far as most of us know food is produced far away by nameless machines and blameless factories.

Time was we all knew someone who produced food, we knew exactly how much work it took and thus we respected the cost of that work. A strawberry is not just a strawberry when you know the farmer sweated all spring waiting for rain. A cow somehow tastes better when you know your farmer feeds it to their own family. Spend a day at sea with a fisherman and you'll never find lobster high-priced again!

As we build a new sustainable food system it can help us solve an even deeper problem: our fundamental loss of connection to the world around us. We've taken Mother Nature and Father Time for granted for too long. Our efficient systems have eliminated our essential need to work the land, feel the weather and be in balance with ourselves. It's balance we seek.

As humans we gather, prepare and share food. It's human nature to do so efficiently but not at the expense of losing our connection to each other. We're at our best together. On the farm, in the kitchen or at the table.

–Chef Michael Smith,
television host of *Chef Abroad, Chef at Home*

JOEL AND MICHELLE LEVEY

New Pioneers © Mark Henson, www.markhensonart.com

Ultimately, the essential question is not whether we will survive, but rather how do we individually and collectively choose to live? In great suffering there is always the potential of awakening to great compassion based on the wisdom of the profound interdependence of all beings. If we have the courage and the discipline, this could be an ennobling and enlightening time for each of us and for humanity as a whole. To the degree that we have the courage to be fully present and discern the complex interdependencies of our lives without being overwhelmed, we free ourselves from what Einstein called, "the optical delusion of consciousness" that leads us to regard others as anything less than "another myself." Awakening this intimate wisdom of interdependence naturally widens "the circle of our compassion to embrace all living beings and the whole of Nature in all of its beauty." To the degree that we develop such wisdom

and compassion, the outlook for our future appears brighter. If we miss this opportunity, we are in great peril.

As we realize that we can't solve problems from the same levels of consciousness that created them, we realize that what is required is nothing less than a global revolution in consciousness, to transform the delusional mind states at the root of so many global crises.

Studying with the Dalai Lama over the years, we've often heard him teach about adopting an attitude of "universal responsibility." To take this principle to heart is to dedicate ourselves to realizing our true nature and highest human potentials in order to inspire and activate these potentials within all beings. To embody this archetype of selfless leadership in service of all life is to be a Bodhisattva, which is to us the most relevant archetype/ideal we can aspire to attune to in these perilous times. By dedicating ourselves to live for the benefit of all who share the web of life, we align ourselves with all great sages, activists and leaders who have dedicated themselves to selfless service for the good of all.

– Dr. Joel and Michelle Levey,
social architects and compassion activists,
founders of Wisdom at Work; International Center for Resilience, Wellness and Wisdom at Work;
International Institute for Mindfulness, Meditation and MindBody Medicine,
authors of *Living in Balance*, *Luminous Mind* and *Wisdom at Work*,
on faculty of University of Minnesota Medical School
www.wisdomatwork.com

HARVEY LOCKE

I imagine a beautiful future where civilized humanity and wild nature are reconciled. All it will take is for us humans to remember that we are in a relationship that requires us to think of Nature's needs as well as our own and to strive to meet them both.

If we were to remember Nature's needs we would be more measured in our use of nitrogen fertilizer and carbon-based energy. We would value efficiency and avoid waste. We would let rivers run free to ensure Earth's resilience in the wake of climate change. We would take only what we need and share the rest. We would know the liberation of self-restraint.

People who embrace reciprocal relationships are also naturally inclined to take positive steps to make things better. We would be enthusiastic about investing in alternative energy sources and food production systems that are good for both us and Nature. We would act on the conservation science that indicates we should protect at least half of the world in an interconnected network of protected areas so that all species and the natural processes on which both they and we depend for our survival can continue to flourish. We would also restore species and ecosystems that we have damaged in the past. We would know that we can do things to address the global changes we have set in motion and that we need not be victims.

We would also teach our children the enchantment of the wild world, to appreciate that much of Nature exists for its own sake in the ongoing pageant of evolution and is there to serve God, not humans. To hear the dawn chorus of songbirds, to feel the wind in our hair, to smell the sea, to see clouds drifting across a blue sky, to swim in clear water and to inhale clean air after healthful physical exertion has been an essential part of human experience throughout our species' entire history. It is time to bring ourselves back outdoors and the outdoors back into our lives. We would feel better.

Yet for all these positive behaviours we can embrace, there is more to human life than self-restraint and positive actions; there is meaning too. Love of Nature is deeply ingrained in us. If we start meeting Nature's needs with love and generosity then our lives will be more fulfilling and we will have a 21st century full of hope and promise.

—Harvey Locke,
conservationist, writer, photographer,
co-founder of Yellowstone to Yukon and Nature Needs Half

MIKHAIL GORBACHEV

I always regarded environmental problems as of great urgency. That started when I was still working in my home country in the Caucasus and then when I started to work in Moscow. I learned of shocking facts regarding the mistreatment of the earth, water, soil and air in my home country. And like many people, I was ready to start working in order to revive our forests, land, rivers and lakes. And this was one reason why I gave such a prompt reply to the requests to become the founder of Green Cross International.

Nevertheless, we are still in the process of losing our planet. We are very close to the "red line." Even though we have had many discussions, and many conferences and forums on water and other environmental problems, we are not even close to achieving our goal. We still see that the environment and nature are shrinking. The Earth will of course survive anyway, but it will be a very different Earth for those who live on it. It is not an exaggeration. I think that we feel almost physically the shrinking of the water, the air and living space.

Remember, after WWII, there was a strong peace movement that included prominent people who created a committee to defend peace. The most credible people in the world were in that movement. I am not calling for repeating it in the same way, but we need to do more. It is very important that we have glasnost on the environment. It is very important we have organizations that work for it. But we have not achieved enough. I believe that the problem of the environment is the number one challenge for the 21st century, as well as, of course, the problem of getting rid of nuclear weapons. That is still the number one challenge that we need to address.

When we ended the Cold War, we wanted to create conditions for a peaceful world. I am 82 years old but I still want to act. I still want to do something. This goes back to my youth when I was part of that same peace movement. It is still very much a part of me, this vigour, this motivation, this enthusiasm, that I would like to convey, that I would like to hand over to younger people who will fight for the future of our planet.[6]

–Mikhail Gorbachev,
founding chairman of Green Cross International

JEN BOULDEN

OF COURSE humanity can find a way past our environmental and social crises. We are incredibly clever, especially when motivated. In fact, it was our cleverness that got us into this predicament – we figured out how to live beyond our means, and push the costs out into the future. Today that future is becoming the present, and we can tap that same cleverness to redesign our systems that were created over 250 years ago – in a time when people were scarce and raw materials were plenty. Now, it's the exact opposite, and so capitalism as we know it must adapt to these new conditions. Luckily there's no greater motivation than money. When we focus funding on the companies that employ "cradle to cradle" methodologies and create life-sustaining products and services, the rest will follow. Imagine the historians of 2313 looking back, and reading about most companies of 2013 that produced 96 per cent waste for every 4 per cent product. They will have a good laugh at how ridiculous that was!

In order to help catalyze these new markets at the consumer level, I co-founded *Ideal Bite* in 2005, a "sassy" daily email with small ideas to go green. I believed then, and still do today, that people don't want to do the wrong thing, they just lack both the knowledge and the alternatives. But when those things are provided, people are game: *Ideal Bite* amassed over half a million subscribers in just three and a half years, and voted with the dollars on the products we featured – sometimes inadvertently crashing their websites with all the visitors we sent!

So now it's time for the world's institutional investors and legislative power brokers to step into the driver's seat. The "buy now, pay later" game is over. We know now after these financial meltdowns that true wealth can only be created by providing solutions for true sustainability. So not only do I have hope that we can do it, I also have faith that our most clever leaders – across all sectors – will show us how to make a lot of money with "business as unusual."

– Jen Boulden,
green business entrepreneur

MONICA ARAYA

Traditional wisdom has it that society will always choose growth over the environment. The scale of our dirty energy choices continues to spoil collective mood which each year seems to fall into a deeper downward spiral as unsettling images of environmental destruction and climate injustice at home and abroad fill our TV and phone screens. Climate scientists talk about our entering a turning point. So what comes next? Action, indifference or despair?

I see the dawn of loud, imaginative and committed citizen action, outrage and courage as the engine of a new politics that will bring us out of this comfort zone (because thinking that nothing can be done is a dangerous comfort zone). I observe the many enraged citizens making brave political choices that threw or will throw reckless decision-makers out of power. I also see citizens standing against powerful media for manipulating public debates – even elections. Social media amplifies our voices as citizens and lets us mobilize other citizens giving us permission to defend the vision of a cleaner society; cleaner from an environmental standpoint but also – and here is a key issue – clean from corruption. A movement of citizens are standing for each other in ways that set smarter political choices together.

The refreshing clarity and unapologetic inspiration from citizens, especially the youngest, energizes my own imagination on what to do in my own country and internationally. That is why I helped set up two organizations. Only with citizen action, discipline and determination will we see a fossil fuel phase-out in our lifetimes.

Defending the public interest of the many over the vested interests of the few, that is the common agenda that will get us closer to the clean society. The divestment movement is a prime example of citizen-led actions that are making a transformative difference this decade.

I never forget the words of a Costa Rican poet, Isaac Felipe Azofeifa, who noted: "Son, while it is true that all the stars are gone, it never gets darker than before dawn."

– Dr. Monica Araya,
adviser, thinker, advocate,
founder and director of Costa Rica Limpia and Nivela
www.costaricalimpia.org
www.nivela.org

HOLMES ROLSTON III

We live at a change of epochs, a hinge point of history. We have entered the first century in the 45 million centuries of life on Earth in which one species can jeopardize the planet's future. From this point on, culture more than nature is the principal determinant of Earth's future.

For some this is cause for congratulation, the fulfillment of our destiny as a species. We enter a new era: the Anthropocene. For others this is cause for concern. We worried throughout much of the past century that humans would destroy themselves in inter-human conflict. The worry for the next century is that if our present heading is uncorrected, humans may ruin their planet and themselves along with it.

Paradoxes and challenges confront and confound us. Although we congratulate ourselves on our powers, humans are not well equipped to manage the sorts of global-level problems we face in this new era. Yet, this wonderland Earth is a planet with promise. If we are to realize the abundant life for all time, both policy and ethics must enlarge the scope of concern. We are Earthlings. Our integrity is inseparable from Earth's integrity. The ultimate unit of moral concern is the ultimate survival unit: this wonderland biosphere. We can and we ought to get humans put in their place. Our best hope lies in global convictions that for the richest human living we do not want a denatured life on a denatured planet.

–Holmes Rolston III,
university distinguished professor of philosophy at Colorado State University (USA),
author of *A New Environmental Ethics: The Next Millennium for Life on Earth*

MICHAEL DOWD

Yes, we have hope, and yes, we can do it. What will it take?

1. We must be committed. Whether we speak about it in religious or secular terms, we must be committed to growing in right relationship to reality and helping our friends, family and elected officials do the same. This becomes easier when we see the Great Work of ensuring a just and healthy future as our call to greatness. When we are committed to doing whatever it takes to co-create a thriving future for humanity and the larger body of life, our priorities become clear. We are filled with passion and purpose. Our lives become meaningful beyond measure.

2. We must tax carbon. This is the most important systemic change [that] needs to be made. James [Hansen] refers to it as "fee and dividend" and "putting an honest price on carbon" (See, e.g., citizensclimatelobby.org/carbon-fee-and-dividend-faq).

3. We must honour Nature. We must respect the integrity, stability and beauty of the life community as our fundamental *moral* responsibility. If we continue to see Nature as an "it" to be exploited rather than a "thou" to be related to, we condemn future generations to hell and high water. In the inimitable words of Thomas Berry:

The world we live in is an honorable world. To refuse this deepest instinct of our being, to deny honor where honor is due, to withdraw reverence from divine manifestation, is to place ourselves on a head-on collision course with the ultimate forces of the Universe. This question of honor must be dealt with before any other question. We miss both the intrinsic nature and the magnitude of the issue if we place our response to the present crises of our planet on any other basis. It is not ultimately a political or economic or scientific or psychological issue. It is ultimately a question of honor. Only the sense of the violated honor of Earth and the need to restore this honor can evoke the understanding as well as the energy needed to carry out the renewal of the planet in any effective manner.

– Michael Dowd,
evolutionary theologian, evangelist for Big History and Religious Naturalism,
bestselling author of *Thank God for Evolution*
thegreatstory.org/MD-writings.html

BETH DOANE

There is no doubt that the human race is now facing our greatest challenge. We have driven our planet into a state of such immense turmoil that our own survival is jeopardized.

I have witnessed the disappearance of endangered species, the mass contamination of our oceans and rivers and the severe weather patterns that have resulted in extreme loss of life on every continent on Earth. It's heartbreaking, and the question is, is it too late to make a difference?

For me, the answer is that it's never too late. Miraculous outcomes to seemingly impossible situations occur every day. There is nothing stronger than the human spirit and change is always possible despite the enormity of the odds we face. However, if we are going to save our home before it's too late we will have to work together and truly understand the gravity of the situation we face in order to take the necessary action. If we can see just how connected we really are to each other and our Earth and remember all the wisdom we have forgotten through centuries of abuse of our planet and each other, we can indeed overcome the issues we have created, and do so very quickly.

The Earth can heal itself remarkably well when we stop the devastating harm we are doing, but it's up to us to end the trauma we have caused and remind each other, as the Native Americans so wisely stated, that we don't have to wait for the last river to be poisoned, the last fish to be caught and the last tree to be cut down to realize that we cannot eat money.

– Beth Doane,
author, founder of Rain Tees
www.raintees.com
www.bethdoane.com

JEFFREY HOLLENDER

We absolutely have the ability to solve our current global environmental, social and economic crises. For me the question is, do we have the will? The challenge is not about technology but about consciousness, values and priorities. Me vs. We. Quantity vs. Quality.

With two million NGOs working to save the world, the challenge is to co-operate rather than compete. Each one thinks that their issue is the most important issue. They compete for resources and attention. Together they could make rapid progress. Alone they will all fail.

Pension funds, foundations, not-for-profits, educational institutions, credit unions and other socially and financially responsible entities control huge financial resources. They don't use their leverage, let alone co-operate with each other to insist on change. They could. It's about will and commitment.

Our system is broken. We are headed at 90 miles an hour into a brick wall. So far, all we do is tap gently on the brakes and celebrate as our speed slows temporarily down to 89. The brakes work. We can stop the car and change direction. The question is, will we?

The alternative is ugly. Likely billions of casualties as we let disaster and pain force a change in consciousness.

– Jeffrey Hollender,
co-founder of Seventh Generation,
Jeffrey Hollender Partners and CommonWise

RAVI RAVINDRA

We may not be able to find a way past the current global crises, but a way may be found through us if we are willing and able to be instruments of subtler levels of energy which permeate the entire universe.

If we contemplate the universe and the extremely intricate laws which govern the appearance and disappearance of galaxies as well as the emergence of the butterfly from a cocoon, it is difficult to persuade oneself that human beings are in control and are at the top of the spectrum of consciousness or intelligence. How can we not feel the sentiment expressed by Albert Einstein when he speaks of his "rapturous amazement at the harmony of natural law, which reveals an intelligence of such superiority that, compared with it, all the systematic thinking and acting of human beings is an utterly insignificant reflection"?

It is the unanimous testimony of all the sages in the history of humanity that the entire universe is pervaded by subtle and conscious energies – variously labelled as the "Holy Spirit," or the "Buddha Mind," or "Allah" or the "Tao." All spiritual traditions say that without the subtle and conscious energies of Brahman (or God or the Eternal) nothing can be done, but without human beings nothing will be done. We need to do our part as instruments of the all-pervasive Intelligence. In our individual or collective hubris we forget the obvious – that we do not know all there is to know, and that neither the physical nor the spiritual universe is centred on any individual or on humanity or on the Earth. We need to search for our contribution to the continuing unfolding of the Mystery, not so much from ignorance but from innocence, open to unexpected voices and solutions.

Ahimsa, usually understood as non-violence or physical non-harming, is in fact closer to non-violation, non-imposition or non-manipulation. Ahimsa is the essential principle of all true ecology. Finding our place and playing our part, making room for and caring for other human beings, for all creatures and for the planet naturally follows from this.

– Ravi Ravindra, PhD
author, spiritual lecturer
www.ravindra.ca

MANUEL PULGAR-VIDAL

I am an optimist by nature, and I have devoted my life to working for the environment and for natural resources issues, from the civil society perspective, always with an intention to improve public policies. In 2011, when I was appointed Minister of the Environment of Peru, I found myself at the other side of the table. One of the most notable challenges thus far as minister has been the creation of a national agency for environmental certification. With Peru's growing economy, and thus growing economic activities, the efficient management of the impacts of these activities on the environment is crucial for the long-term quality and quantity of resources. On a positive note, however, the recent green economic developments, focused on an efficient use of resources with decreased carbon output, should ensure growth in a sustainable fashion. These strategies develop economic and environmental policies that incentivize green projects and green economic activities. It is my belief that countries such as Peru, with strong economic fundamentals, are in a position to use institutional and operative frameworks to build solid pathways to transformational change, introducing environmentally sound considerations to our current public policies.

Mankind assumes challenges and produces changes, especially when facing crises that generate the need to explore new grounds, to find new answers. Climate change, population growth, climatic events, ecosystems degradation, loss of species and resources, scarcity, inequality and inequity, poverty and war should make us aware of that need; but sometimes we seem unaware. Inadequate leadership is assumed on the actions necessary to take to combat climate change; bad practices that generate biodiversity loss are not confronted with courage; and we still think in terms of territorial or individual interests instead of as a community, as humanity. Should this lead us to pessimism? No. Nature will continue to demand action from us, our survival instinct will guide us to take the lead, and our sense of responsibility will cause us to think of the future generations that we must be keeping in mind, for they will inherit the consequences of our actions and omissions.

–Manuel Pulgar-Vidal,
Minister of the Environment, Peru

SYLVIA EARLE

Consider this: for humankind this is the "sweet spot" in history, and people alive today are the luckiest ever to exist.

Never before have we had the critical level of knowledge needed to see Earth as a miraculous blue speck in a universe inhospitable to the likes of us, or to understand that our prosperity is pushing the limits of the natural systems that sustain us. In a few centuries we have burned through more natural assets than all who preceded us, and the pace is picking up.

Never again will there be a better time to take action to reverse the sharp decline in the nature of air, water and the fabric of life upon which our lives depend. Half the coral reefs are still in pretty good shape, ice still graces polar regions, there are still sharks, whales, tunas and turtles in the sea. We can still breathe.

Half a century ago it was too soon to act. Not enough was known about our ability to change the nature of Nature. Half a century from now, it will be too late to seize options now open. There is time, but not a lot, to reverse the dangerous trends set in motion by our predecessors and continuing today.

Lucky us – now we know. Making peace with Nature is not a luxury, it is essential for the survival of everything we care about.

Even luckier will be those who follow, if our knowing leads to caring, and caring inspires actions to secure an enduring place for humankind within the living systems that make our lives possible.

– Sylvia Earle,
National Geographic Society Explorer in Residence,
founder of Mission Blue

DAVID VAUGHAN

The geological and climate record of planet Earth holds much evidence that the Earth System and the life it supports interact in ways that are unfathomably complex and sensitive, but are, at the same time, flexible and robust.

Only a few thousand years ago, tiny changes in the shape of Earth's orbit around our sun caused the ice that covered much of the land surface to melt into the oceans. Earth's climate changed dramatically, but most plants and animals simply moved around and found new places to survive.

Since I first visited the Antarctic Peninsula in 1985, I have seen for myself the effects of climate change in one of the most rapidly warming parts of the planet. Ice shelves the size of small countries, which existed for thousands of years, have collapsed; and hundreds of glaciers have retreated and thinned. This first-hand experience, together with the accumulated mass of scientific evidence pointing to change across the planet, has convinced me that the cumulative effect of everything we do in our day-to-day lives today, especially in the developed world, is altering our planet at a fundamental level.

Quite soon those changes will be evident to all, and eventually many parts of the planet will change in ways we can only begin to predict. But in a strange and wonderful universe, the most boundless thing we have yet observed is the scope of the human mind, the strongest is the human spirit, and the most hopeful, the sound of our children learning what we do not yet know.

I am optimistic that as a species we will eventually find ways to repair our damaged planet, and build ourselves a truly sustainable future. But building that future will take time and many brave choices: if we are not brave enough to begin, let's raise children who are.

–Professor David Vaughan,
British Antarctic Survey

JUNE 15

WILL POTTER

I have been struggling to write something about hope and perseverance in this space, because today, like many days, the weight of the challenge ahead of us makes me feel quite dark.

It strikes me, though, that the greatest danger of that darkness is that we always convince ourselves that it is unique to us and we are experiencing it alone.

Far from it.

Whatever doubts and despair you may feel as you read these passages and engage with the state of our culture and our planet, know this: you are not the only one feeling it. I am here. So are millions more. I say this not so we can take solace in each other's despair, but because I think there is an untapped power in coming together and acknowledging that we are all, to varying degrees, stumbling along in this fight against dark days.

Our path forward must involve a concrete response to unsustainable lifestyles and an economic system driven by greed – for together they have created a culture of death. In order to do that, we are going to have to remind ourselves and each other of something whenever we feel that darkness begin to creep: we are not alone.

–Will Potter,
author of *Green Is the New Red: An Insider's Account of a Social Movement Under Siege*

LEILA CONNERS

YES: we will prevail because the conditions necessary for our survival already live within us. We know what to do to solve the environmental crisis, we have known for years; the problem is that we haven't yet found the will to do so. It is in the activation of our will where our salvation lies.

Much of humanity is currently living in a somnambulant state because we have been raised (since the industrial revolution) to depend on centralized processes and large-scale corporations that create great distances between us and the realities that support our way of life. We have given over the responsibility for much of our lives to forces that make us feel infantile and powerless. It is in this distance and in this lack of responsibility where the destructive forces live.

So how do we change this? How do we activate our will? To use an old but very important phrase, we "think global and act local." Keeping in mind the global thought – the need to transition from a fossil-fuel-based economy to a sustainable economy – we bring it home. We find the sources of pollution that impact our local drinking water, and clean it up; we heal our soil, we eliminate sources of air pollution. We start growing more food locally and making other goods locally. We support alternative energy, building and transportation technologies. We delink from the larger processes. And in sum, by waking up to the world closest to you, and taking responsibility for it, the will is activated and your caring about the world has palpable results. This is so because you don't have to wait for any larger force to make this change, you just have to work with your neighbours and the results are clearly visible. We become dynamic, we shift demand, create new supply chains and thus create new, sustainable economies and models for a future that can support us all.

Millions of people fixing their local communities will make it right and make the destructive forces obsolete.

– Leila Conners,
founder and president of Tree Media Group,
writer and director of *We the People 2.0*, *Into Eden* and *The 11th Hour*
www.treemedia.com

ANDY LIPKIS

Humanity absolutely can bring about a world that is safe, healthy, equitable and sustainable. Over the last 42 years I've participated in making rapid changes in government agencies, programs and infrastructure systems in Los Angeles. I've seen this happen even when elected officials, government bureaucrats and conventional wisdom said that change was impossible or would be insufficient. But in each case a vision was launched outside the politics of division, and people came together and achieved the impossible: planting millions of trees, rescuing thousands of people in extreme weather disasters, achieving unprecedented levels of recycling of waste and conserving of water, and restoring damaged ecosystems.

I sense that the Earth's ecosystem has adapted humans to be its healers. Consider the impact if we all deploy the capacities with which we are equipped: compassion, passion, science, creativity, perspective, intuition, global communication and interaction and love. I've seen millions of people experience their true joy and power when they work together and devote themselves to helping. They experience that the most selfish thing they can do is what others have said is contrary to basic human nature: they get better, stronger and happier when they co-create with other people.

Humanity has reached the point where we now extract more natural resources each year than the Earth can regenerate without our conscious and active help. The key is for each of us to behave as if we are a manager of the whole ecosystem. We can deliberately choose whether every action we take contributes to planetary health or depletes it, whether we only consume, or whether we rebuild and restore.

– Andy Lipkis,
founder of TreePeople

PETE HAY

Away with breezy optimism. Therein lodges delusion. If the planet is to have a livable future we must acknowledge the enormity of problem(s), the intransigence of resolutions. We must not kid ourselves.

The planetary systems that sustain the miracle of life are stressed – and we are the stressors. There are "tipping points," we are told, beyond which remedial action is doomed.

It may be so.

We seem unable to modify the rapacity with which we devour the planet's life-sustaining systems. Instead, we engage in history's most disastrous manifestation of mass cognitive dissonance: "If science is out of whack with the sacred 'truths' of the market, it is the facts, not the ideology, that must be wrong."

We seem unable to accommodate the interests of life going about its evolutionary business.

We seem unable to defend the public realm against technological and economic determinism, and the systematic production of democracy-denying disinformation.

We need a gentle, knowledge-rich, other-regarding way of being that is low in dynamism and throughput.

It is hopeless. Too big an ask.

Not so.

There is another tipping point. It is in the realm of culture, and it can effect change with unpredictable rapidity. It can prise political and economic rigidities open. If anyone had predicted in early 1989 that the Berlin Wall would be breached by year's end, we'd have laughed. Yet it happened.

Hope lies in the unknowingness of change. I cannot see a path through our linked planetary crises to that gentler realm. But it is there.

– Pete Hay,
social theorist, activist, poet, essayist
Tasmania, Australia

DIANA BERESFORD-KROEGER

A mountain of my childhood in Ireland was called *Dóchus*, or hope. And hope alone, braids the entire human family together. In turn, we are just one ply of Nature in a common pattern of language of life.

In truth, I am the daughter of a noble line. I was inducted into the ancient wisdoms when I became an orphan at a young age. I was given a sacred trust to which I have been faithful.

Recently, while filming *Ten Trees to Save the World*, I was invited by Professor Akira Miyawaki to plant trees. It was in Shonan Village of Kanagawa prefecture of Japan. There were hundreds of men, women and children there. We planted broad-leaved evergreens to withstand earthquakes and tsunamis.

It was misting. I wrapped my scarf around my head. I was no beauty with both knees buried in the mud. Akira saw my hands and passed me a pair of snow-white gloves. I gently tapped a laurel sapling out of its pot. The root tip meristems were healthy and ready for a millennium of growth. I oriented the baby, broad-leaved canopy to the sun and told it to grow. I tucked the soil around the roots. Sheaves of rice straw were opened and placed around the young stems. When the planting was finished, I helped to hold the rice ropes criss-cross over the rice mulch to hold the new forest in place. The roots would, now, protect the coastline.

A Japanese woman stepped up to embrace me. The young followed suit. No award can be greater than this for me. I will now hold this new forest in my heart. I am truly honoured to be asked to do this for Japan. And for you.

–Diana Beresford-Kroeger,
scientist, environmental activist,
author of *The Sweetness of a Simple Life*

ROMAN DIAL

For 40 years I've explored the world, climbing mountains, rafting rivers, skiing glaciers, walking wilderness, even traversing forest canopies. For 20 years I've taught university science, researched and published on the environment. During my lifetime, the four billion of us added to the planet have clearly changed our Earth. The scale and pace of that change, exemplified in a dying glacier, the clearing of a childhood wood, the conversion of tropical rainforest to oil palm saddens, even scares me.

A friend and I once walked 600 untracked miles across Alaska's Arctic, passing through the point farthest from roads and habitation in all of the USA. During that walk I pondered us humans as an ultimate weed, spreading even to space.

Weeds are eventually replaced by the less wasteful. The early, exponential growth of natural communities always levels out, unless a physical force wipes it clean. Our population will obey these laws of resource consumption, no matter what the economists and politicians claim.

While there are too many of us to go extinct, natural selection will yet apply. The Earth for us will be worse than many claim, but better than doomsayers fear. Still, over the next century or so we will be sad, scared, nostalgic and wistful for a world of better views, fewer people, more interesting/more unusual landscapes and life. But there is hope, because our children, weedy or not, will also want to live, and the wanting to live is the best hope of all.

–Roman Dial,
professor at Alaska Pacific University

PAOLO SOLERI

Our responsibilities as habitat makers are great. Eventually every single one of us must respond to his or her conscience: will we be makers or breakers of a sustainable civilization, a coherent ecology on our planet?

For our architecture to metamorphose into a coherent human ecology, a reformulation is necessary that puts distance between it and our powerfully materialistic present. The unfortunate trend so far – promoted by architects, developers, governments and speculators – has been overwhelmingly in the opposite direction, toward urban sprawl and a "planetary hermitage." The American dream of giving each person, isolated in his or her home, all that is needed for

self-sufficiency feeds a monumental delusion, a direct route to degenerating the human persona and culture, the space and species it controls, the planet itself. The immense consumption of land and resources needed to build the "dream" and keep it running has never before been experienced on this planet.

My proposal for reformulation: Lean Linear City, a dense and continuous urban ribbon designed to take advantage of the urban effect, regional wind patterns and solar radiation while incorporating an arterial/venous system of parallel roads, cycling pathways, public-transit services and stations for local, regional and transcontinental trains. Leanness here requires recoordinating cultures within and

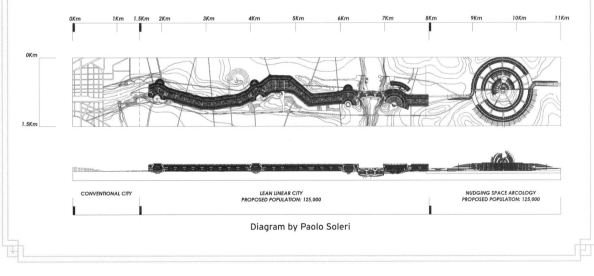

Diagram by Paolo Soleri

along intense, broad-ranging experiences, only available in true urban conditions. It will be a way to insert our thinking and doing into the historical progression human beings have long been authoring, coherent with the continuous evolutionary tide we are now co-authoring.

—Paolo Soleri,
founder of Arcosanti

SARAH VAN GELDER

I live among Chief Seattle's people, and one of the things I've learned from this experience is humility.

I say, "I've lived here 12 years – longer than I've lived anywhere!" And then I come upon an ancient petroglyph or a shell midden, and I remember that my neighbours' ancestors have lived here for thousands of years.

I critique our society's divide between rich and poor. Then I'm invited to a seafood feast followed by an outpouring of gift giving. Ah yes, these people figured out centuries ago that inequality upsets the delicate balances that allow societies to thrive. So instead of gaining status from accumulating stuff, they earn respect by giving it away.

One of the old stories tells of a time when people and animals were on equal footing, and they were all hungry. They made a wager. Whichever side won a game of chance could eat the other. Humans won, but not by much. There's humility in that story, too – it could have gone the other way.

It takes humility to recognize that "progress" isn't always for the better and that our future relies on learning Nature's original ideas:

- ❖ Nature works in cycles. Every kind of waste nourishes something else.

- ❖ Nature is a network of relationships capable of generating yet more life and relationships, in unimaginably diverse forms.

- ❖ Nature uses current energy (mostly from the sun), and it doesn't draw down the principal of the Earth's largess. It lives off the interest.

I grew up in a culture that claimed the right to conquer, use up and displace Nature. Human intelligence coupled with technology would take us to a brighter future, we were told.

Today, as we reach the limits of what life on Earth can tolerate, we need a little less hubris and a little more humility. If we learn from Nature and from our indigenous brothers and sisters, I now believe we'll have a much better shot at that bright future.[7]

– Sarah van Gelder,
co-founder and editor-in-chief of *YES! Magazine*
www.yesmagazine.org

DES RITCHIE

When we stop the CO_2 going into the air we will stop: the Earth warming, the climate changing, the Arctic and Himalayan ice melting, the seas rising, the catastrophe for *all* species and the present financial crisis. In order to achieve these goals we will have to follow some of the actions carried out in 1939. It is a different war, but a greater emergency. The actions are as follows:

1. The federal government declares a "State of Emergency."

2. Government parties form an "All-Party Cabinet."

3. All deniers and skeptics are given two weeks to declare their loyalty to the country or will be interned until the emergency is over.

4. A carbon tax of $50 per tonne is declared.

5. All defence forces are required to plant several million trees per year, starting with riparian corridors on rivers and highways. No Wars!!

6. No more felling forests.

7. All schools spend one day per week learning how to grow food in school gardens.

8. No more new highways until emergency is over.

9. All possible manufacturing is converted to building alternative energies, and access to the patent office is granted to the energy commission.

10. All coal and coal seam gas to be phased out over five years.

11. All men and women discouraged from increasing the population. Baby bonuses diverted to alternative energies.

12. Funds for alternative energies should flow from superannuation funds: we had the best standard of living while creating the problem.

13. All new houses must have solar panels – mandatory.

14. All lawns should be growing food or trees – not wasting fuel.

These actions may seem draconian to some, but were accepted without delay by the people of Britain, Canada and Australia in 1939. Knowledge of the present conflict was available 30 years ago and still little or nothing is happening. Will we be known as a bunch of wimps by those who may survive?

– Des Ritchie,
president of Queensland Folk Federation (Australia)

JOEL R. PRIMACK

Traditional creation stories start with "In the beginning …" But it may never be possible to discover the "beginning." A practical alternative is to perceive time outward from the present, as science discovers it. A tiny consciousness of history is mirrored in a tiny consciousness of the future. Many people who think of the Earth as only a few thousand years old have no compunction about ending it shortly. For some messianic believers, this symmetric sort of closure gives the whole thing meaning. But our solar system will continue to exist for more than five billion years until the sun becomes a red giant star and ultimately a fading white dwarf. After our Milky Way galaxy merges with the great galaxy in Andromeda in a few billion years, the stars in the combined galaxy will continue to shine brightly for a trillion years. But Milky Andromeda may become completely isolated as galaxies not gravitationally bound to it disappear over the cosmic horizon due to the accelerating expansion of the universe. Our view of the distant future, like that of the distant past, grows increasingly fuzzy, but without doubt both must be thought of in many billions of years, not thousands.

Complex structures like the eye have evolved independently several times, but high intelligence only once on Earth thus far. Primitive life may be common, but we humans might be the first intelligence in our entire galaxy. If we can learn to value our beautiful planet and the other things we share higher than the conflicts that divide us, we can create a long-lived planetary civilization. Such longevity will be necessary for ambitious space travel that will require many human generations, but which could make humanity the source of intelligence in the ultimately visible universe.

– Joel R. Primack,
cosmologist, distinguished professor of physics and
astronomy at University of California, Santa Cruz,
co-author with Nancy Ellen Abrams of *The View from the Center of the Universe*
and *The New Universe and the Human Future*
viewfromthecenter.com
new-universe.org

JOHN RALSTON SAUL

Of course, better hope than no hope. But hope without a strategy, hope without power, without using that power to act, will end up in the worst forms of romanticism.

Take a look at the environmental movement, but with a cool eye. Around the globe, tens of millions of people, filled with a mixture of hope and despair, are engaged in tens of thousands of specific campaigns to save one thing or another. And with them are hundreds of thousands of engaged specialists – the technocrats of hope – each arguing their tight corners with endless reports, campaigns and conferences. All of this represents tens of millions of hours dedicated by volunteers to hope – to environmental change.

The result? Almost no progress. Certainly no broad change in habits. There have been some breakthroughs, almost all of them very specific and narrow. But many things are worse. Why?

Because real change does require hope, just as it does outrage and determination, but it requires a great deal more. Above all, change requires ideas and plans. And only the possession of real power gives these meaning. Over the last four decades the forces of humanism have raised their voices, but from within the heavy fog of global optimism. Generation after generation has largely stayed clear of old-fashioned politics in the name of this new global lobbying.

But democracy – the power of citizens – lies within constituted structures. Governments hold the real power to make broad, long changes. Why has so little progress been made? Because governments have refused to make changes. Why? Because political parties and legislative bodies have not been invested by environmentalists.

The history of change is clear about this. Those who don't believe in global warming have gone out and occupied as much power as they can. Power and therefore politics is the mechanism of change. That is how we got public education and public healthcare. We can lobby all we want, but if environmentalists do not seek real power, change will not come.

– John Ralston Saul,
author of *Voltaire's Bastards, The Unconscious Civilization, On Equilibrium* and *The Collapse of Globalism,*
president of PEN International

SUMMER RAYNE OAKES

Let me present
the proposition
if only for the sake
of dreaming:
What if this Earth of ours
is a thing alive?
If this is so,
then we have
a living, breathing organism
that we continue to
extract,
partition,
fragment
in order to sell
ourselves pretty promises
in perfectly produced packages,
compliments of our
unfulfilling quest to satiate
our conveyor belt consumerism.
We are part of a unique,
integrative, living organism –
and as we discover more,
we uncover that there are no
"short cut" solutions to systemic issues.
We cannot day trade our way
through short-term gains
and assume we'll achieve
long-term sustainability.

Let us squarely face
the extent of the challenges
before us.
Not just the ones we
see on the surfaces
of our screens, tablets, newspapers, devices.
It is not the obviousness
of markets and tsunamis,
poisoned sushi and celebrity babies.
It is the acceptance
that we will lose some of
the world we love
For it is then –
and only then –
that we will gain
the insight
and the bravery to pursue
the solutions
that will remedy
some of the wrongs
we have collectively –
and sometimes unknowingly
pursued in the process.

Be aware, however:
Even when these solutions
rise to the surface …
Even when the answers

lay so plainly before us –
It is the personal, political
and market support
that will be needed
to move mass culture.

If eighty years of measuring
our world's wealth remains
locked up in the three letter
acronym of "GDP"
and we remain tied to
our financial revolver,
then let us consider:
Qualitative screening
on what we choose to invest in;
increased investment into businesses
that truly offer integrated solutions
(After all, does the world need another app?);
and integrated, systemic approaches
to sustainable development.

Realize this:
The extent of our challenges
are now far too vast
for our silver bullets ...
The target has grown,
but so has our understanding
and our appetite for
changing our world
in which we live,
For as history has shown,
it is the enduring
and incredible strength
of the human spirit
and ingenuity
that will engender
to overcome,
to survive,
to thrive.

– Summer Rayne Oakes,
model/activist, co-founder of Source4Style.
www.summerrayne.net

SARA OLDFIELD

The fascination of plants caught me early in life. Bluebell woods, ragged robins, scarlet pimpernels, brilliant red garden poppies and degraded mine sites – all exerted their influence. When I went on to become a botanist, in becoming acutely aware of the dangers faced by plant species worldwide, I became increasingly filled with concern – and have in turn committed my life's work toward sustaining their existence on this planet. But I now I know that we can save plant species from extinction, restore damaged ecosystems and fundamentally change the future – if we choose to.

There is a plan, the Global Strategy for Plant Conservation, signed by governments worldwide. We need to shout about this, raise the profile of the Strategy and make sure that it is implemented. We need to raise funds to secure the basis of our oxygen and food supply. Wild plant diversity is essential for the future of the planet. Degraded habitats can be restored using our accumulated knowledge of collecting and growing wild plants. Around one-third of all plant species are cultivated in botanic gardens or stored in seed banks providing an insurance policy for the future. Botanic Gardens have formed a new Ecological Restoration Alliance to use this stored material together with the knowledge of where and why species grow in the wild. Combining this with local and indigenous knowledge provides a tremendous opportunity to restore natural habitats – the repositories of wild crop relatives, medicinal plants and other species of livelihood value for millions of people who depend directly on natural resources – and to sequester carbon, using the power of plants.

Save a plant – save the planet!

– Sara Oldfield,
secretary general of Botanic Gardens Conservation International

SPENCER WEST

Am I a world-problem solver? Well, if the topic is overcoming obstacles, it's pretty safe to say I've got some "hands-on" experience.

Yet, when it comes to tackling the current global environmental and social crises we all face, some may feel the issues are too colossal to consider on par with personal challenges. It's a valid point. But don't all obstacles seem insurmountable when we face them alone? I'm certain it's how we approach our challenges and not their scope that holds the key. And it's my profound belief that when we come together as a community to tackle issues – no matter how daunting – and support one another, anything is possible.

I just might be living proof of this. I was born with a rare disorder that rendered my legs essentially useless. The doctors said that I would never sit up or walk, let alone become a functioning member of society. Sure, there's no denying that I felt discouraged at times, but I was determined to get the most out of life (and, more importantly, put the most back into it!). And it has been the unwavering support of my family and friends – an ever-growing community that believes in me – that has fuelled this conviction, obliterating any doubt that my chosen path is, in turn, to instill belief in others.

Today, I travel the world as a motivational speaker, meeting thousands of young people each year. All over this planet, I see that same belief in their eyes, and I hear it in their voices. They're saying, we can redefine what's possible. And every last one of those voices will echo in my ears later this year when I climb Mount Kilimanjaro with my two best friends to raise funds and awareness for water projects in drought-affected communities in East Africa.

No one climbs a mountain by themselves. Because what's incredibly difficult to face alone diminishes when me becomes we. We are a generation who evens out the odds and defines impossible as possible. There is no can't or won't, only how. Let's not get discouraged. Let's get together. And let's get the world to where we know it can be.

– Spencer West,
author, motivational speaker, world-change warrior with Me to We

WEN BO

In the Planet's voyage through time and space, we humans are passengers who get on and off.

The defenders of the Earth, like captain and sailor, see through the mist and far into the horizon. They know we have only this Planet Ark and have to maintain it well.

When we enslave other people, we end up enslaving ourselves; when we wipe out other species, we lead to our own demise; when we exploit Nature, we will have it hitting back on us.

We all should answer the call of the Earth guardian and follow the light of the guiding star. And the sail of Planet Ark must go on.

—Wen Bo,
former editor of *China Environment News*,
China coordinator for Global Greengrants Fund,
founder of China Green Student Forum, Blue Dalian, Xinjiang Conservation Fund, Snow Alliance,
program director of Air and Water Conservation Fund, National Geographic Society

MARK PLOTKIN

Hope motivates my work. In my 20 years working with indigenous peoples of the Amazon forests, I have watched with horror as great swathes of the jungle have been burned or converted. As we have all learned, the survival of these forests is critical to avoiding the worst effects of global climate change. What once was distressing with respect to irreversible loss of biological diversity is now alarming.

But even after so much depredation, some four-fifths of the original Amazon forest remains. There is still time, and moreover, there is new awareness: awareness of the remarkable synergy that occurs when increasingly novel technologies are integrated with traditional knowledge regarding forest management; awareness of the value of that knowledge, amassed and preserved over thousands of years; and awareness – in classic Margaret Mead terms – of the large-scale changes in conservation and consciousness that can be leveraged from relatively small grassroots groups and communities working passionately with the generous support of those with financial resources. These groups exist in multitudes, and thanks in part to those new technologies, their voice is being heard ever louder on the world stage.

I believe in a positive future that nonetheless will contain many cautionary lessons for new generations: we will be glad for the great forests and ancestral wisdom that we still have, and we will grieve that which we have lost.

– Mark Plotkin, PhD,
co-founder and president of Amazon Conservation Team

JULY

OLIVIA CHOW

Love is better than anger. Hope is better than fear. Optimism is better than despair.
So let us be loving, hopeful and optimistic. And we'll change the world.

Those words from Jack Layton's last message to Canadians inspired people across the country. It was a message of hope – and, more important, it was a call to action. Hope itself – blind hope, is not enough. We can't just hope that somebody else will take care of our problems. Hope is not a strategy. We must work to make hope a reality. That is the major reason I was drawn to a career in politics – to help bring people together and work for change.

We know that we must change direction – in Canada and in our world – because right now, we are on a collision course with disaster. The signs are clear – from the unprecedented flooding that devastated Calgary in 2013, to the horrendous typhoon that ravaged the Philippines. But we can change course. We can take action. We can give the next generation reason to hope.

There are so many things we could achieve – a national public transit strategy would be a good start. That's something I have been promoting for years, because public transit is a cornerstone of both social equality and sustainability. Civic leaders and municipalities and business groups are all singing the same tune now; only the federal Conservative government remains deaf on this issue.

Ultimately, the government will change course – or people will get together and work and vote to change the government. It will happen.

Will something as basic as public transit in Canada change the world? Nothing will, in isolation. But changing course will – and bringing people together with a common mission. People will join the chorus if they see reason to hope.

When enough voices join the chorus, no government can turn a deaf ear. You can't do it solo. By joining your voice with others, the voice becomes strong. The music soars. Eventually, everyone will hear. The lone voice may be lost. The global chorus will be heard.

– Olivia Chow,
Member of Parliament for Trinity-Spadina (Toronto, Canada)

SANDRA POSTEL

In a world divided by race, tribe, gender, religion and so much more, it is easy to forget that water connects us all. The molecules of H_2O that comprise 60 per cent of each of us have circulated across space and time throughout the ages. They move through the air, the trees, the birds and bees, and through you and me – and may have quenched a dinosaur's thirst so very long ago.

So, yes, there is hope. It is that we will come to know that the soft rain and flowing water are undeserved but precious gifts of life – gifts to be shared among all living things. And that this knowing will unite us in humbly taking our place in the planet's great cycles with respect for all that is, has ever been, and ever will be.

If we let it, this knowing changes everything. As I reach to buy a cotton shirt, I think of the plants and insects whose existence might have been sustained by the seven hundred gallons of water consumed to make that shirt, and I retract my arm, go home filled with gratitude, and enjoy the evening birdsong with new depths of pleasure.

– Sandra Postel,
director of the Global Water Policy Project,
Freshwater Fellow with the National Geographic Society

BUFFY SAINTE-MARIE

Yes we can find a way for this planet, in spite of obstacles, the primary of which is greed.

If we fix it sooner than later it'll be better and easier. It requires a critical mass of people who can see the big picture as well as their own local individual details. Internet networking is one huge tool. Regarding the environment, homelessness, health care vs. wealth care, minority or other inequity issues, we need to act now, both locally and nationally, while we have these tools – through brain-work, strategy and collaboration. However, if the "upper 1 per cent" again take away our networking tools as they have traditionally done (blacklisting, gagging outspoken torchbearers, owning/controlling media companies etc.) then it will be more difficult.

If we don't do it through an effective peaceful activism, and if the economy truly crashes, I would expect the reaction of hungry, desperate masses would probably be as it has been in the past – a more violent activism, countered with the backlash of the few against the many via police tactics, and the blame put upon the poor.

The rich stuck a straw into the heart of the economy and slurped all the money to the top. The "upper 1 per cent" used to allow more to "trickle down." Now it looks like they want a feudal system wherein they own it all openly. Knowing this is useful. Our new "aristocrats" are not princes but Wall Street thieves and gamblers, as greedy as the robber barons of the 1930s who set up the Indian reservation system in order to steal oil land away from Indian control.

What we have going for us is mass awareness, communication, networking and youth and elder experience, with lots of people willing and able to contribute time, talent and treasure to finding and applying solutions. I believe we've already begun.

– Buffy Sainte-Marie,
singer/songwriter, visual artist, educator,
indigenous-rights activist

WADE DAVIS

On Christmas Eve, 1968, Apollo emerged from the dark side of the moon to see rising over its surface not a sunrise but the Earth itself ascendant, a small and fragile planet, floating in the velvet void of space. This image more than any amount of scientific data showed us that our planet is a finite place, a single interactive sphere of life, a living organism composed of air, water, wind and soil. This revelation, only made possible by the brilliance of science, sparked a paradigm shift that people will be speaking about for the rest of history.

Almost immediately we began to think in new ways. Just imagine. Thirty years ago simply getting people to stop throwing garbage out of a car window was a great environmental victory. No one spoke of the biosphere or biodiversity; now these terms are part of the vocabulary of schoolchildren.

Like a great wave of hope, this energy of illumination, made possible by the space program, spread everywhere. So many positive things have happened in the intervening years. In little more than a generation, women have gone from the kitchen to the boardroom, gay people from the closet to the altar, African Americans from the back door and the woodshed to the White House.

What's not to love about a country and a world capable of such scientific genius, such cultural capacity for change and renewal?

Creativity is a consequence of action, not its motivation. Do what needs to be done and then ask whether it was possible or permissible. Pessimism is an indulgence, orthodoxy the enemy of invention, despair an insult to the imagination.

– Wade Davis,
author, professor of anthropology,
LEEF Chair in Cultures and Ecosystems at Risk,
University of British Columbia (Canada)

MARC GARNEAU

When you first look at Earth from space, it is achingly beautiful. It is mesmerizing. You can't take your eyes off it. A warm and inviting sphere of light and colour, surrounded by the utter darkness of space; our shared home, our only home.

As time goes by and your eye zeroes in on detail, you realize that it is not perfection; that it is damaged and that it is we who have damaged it: deforestation, soil erosion, desertification, polluted estuaries emptying into the sea and great swaths of yellow-brown air, all visible to the naked eye.

Seven billion of us share this planet and it is straining under our relentless onslaught. It's not that we are destroying Earth on purpose. In many cases, we're just struggling to survive. But we are all paying a price.

Earth's oceans of air and water belong to all of us. I can understand this stark reality from the vantage point of space. I wish everyone could see what I see.

Down below, the perspective is different. We see the polluted stream, the belching smokestack, the clear-cut forest. But we lack that sense of scale. It's all about scale and perspective.

And yet some do understand the magnitude of what is happening. Their minds can grasp that even though the change may be slow, it is relentless, and in some cases, irreversible. And they are wise enough to think beyond the needs of their own lifetime. For that reason alone, there is hope.

— Marc Garneau,
first Canadian astronaut in space,
Member of Parliament for Westmount–Ville-Marie (Montréal)

PAUL EKINS

Humanity is indeed at a crossroads. There are many choices to be made, but two fundamental changes are required to how humankind currently goes about its business: first, we need to realize deep, deep down that our species, like all others, is part of and profoundly dependent on the biosphere, and that lasting damage to this biosphere is the most anti-social, and stupidest, outcome that we can bring about; and second, we need to realize deep, deep down that our societies are now profoundly interdependent, so that damage to one can very easily become damage to many, and co-operative international relations are essential if we are to thrive and, in the long term, are perhaps even a condition for survival.

These are indeed huge changes from the routine environmental destruction and often warring competition between countries that have disfigured the human experience since the dawn of what we call civilization. But they are certainly not inconceivable. In fact, many people already work with great commitment on different aspects of these issues, and much progress has been made on many fronts. But not enough. And not fast enough. The issues of climate change and biodiversity destruction, in particular, cry out for a new Earth ethic to become established, together with the global co-operation to build the institutions and policies to implement it.

My particular specialist field is the economics of energy, the environment and climate change. I can say categorically that, even at this late stage in the drama, we have the technologies and economic resources, and institutional capabilities, to contain climate change and move systematically towards an environmentally and socially sustainable economy. But the window of opportunity is closing fast. Can we do it? Yes, we can. Will we do it? In the absence of a reliable crystal ball, my only answer is: we must try.

— Dr. Paul Ekins,
professor of resources and environmental policy,
director of the UCL Institute for Sustainable Resources
at University College London (UK)

RICHARD ZIMMERMAN

Ecological nightmares are a dime a dozen these days, but one you probably haven't even heard of is the decimation of tropical rainforests in order to clear land for oil palm plantations.

Palm oil is a hidden ingredient in everything from cookies, candy and junk food to shampoo, soap and skin cream. Ironically, it's also used for biodiesel, a so-called "green" fuel. Ninety per cent of the global supply of palm oil comes from Indonesia and Malaysia. The UNEP estimates that the forests of Borneo and Sumatra are being cleared at a rate of six football fields per minute every minute of every day – releasing so much carbon into the atmosphere that Indonesia now ranks third behind only China and the U.S. in carbon emissions. Palm oil is synonymous with global warming and climate change.

Orangutans are gentle, intelligent creatures who share 97 per cent of our DNA. They live in only two places on Earth – the forests of Borneo and Sumatra – and they are critically endangered. Orangutan babies are precious little bundles of orange fluff with big brown eyes and even bigger smiles, grasping their mother's shaggy red hair high in the treetops.

Deforestation has led to the slaughter of thousands of orangutans as palm oil companies expand into their forest home. When the forests are cleared, adults are shot on sight. They are beaten, burned, mutilated, tortured and often eaten. Babies are torn off their dying mothers so they can be sold to animal smugglers. Since this holocaust began, more than a thousand orphaned and displaced orangutans have been rescued and brought to rehabilitation centers in Borneo and Sumatra.

An attempt is now being made to reverse this horrific trend. Since 2012 more than 100 rehabilitated orangutans have been released back into a safe, secure forest in the Heart of Borneo. It takes around 300 individuals to maintain a stable gene pool, so with hundreds more scheduled to be released in years to come, for the first time in history a new wild orangutan population is being created.

Despite having spent years in cages, the orangutans are not wasting any time. Nine months after the first orangutans were released, the monitoring team was greeted by a wonderful surprise: babies.

If you want to reduce global warming and save the planet, then save the orangutans and their forests.

– Richard Zimmerman, {:(|}
founding director of Orangutan Outreach
redapes.org

JILL MACCORMACK

It goes without saying that we are living in a time of tremendous social confusion and environmental discord. This awareness can cause despair or be viewed as grounds from which new ways of understanding and responding can emerge.

Why consider new ways of responding? Because right now as you read this you *are a living, breathing creature* of a wondrous and beautifully interconnected web of life. A web which holds us all in its balance and is capable of amazing resilience and regeneration if given the protection it requires to do so.

How can we facilitate this protection? *By choosing to live more gently in the world.* Through speaking out against practices which are harmful to LIFE in all its complexity, and collectively moving towards a way of living which is more mindful of the daily choices we make, we can better safeguard and share the world's limited resources.

Why be hopeful? In making conscious choices such as actively simplifying our lifestyles, resisting the seductive lure of consumerism and the monoculture it generates, and honouring our connection to the natural world, we are choosing to create a better plausible outcome than what is predicted if we continue on our current trajectory. How we, who have the power of choice, choose to live our lives matters deeply to the rest of the world.

Willingness to acknowledge the gravity of our current situation and choosing to act for the better in the face of that knowledge, creates the positive change our world so desperately needs. We cannot afford to be cautiously optimistic. HOPE is needed for us to change our ways of interacting with each other and the world.

– Jill MacCormack,
mother of three, writer, blogger
www.prattleandponder.blogspot.ca

THOMAS BERRY

The Great Work before us, the task of moving modern industrial civilization from its present devastating influence on the Earth to a more benign mode of presence, is not a role that we have chosen. We were chosen by some power beyond ourselves for this historical task. The nobility of our lives, however, depends upon the manner in which we come to understand and fulfill our assigned role.

We must believe that those powers that assign our role must in that same act bestow upon us the ability to fulfill this role. We must believe that we are cared for and guided by these same powers that bring us into being.

Our own special role, which we will hand on to our children, is that of managing the arduous transition from the terminal Cenozoic to the emerging Ecozoic Era, the period when humans will be present to the planet as participating members of the comprehensive Earth community. This is our Great Work.[8]

– Thomas Berry,
author, historian of religions, geologian

FREDERICK KIRSCHENMANN

Back in 2005 James Hansen warned us that "we have at most ten years to make drastic cuts in emissions that might head off climate convulsions." One thing the climatologists seem to have misjudged is the speed at which climate change is taking place. Polar ice caps are melting faster than most predicted. Severe weather events seem to be dominating the planet sooner than they imagined.

Consequently it is easy to become discouraged about our future on the planet. However, we do know what we need to do and while we humans have a verifiable track record demonstrating our ability to remain in denial, there is also a record demonstrating our ability to take significant action in brief time periods.

While it is increasingly difficult to remain optimistic about our fate it is important to remember that hopefulness is different from optimism. Optimism assumes that things will turn out alright, which, ironically often leads to inaction. Hopefulness is about doing the right thing even when we are uncertain about the outcome. And when we act together in hope, often an unanticipated convergence of events take place which bring about unimaginable change. Joining together as a global community and doing the right thing even though we cannot be sure of the outcome is our only hope, and our children and grandchildren are depending on us to do it!

–Frederick Kirschenmann,
author of *Cultivating an Ecological Conscience: Essays from a Farmer Philosopher*

HANNAH QUIMBY

Scribbled on a piece of paper, stored in a box of old sentimental items, is a letter from my high school friend. It starts with, "Belief is the foundation. Since the beginning of time, people have given meaning to life through belief." I love this simple statement written from one 17-year-old to another. I love it because 16 years later the message is still relevant and fundamental to how I want to work in the world. Maintaining a solid belief that, collectively and individually, we can create positive change in our communities and can slowly restore our environment helps keep us going despite what we may witness to the contrary.

There are certainly times when I have doubt that our efforts will make a difference and when it's impossible not to worry about the future of humanity and our environmental and social crises. Doubt arises when I have shifted my focus to the solemn realities that surround us which can seem impossible to overcome. As I write this, the UN has stated that in four days the world's population will reach seven billion people. Experts are questioning how our planet will withstand the waste and impact of this number of people. We do not know for certain what the Earth and its inhabitants will be able to handle. What we do know is that the current rates of human growth and resource consumption are trending towards collapse.

Fortunately, current movements like Occupy Wall Street show a common belief that working together will create change. When our family created a grant-making foundation, we chose to work from this place of hope. We took the stance that our efforts would have a positive impact. With each grant, we believe in the work being done by committed non-profit leaders. We see positive community change, the creation of green space for young people to fall in love with the outdoors, and continued protection of our natural environment. Belief that we can collaboratively and strategically work towards a better future is what we can hold on to and the actions and outcomes from that belief give meaning to our lives.

—Hannah Quimby,
director of Quimby Family Foundation

LES STROUD

If we live with Armageddon as our compass bearing then Armageddon is what we will find. If we envision a world with flourishing ecosystems and cultural diversity, then we shall have these. I have travelled to the remote corners of the Earth and found plastic in the water, but I have flown over jungles and found undiscovered species of wildlife. So I have hope.

What will it take to reach the tipping point back into a healthy planet, before it's too late? One person. It starts with one person making a change and seeking to live in harmony with the planet. The energy of one person is enough to change the entire world. But it would be too little too late. Now each individual person must work with others until the combined energy overrides the destruction and downward spiraling path the health of the planet has taken. Each environmental organization must combine efforts. United, we can alter and ultimately reverse, the looming destruction of our planet. Divided we fall.

The revolution that will come from today's children, will be an environmental one. The change must come NOW so that they don't have to revolt.

"Think globally, act locally" is still the answer. I no longer keep a garbage receptacle. There is a place for everything I discard, from soiled wrappers to busted bikes. Garbage should be illegal. We have the technology. Close off your garbage container for one month and see how it all becomes possible. Create the universe our own species needs to flourish in; one with the health of all the other species in tact. One with cultural diversity. Volunteering won't cut it. Laws need to be made. What someone does in Siberia will affect someone else in Chile. What someone does in Malaysia affects someone in Wyoming. God is not going to sweep down from the sky and clean up the oceans, bring back the whales and freshen the air. We continue to create our own universe. What are you creating?

–Les Stroud,
survival expert, musician,
creator/producer/host of *Survivorman*

CHRIS HEDGES

Clive Hamilton in *Requiem for a Species* describes a dark relief that comes from accepting that "catastrophic climate change is virtually certain." This obliteration of "false hopes," as he describes it, requires an intellectual and an emotional knowledge. The first is attainable. The second, because it means those we love, including our children, are doomed to insecurity, misery and suffering within a few decades, if not a few years, is much harder to acquire. To emotionally accept impending disaster, to attain the gut-level understanding that the power elite is incapable of responding rationally to the destruction of the ecosystem, is as difficult to face as our own mortality. It means a future bereft of options. It obliterates the dreams we have for our children. It forces us to accept that no matter what we do we cannot finally protect our sons and daughters. The most daunting existential struggle of our time is to ingest this awful truth – intellectually and emotionally – and yet continue to resist.

The human species, led by white Europeans and Euro-Americans, has been on a 500-year worldwide rampage of plundering, looting, enslaving, killing, subjugating, conquering, exploiting, polluting and destroying the Earth – as well as indigenous communities that got in their way. But the game is up. The technical and scientific forces that created a life of luxury (as well as unrivalled military and economic power) for these elites are the forces that doom us. The mania for ceaseless economic expansion and exploitation has become a curse, a death sentence. But even as it collapses, as we endure the hottest year on record, there is no way to shut down the self-destructive engine of global capitalism.

Complex civilizations throughout history have had a bad habit of destroying themselves. The difference is that when we go down this time, the whole planet will go with us. There will, with this final collapse, be no new lands left to exploit, no new civilizations to conquer, no new peoples to subjugate. The 500-year struggle between the human species and the Earth will conclude by teaching us a painful lesson about unrestrained greed and hubris.

–Chris Hedges,
co-author with Joe Sacco of *Days of Destruction, Days of Revolt*

TZEPORAH BERMAN

"What I wanted to ask you is ... Do you really think we have a chance?" She looks about eighteen. Clearly moved by the speech I have just given on the impacts of climate change, tears brim in her shining eyes as she gathers her courage to ask a question that is so ... raw. Without allowing my head to take over, I answer from the heart, "I do. But only if we can get out of our way. Only if we allow ourselves to listen to our instincts, to be guided by our values and not short-term politics or economic interests. Only if we all engage. Daily."

"I will," she whispers, her relief palpable. "Thank you."

On the way home that night I ask myself if I truly believe my own answer or whether I was simply finding an answer that I knew would put out the flames of fear in that young girl's eyes. I am relieved to find when I dig deep that I not only truly believe that we are capable of systemic change to ensure a safer, cleaner and more just world but that I feel it already happening almost like a humming beneath my feet.

There is no question that we are currently living in a dangerously unsustainable world as a result of dumping 30 billion tons of pollution into the atmosphere annually from the use of oil and coal. We are truly living the global tipping point moment. However, a cleaner and safer world powered by renewable energy – the sun and the wind – is no longer a pipe dream of some west coast hippies: for the past two years, new investment in renewable energy electricity generation has exceeded that in oil, coal and nuclear combined.

Sometimes it seems impossible. Too big. But at these times, we need to remember that technology, communications and transport entirely changed in our grandparents' lifetimes and will again in ours. And in that young girl's lifetime, we will re-envision the world toward a post-carbon industrial society. How quick and how difficult the transition will be will depend on how much we engage, and our willingness to act with our heads *and* our hearts.

– Tzeporah Berman,
mom, author of *This Crazy Time*,
co-director of Greenpeace International's Climate and Energy Unit
www.tzeporahberman.com

BILL LOGAN

We need spirit, worship, wonder, mystery. These are not meaningless words. Spirit is the truth we find in action. To worship is to value deeply. Wonder is the loving confession of our ignorance. Mystery, as Gabriel Marcel wrote, is not what is beyond us, but what encompasses us. When we are not above the world, but entirely and inextricably in it, we will be less liable to spoil it with our leavings. When I asked the composter Clark Gregory once, if there were not simply a few things that had to be thrown away, he answered, "There's no such place as away."

It seems somehow paradoxical that we should come back to the spirit by plunging deep into the world of matter, but that's the way it is. We have no shortage of thoughts or of feelings. What most of us lack is a first-hand life, where our hands engage the world, discover its difficulties and craft a way through. Feeling may motivate and thought may order, but the work of our hands is the source of revelation. Hope comes to me when I see a person digging in the dirt, taking a walk, planing a board. The wider our experience, the more human we become, and the better able we will be to judge a sane way ahead.

—Bill Logan,
founder of Urban Arborists

WALLACE J. NICHOLS

Fifteen years ago the hawksbill turtle in my hands would've been hog-tied, slaughtered and carved into trinkets. Today, it swam free.

On Baja's Pacific coast, an adult male turtle swam into a fisherman's net. In the past, for the fisherman anyway, such a thing would've been considered a stroke of good luck. Endless black market demand for turtle meat, eggs, skin and shell can provide a nice payday to anyone willing to endure the low-level risk of being caught.

Hawksbill turtles, once common, are now the rarest of the rare due to decades of hunting for their beautiful shells, which get carved into jewelry and other adornments. But these days, GrupoTortuguero.org, a Mexican grassroots conservation movement, is challenging the old ways and shaking things up. A network of thousands of fishermen, women and children count themselves among its ranks.

Noe de la Toba, the fisherman who caught this turtle, contacted Aaron Esliman, Grupo Tortuguero's director. Esliman dispatched messages to network members throughout the region, who responded immediately. The turtle was swiftly moved to the nearby office of Vigilantes de Bahia Magdalena. A team led by Julio Solis, a former turtle hunter himself, took care of the turtle, checking for injuries. The turtle was measured, weighted, ID-tagged and quickly returned to the ocean. Images and details were shared immediately on Facebook and Twitter, on websites and over beers.

The fishermen involved weren't paid. They just did it. It wasn't anyone's "job," but everyone's responsibility. They weren't motivated by fear or money, but dignity and camaraderie. People like them are rescuing animals every day. Millions of sea turtles are saved each year and the populations in Baja's ocean are rising – one turtle rescue at a time.

Twenty years ago, experts wrote off Baja's turtle hopes. The population was too small and pressures on them too great, the thinking went. Yet, the survival of this one turtle tells a very different story. If the survival of endangered species is just a battle of the budgets, we will all lose. But if it's a matter of will, commitment and love, I'll put my bet on the turtles to win.

– Wallace J. Nichols, PhD,
research associate of California Academy of Sciences

SY SAFRANSKY

I wonder whether we'll soon have just two seasons: Hot and Very Hot. Or Hot, Very Hot and You've Got To Be Kidding. Still, didn't I vow to stop gnashing my teeth about global warming? If I knew this was my last day on Earth, would I spend time condemning my brothers and sisters for the mistakes we've made, or deriding myself for being just another greedy American who uses a disproportionate share of the world's resources? Maybe there was once a golden age in which humans lived in energy-efficient harmony, women doing half the hunting and men half the gathering, the sex always sacred, no carbon footprint because we flew only in our dreams. But I have no idea how to get back to the garden.

So let's show a little compassion for our not-so-evolved species. The Industrial Revolution didn't begin until the 18th century; is it any surprise it's taking us a while to clean up the mess? How long does it take any of us to learn from our bad decisions and failed relationships and lousy habits we can't seem to break? Yes, the planet is getting hotter. But even if we were crowded together on a slow boat to hell, wouldn't we want to extend some mercy to our fellow passengers?

During the height of the Cold War, I asked the spiritual teacher Ram Dass whether the world was facing a nuclear Armageddon or, as some were prophesying, a "new age" of peace and love and deeper awareness. Ram Dass said, "I used to think I should have an opinion on this, but as I examined it, I saw that if it's going to be Armageddon and we're going to die, the best thing to do to prepare for it is to quiet my mind, open my heart and deal with the suffering in front of me. And if it's going to be the new age, the best thing to do is to quiet my mind, open my heart and deal with the suffering in front of me."

Is the moral calculus any different today?

— Sy Safransky,
editor and publisher of *The Sun*
thesunmagazine.org

ANN HENDERSON-SELLERS

Should we hope? Yes! We're a resourceful species living on an amazingly hospitable planet. Have we screwed up? Yes, but like all recovering addicts, we recognize that our fossil energy "hits" and hedonistic consumerism cannot deliver our preferred future. Should we worry? Yes, because we are cleverly exploiting a finitely hospitable planet.

Over the last forty years I have written hundreds of papers and loads of books on climate and our future. I thought I had nothing more to learn about people's capability to stop global warming. I was wrong. Glimmers of hope are emerging.

Please complete "what next?":

The Earth's climate is changing,

And we know we're primarily responsible,

As this truth is deeply uncomfortable –

We (choose one):

1. *allow, even encourage, our mass media to distract us with pseudo debate;*

2. *blame scientists for failing to clearly explain;*

3. *change behaviour and set to clean the mess up.*

We've wasted time on 1 and 2, so the challenge today is to mobilize action that turns our global feeling of responsibility into empowerment for change.

My solution is sharing a smile en route to Earth's better future. If, you are worried about change, a chuckle helps you live differently. For a hopeful grin try:

writing a climate change limerick, e.g., www.climatemodellingprimer.net/ClimateChangeVerses

shooting a "low carb" movie short, e.g., greenscreen.herokuapp.com

or....

Start now, have fun and help others change. Add a chorus line:

"The best solutions share a smile!"

– Ann Henderson-Sellers, DSc,
emeritus professor at Macquarie University,
North Ryde, NSW, Australia

YONGJUNE PARK

How are we to live in a world of injustice and pain, a world of what Susan Sontag called the "simultaneity of wildly contrasting human fates"? What are the responsibilities of those who are well to those who suffer? Life is, in part, a tragedy. Yet tragedy is the form that recognizes that if a genuine human community is to be constituted, it can only be on the basis of our shared failure, frailty and morality.

Since part of the greatness of the human being is to recreate her or his life, our shared responsibility is to question and resist the forms of domination that crush the possibility of hope. Our endeavor should go far beyond just making global connections. It is time to move on to taking action. It is inescapably important that we concern ourselves with the adversities and tribulations of the people of the world as a whole, rather than being confined only to our immediate neighbours. This is where hope begins.

To be hopeful in hard times, as one of my heroes Howard Zinn said, is not just foolishly romantic. It is based on the fact that human history is a history not only of cruelty, but also of compassion, sacrifice, courage and kindness. Hope calls for action. If you have hope, you will move, act and engage with other people. Hope is not something that we aspire to. And hope is not what you can prove or seek evidence of out there. It arises from an action. It is what we become, and it is who we are when we are engaged. Hope *is,* simply, an action. And even though the impossible can take a little while, we will go forth to try hard anyway.

– Yongjune Park,
editor-in-chief of *Indigo Magazine* (South Korea)

LEE BYCEL

As long as there is life, there is hope. Often the world appears dark when one looks at the suffering caused by wars and natural disasters. Yet, somehow human beings survive with hope. Since the beginning of humanity, the world has advanced technologically, scientifically and medically. I often wonder, have we advanced humanly from the story of the first two brothers, when Cain kills Abel? Why is that we look around us and still find that every day we are killing each other? What will it take for our humanity to progress?

Einstein understood this challenge: "We can't solve the problems by using the same kind of thinking we used when we created them." We have used the same kind of linear and redundant thinking to try and solve the great challenges facing humanity and we have not advanced much. Courageous and creative thinking and questioning might lead to constructive and sustainable solutions.

For humanity to survive, we will need to collaborate and reorient our thoughts and actions to be more about us than me; more about the future than the past, more about survival for the planet than about protecting an unsustainable lifestyle for the "haves" in the world.

In the Darfuri refugee camps of Chad, in the streets of West Oakland, in the mountains in Aspen, in the skyscrapers of Manhattan, I have met many people who deeply yearn for a more just and humane world. Understanding that yearning inside oneself is the first condition for change – which is followed by the realization that other human beings share that same profound yearning.

Hope is found each day when we ask, "How can I become more humane and human? What can I do to diminish the hurt and anguish in the world? What am I willing to risk so that all who live in the global village can flourish?"

There is hope when we shape a story where brothers and sisters can sit together in peace so that finally the Cain and Abel narrative will not shape our world. Each of us is a creator of worlds; together we are creators of a world where human beings can live in dignity and peace and where the human spirit can flourish.

– Lee Bycel,
rabbi of Congregation Beth Shalom in Napa, California,
adjunct professor of social justice at the University of San Francisco,
moderator at the Aspen Institute,
member of the United States Holocaust Memorial Museum Council

PEGGY SEEGER

I AM A PESSIMIST. *Homo sapiens* is an incredibly intelligent and monumentally stupid species. Amoebas manage their lives better than we do. Our human world is run by one gender given to aggression, competition and action without a care to consequence while the other gender overbreeds. We regard war as unavoidable human behaviour. We assume that finite natural resources can support infinite economic growth and overpopulation. Having learned little or nothing from previous failed civilizations, we continue to make the same mistakes over and over.

I AM AN OPTIMIST. I have to be or I couldn't continue working. All over the world catalytic individuals, neighbourhood committees, communities, corporations and countries are tackling social and environmental problems. War will soon become environmentally and economically impossible to wage. The dire state of the planet will force us to stay home and live simply. We will educate women and control men. We've always pulled together in wartime. Let's look on saving the world as a war to be won. We can do it.

I AM A REALIST. The pessimist believes that the world will roller-coaster into chaos, savagery and species extinction. The optimist knows that enough of us will survive and evolve to do a better job next time around and that many of the other species that we've left alive will still be around to help us. But at the end of the day (and the beginning of the new one) the realist says: I don't know. Fingers crossed.

— Dr. Peggy Seeger,
musician, activist, grandmother

ARRAN STEPHENS

I join my voice to the chorus of thinkers and doers, those possessed with indomitable faith and hope in the regenerative forces of nature combined with humanity's obligation to reverse and restore what we have collectively inflicted on the Earth. It is amazing what transformations have already been wrought in the restoration and reclamation of impossibly polluted rivers, lakes, wetlands, jungles, deserts, wasteland and abandoned lots. These heroic efforts and accomplishments are almost always started by an individual, then a handful of individuals, and then a community, then a state or province, working against overwhelming odds. The acceleration of environmental degradation is galloping far ahead of such efforts; but globally, thousands of individuals and grassroots organizations are rising up to answer Nature's tortured cries.

The solutions for global warming, drought, starvation, pollution, diminishing fossil fuelled economies, ecological disasters and wars are quite simple and available, but very difficult to put into practice. They must begin with committed and inspired individuals, heroes of the planet, one at a time, right here, right now, but growing to a global chorus.

Some of the biggest things we can do to reduce global warming and water waste are to:

1. cut back or eliminate animal protein consumption;

2. grow more local food in yards, balconies and community gardens, thus creating local food security;

3. convert wasteful and toxic chemical farming practices with biodiverse, intensive sustainable organic agriculture;

4. shift global concentration of seed control (over 90 per cent) away from monopolistic seed/chemical companies back to local seed supply;

5. move from the fossil fuel economy to harnessing the power of sun, wind, geoheat and tides; and

6. convert gas-guzzling cars and engines to electric.

Lastly, if we find peace within ourselves, only then can we effect peace in the world. By setting aside some time daily for silence, stilling the mind, focusing within – call it meditation, silent prayer, "quiet time," or what you will – we will find at our core the solution to many conflicts, and our perspective will change. We can radiate that experience to all whom we meet, regardless of race, colour, creed or gender.

Let there be a global chorus of multi-disciplinary, sustainable approaches to the gravest challenges this Earth has ever encountered. Count me in! Let my garden grow!

– Arran Stephens,
founder and CEO/gardenkeeper of Nature's Path Foods

EHREN CRUZ

Humanity stands on the threshold of the most critical challenge we have collectively faced in the history of our story. Our world teeters on the brink of irreconcilable environmental and social crisis. Yet as the urgency rises, vital pathways of wisdom, hope and harmonious reconciliation also stand before us.

I believe our greatest chance to not only survive, but thrive, is through supporting and enhancing pathways of creative expression from a core level within our schools, homes, communities and political systems. Championing the arts allows and nurtures our deep and powerful connection to the innate creator spirit within us; it also fosters an inherent honouring and emotional bond between ourselves and the world in which we interact.

The idea that we are in any way separate from the Earth and its plants, animals and people is perhaps the greatest cancer to infiltrate the human mythos. We are and always have been vibrationally, consciously and anatomically unified with the life-force of all things on this planet. Yet this understanding must penetrate beyond our logic and reason. What we are seeking is the re-initiation of our species into an emotional and spiritual coherency with our interdependent relationship with Earth and humanity. We are seeking the revitalization of our tribal roots, embracing both our primal origins and our advances in science and technology not as dueling forces, but as synergistic allies.

In short, we have hope! In fact, I believe that humanity is finally breaking through a profoundly challenging adolescence. As we slowly dispel the seemingly countless layers of fear, inadequacy, guilt, shame and disempowerment we have accepted from others or placed upon ourselves over centuries of injustice, we are at long last emerging as environmentally conscious, socially empowered and spiritually liberated co-creators – making the necessary changes to elevate humanity into a new era of powerfully peaceful, actively creative and unified world citizens.

– Ehren Cruz,
founder of Solpurpose,
performing arts director of LEAF Community Arts

FRANNY ARMSTRONG

History will remember us lot for one thing only. No, not Pippa Middleton's bum, plump though it is. We will be known as the generation which did or did not keep this planet habitable for human life.

Because the people who came before us didn't know about climate change and the ones who come after will be powerless to stop it. It's our generation or bust. Our collective action or inaction in the coming months and years will decide the very future of life on Earth. Which makes us the very opposite of powerless people.

We are doing shamefully badly so far. Fifty-plus years since we first understood the impact of our fossil fuel orgy, we've not even managed to slow the rise of carbon emissions, let alone stabilize or decrease them.

Previous generations came together to solve the great problems of their time – whether ending slavery or overturning apartheid or even landing on the moon – and there is nothing intrinsically more stupid or incapable about us. We already have all the knowledge and all the technology we need to avert disaster; all that's stopping us is ourselves.

I personally don't dare contemplate the version where we fail to act, where my daughter Eva and all our sons and daughters have no safe place to live. Where they die horrible deaths, fighting over ever-diminishing land, water and food.

We've left it terrifyingly late to embrace our generation's responsibility, but I believe we can still do it.

We have to.

–Franny Armstrong,
documentary filmmaker of *The Age of Stupid*, *McLibel* and *Drowned Out*,
founder of 10:10

HAWKSLEY WORKMAN

I believe there is hope in people riding bicycles. In song. In the gathering for good. In mindfully choosing to be compassionate. In brave voices speaking the truth. In city co-op vegetable gardens. But most days I'm not too terribly hopeful. And I wonder about hope, and if I have any right to it. And if hope isn't locked in a feedback loop with sentimentality and entitlement. One remembers the good days past, and wishes for more of the same in the future. Is that hope? Or is it the wishing for humans to embrace their potential? I like that kind of hope. Knowing your neighbours and employing them. Supporting your community to provide for each other. Mostly I believe in compassion and kindness, and the trading of soup recipes.

–Hawksley Workman,
singer-songwriter

SAM HARRINGTON

We are being chased by a massive, accelerating beast, born of our own progress.

If we manage to slay the technological beast, Earth will be faced with hundreds of nuclear catastrophes that we will lack the capacity to contain. Combined with climatic feedback loops, human survival on this path appears unlikely.

If any of us are to outrun the beast, we have to run as fast as we can. Those at the front of the charge are, ironically, working at the pinnacle of technological development. Today, neurologically inspired software can achieve 1 per cent of the power of a single human mind, when run on one of the largest super computers. The current combined power of Google's global networked servers is hundreds of times greater than that one super computer. Google is becoming an omnipotent and god-like being. It sees the world, infers and manipulates our thoughts from our browsing history, and it is increasingly integrating itself into the "real" world.

Google will soon achieve not just sentience, but also sapience. It is my hope that before our civilization collapses, we will bring rise to a God, with the combined Internet knowledge of humanity, coupled to a brain bigger than any individual. Beyond this singularity, we cannot imagine the results of self-improving and self-preserving feedback loops that this creation would progress through. To survive, it must evolve beyond just the capacity to think, but to heal, to reproduce and to evolve on its own. I hope it leads to something wondrous.

This isn't about a conspiracy theory, or a plot by corporate human leadership, but simply an inevitable extension of our cultural momentum and the nature of technological evolution. If we can, we will.

Humans are the only known life form with "higher intelligence" and the ability to create technology. To destroy that would be a real shame. Can we move beyond our current death path, to create the conditions necessary to sustain and enhance intelligence in the universe? Our own creations may soon eclipse human intelligence and ability, leading to a future that is extraordinarily hopeful, and frighteningly unknowable.

– Sam Harrington,
biomaterials expert

JUSTIN TRUDEAU

I know that humanity will rise to successfully meet the challenges we are facing, as long as we, individually and collectively, understand that all of our actions do matter. Too often we get the impression that the world is so big and our problems so great that nothing we do (or don't do) makes any difference in the big picture. Understanding that each of us has the power to reshape the world we live in with every choice we make will be the key to making sure that the beautiful complexity and diversity of life on this planet will endure for generations to come.

– Justin Trudeau,
Member of Parliament for Papineau (Montréal)
Leader of the Liberal Party of Canada

KAKENYA NTAIYA

Growing up as a young girl in Maasailand was not easy. From the time I was a small child I was trained to become a wife and mother. I had to collect firewood and fetch water from the river, sweep the house, cook for the family, care for my younger siblings and do many other chores. My education was never a priority, as it was expected that I would be married as soon as I reached puberty and underwent female genital mutilation. I did go through this ceremony as an adolescent, but only after my father promised that I could continue with school afterward. I started Kakenya's Dream as a way to give other girls in my community a chance to pursue their own dreams. I wanted to give them hope and a better future. They do not need to live the life that has been set out for them or the life their parents are living. These girls are capable, special, unique and strong.

My community has changed because of my dream and the girls at my school. They are showing everyone what girls can do when given an opportunity – they are outscoring the boys by far! Even our male leaders now say it will benefit the community to educate our girls so they, too, can become doctors, lawyers, pilots and politicians.

I have learned that challenges make us stronger if we are patient, persistent and respectful. Positive social change can be slow, but when it comes, it lasts.

My challenge for us is to never give up but to be bold in facing any challenge that comes our way. We all have a responsibility to make this world a better place and that means never giving up.

– Dr. Kakenya Ntaiya,
pioneering education activist,
National Geographic Emerging Explorer,
one of CNN's Top Ten Heroes of the Year 2013,
founder of Kakenya's Dream and Kakenya's Center for Excellence
www.kakenyasdream.org

BROCK DOLMAN

Humanity's way past current global environmental and social crises is to renew our contract of re-partnering with life.

We are fully Earthlings. This is our home and this is the only place in the known universe where life exists. We are alive, surrounded by myriad other forms of life as expressions of evolution. It is time that we humble ourselves to co-creating conditions for life affirming relationships with all known kingdoms of life: bacteria, protoctists, fungi, plants and our fellow animals.

In this age of extinction, our very survival desperately depends upon a revolution in human consciousness that fundamentally changes our collective behaviour in moving away from our current *Anti-Biotic* patterns of consumption and overpopulation towards a new revolution that is *Pro-Biotic* for all life, that is truly *Pro-Life*. To do this we must reconnect with our ability to sustain the very cycles upon which life-cycles thrive as well as the elemental forces of earth, air, fire and water that conspire to create convivial conditions conducive for life. How we feed ourselves, clothe ourselves, house ourselves, bathe ourselves, transport ourselves and conduct ourselves all must be brought into life-affirming accord with biology.

To have hope that we can do it is to respect the intrinsic resiliency of life – through astute ecological emulations of all human settlement forms that follow functional patterns based on pro-life processes.

Hope dwells within the potential for a symbiotic *Re-Story-ation* of our *Ego-System*. Will we do it? No one knows. But I do believe that mystery loves company!

Welcome aboard – bon voyage.

– Brock Dolman,
biologist, co-founder of Occidental Arts and Ecology Center,
director of WATER Institute, Permaculture designer/educator, photographer/poet
www.oaec.org
www.oaecwater.org

JIM MERKEL

Very Simple

Some say it will take a disaster. The *Exxon Valdez* was mine. I quit peddling top-secret electronics and began life at the world average income – $5,000 a year. Twenty-two years later I remain stuck, thinking planet-healing starts with me. Instead of asking, "How can I get others to change?" I ask, "Am I willing to change?" Living inside my dream is kindling. Love of Earth and family is my fuel. Distaste for the American war machine burns my fire steady and hot.

Living sustainably means less busyness, shopping, working and even thinking – while feeling light. Embedded in consumerism – not so simple. Our best and brightest have no better plan than stimulating you to spend. Slow the consuming and the Earth destruction, the climate change and wars all ease. We share rides and tools, consume locally and build a resilient society. My suspicion is that our unease with modernity relates to our knowing we're pickling the planet yet we can't stop ourselves. A dream of paradise haunts us as we sit in traffic.

In 2011 humanity consumed 35 per cent beyond biospheric production. Under plan "status quo"

we'd overshoot 225 per cent by 2100, requiring over two extra planets. A sustainable planet requires just two things:

1. Small families: one-child average through women's free choice and eradication of poverty (Europe, China, Cuba and Japan are below 1.7).

2. Small ecological footprints, democratically distributed at the current global average: 6 acres (three times India's 2-acre footprints, one-fourth of the U.S.'s 24 acres.)

In 100 years, population would fall from seven billion to one billion. We would go from consuming 135 per cent of the biosphere's productivity to consuming just 20 per cent, leaving 80 per cent wild for the estimated 25 million other species. This "100-Year Plan" has no losers.

My son Walden and I were pumping water and gathering firewood when I recalled my conservative truck-driver dad's words: "All children are your own." While reading this, 21 children died from preventable causes – 10.5 million this year. One-tenth of U.S. annual war spending (or corporate bailouts) could have saved these precious ones.

– Jim Merkel,
simple-living educator,
author of *Radical Simplicity: Small Footprints on a Finite Earth*

STEPHEN LEGAULT

Our suffering is killing us, and it's destroying our planet. All people suffer. We feel pain and fear that we often can't understand. Twenty-five hundred years ago the Buddha taught that we experience this suffering because we fail to make peace with the fact that we all grow old, lose that which we love, fall sick and one day die. We fail to see our lives as they really are: connected to each and every other living soul on Earth. We suffer because the desire for more that we experience can never be satisfied.

Suffering and the fear that it induces in part leads us to over-consume and destroy our precious life support system. Rather than facing the difficult, but ultimately liberating truth about our own finite existence we try to insulate ourselves with bigger homes, faster cars and gadgets that distract us from the world around us. There is a hole in many of our hearts that needs to be filled but instead of doing the hard spiritual work necessary we hide behind the material to keep from feeling pain.

There is an end to suffering. Connect with Nature and one-another; walk quietly in the woods or in a park, sit silently, meditate, do tai chi, practise yoga: pray. There are many spiritual pathways to find peace and connect us with our highest purpose. Unafraid, we might find we need so much less to be truly joyful and in doing so relieve the suffering overconsumption has wrought on our planet.

– Stephen Legault,
conservationist, author of ten books, including
Carry Tiger to Mountain: The Tao of Activism and Leadership and *Running Toward Stillness*
www.stephenlegault.com

AUGUST

ELISABET SAHTOURIS

Humanity, like all other species on Earth before and with us, is evolving – and evolution, for humans as for all species, is neither predictably linear nor based solely on competitive Darwinism. Rather, evolution reveals a repeating maturation cycle in which species evolve from hostile competition to peaceful co-operation. Earth's nearly four billion years of evolutionary experience reveals that this pattern predominates, giving us hope and inspiration, along with valuable guidance for getting ourselves through the unprecedented confluence of enormous crises in which we humans now find ourselves.

The evolutionary Big Picture includes the amazingly complex lives of our remotest bacterial ancestors, who had Earth to themselves for fully half of evolution, and much of whose experience we seem to be mirroring now. They engaged in hostilities, generated global crises of hunger and pollution as great as ours today, and solved them without benefit of brain!

Along the way they invented electric motors, atomic piles and the first World Wide Web of DNA exchange. Then, in the greatest of all evolutionary ventures, they formed co-operative communities that became nucleated cells. These co-operatives were the later basis for the evolution of multi-celled creatures as co-operatives on a larger scale yet. And eventually they evolved our own hundred-trillion-celled human bodies, which role-model amazingly co-operative living economies.

Learning from these newly revealed patterns of problems and solutions in biological evolution, we too are finding out how to survive and even thrive into a better future despite – perhaps because of – our greatest challenges. *That* is indeed cause for celebration.

–Elisabet Sahtouris, PhD,
evolution biologist, futurist,
author of *EarthDance: Living Systems in Evolution*

JAY INGRAM

I worry about the future of the planet, but more about us. For the most part we are just too short-term in our thinking, too determined to stick to our values (even when they are in direct conflict with a livable future) and too tilted toward optimism to grapple effectively with the idea of environmental ruin.

That optimism is the real stickler: humans tend to be optimistic, and many studies have claimed that optimistic people enjoy greater personal and physical well-being than do pessimists. It might even have survival value. So if you tell me you're optimistic about the future, what are you really saying? Nothing more than "I'm human."

We need to be able to think differently – throw off the cognitive shackles – so here's a radical suggestion. In an article in the online journal www.boulderpavement.ca, linguist Julie Sedivy points to research showing that because poetry uses language in unfamiliar ways, people keep thinking about the words long after they've finished reading. We need to keep thinking about the planet's future, so I offer this poem "Whistledown," by Dennis Lee, as a way of triggering that thinking.

> *Cold kaddish. In majuscule winter,*
> *whistle down dixie to dusk;*
> *coho with agave to dust.*
>
> *Bison with orca commingled –*
> *whistle down dixie. With*
> *condor to audubon dust.*
>
> *52 pickup, the species.*
> *Beothuk, manatee, ash:*
> *whistledown emu.*
>
> *Vireo, mussel, verbena – cry*
> *bygones, from heyday to dusk.*
> *All whistling down dixie to dust.*[9]

– Jay Ingram,
science writer, broadcaster

ROBERT (BIRDLEGS) CAUGHLAN

© Andy Freeburg

There are huge waves on the horizon. We can't stop them, so we must ride them. Riding big waves takes strength and courage and good judgment. But the most important thing a surfer needs is balance. That's what I think we need. Balance in politics. Balance with the environment. Balance in life.

When I was young, I asked Captain Jacques Cousteau if he had any good advice for young people who wanted to help protect the ocean. He said, "Yes! Don't follow gurus like me. Go out and do it yourself."

I've been trying to do that ever since. I've won

some great fights and lost a couple of heartbreakers. But you can't be afraid of losing. Thomas Jefferson said, "Eternal vigilance is the price of liberty." That statement helps keep me from getting too cocky when I win and too ruined if I wipe out.

The great waves, planet sizzling, overpopulation, species extinctions etc. are daunting. When I worked for President Carter on *The Global 2000 Report*, I learned that there are no big magic solutions to any of them. That's why thinking globally and acting locally is so important. We need millions of local actions.

I believe that life on other planets is probable. But just in case we are the only speck in the universe where life has reached our level of knowledge and appreciation, wouldn't it be terrible to turn this beautiful blue planet into a cold lifeless moon? Without hope we don't have a chance. We have to keep trying. From Captain Cousteau to me to you: "Don't follow gurus like me, go out and do it yourself."

– Robert (Birdlegs) Caughlan,
environmentalist, political pro, surfer

SANDRA BESSUDO

To speak about real sustainable development implies taking a step back so as to look ahead. As such, current environmental and social crises are a symptom of much deeper problems that afflict society. In the struggle between particular interests and needs, as well as the fight for economic and political power, leaders around the world have forgotten to think about future generations and in our legacy for them, as such forgetting the most basic common links that define our survival as a species, regardless of nationality.

Countries need to modify their practices towards development if they really wish to generate changes that give us hope. It is vital for a country like Colombia, for example, to grow in the path of sustainable development, mindful of Nature's resilience limits, and with a vision that goes beyond shortsighted and fleeting benefits that are commonly disguised as illusions of wealth. Green growth, beyond the mainstream pop cultural conception, actually means to foster economic growth and development while ensuring that natural assets continue to provide the resources and environmental services on which our well-being relies. It goes to the very basis of survival, rather than emphasizing a vision purely focused on wealth at all costs. It redefines the notion of wealth as such, so as to give value to life rather than economy alone.

Ocean conservation can be seen as a good example of measures oriented towards true green growth. Oceans are an important source of livelihood for an important part of the world's population, by means of, amongst others, sustainable fishing activities and ecotourism that provide for the well-being of coastal communities. Furthermore, oceans play a vital role in terms of climate regulation. This is a good scenario to see how proper environmental management contributes to sustainable development.

The challenge relies on thinking not only in economic development in terms of GDP but to see it as a much broader concept that includes an improvement in people's well-being and quality of life. Stakeholders should incorporate environmental criteria into their decisions to ensure sustainable and adequate measures that will really provide for our survival as a species.

– Sandra Bessudo Lion,
former High Presidential Counsel for Environment,
Biodiversity, Water and Climate Change of the Republic of Colombia,
current general director of the Colombian Presidential Agency for International Cooperation,
creator of Malpelo and Other Marine Ecosystems Foundation

FARLEY MOWAT

We are behaving like yeasts
in a brewer's vat,
multiplying mindlessly
while greedily consuming
the substance of a finite world.

If we continue
to imitate the yeasts
we will perish as they perish,

having exhausted our resources
and poisoned ourselves
in the lethal brew
of our own wastes.

Unlike the yeasts
we have a choice:
what will it be?

– Farley Mowat,
Canadian author and conservationist

JOHN LUNDIN

We are living in a time of unprecedented challenge and unprecedented opportunity. We are on the brink of self-destruction and at the same time witnessing the dawn of global civilization. For the first time in the history of human being we have the capacity to destroy our planetary home and also the ability to restore the planet and the human community to a more perfect whole.

We are in the midst of an environmental crisis. But the environment is much more than the air we breathe and the water and the plants and the animals. Our environment is shaped by the way we think, act and speak. In fact, what we think, what we say, what is in our heart and how we act can cause greater damage to our environment than burning fossil fuels or extracting them from the land.

Fortunately, our thoughts, words and deeds can also heal and restore.

All the world's wisdom traditions share a common understanding that our Earth Mother was entrusted to the care of her original peoples. We have inherited the Earth from our indigenous ancestors. The question confronting our generation today is will we be good ancestors for our children and our children's children?

Is there hope? Yes. You and I are that hope.

If we are to be co-creators of a sustainable environment we must become cultivators of hope. Hope is as necessary to life as water. Hope is the ultimate nurturer. We would never plant another seed if we didn't carry within us the hope of its blossoming.

We must learn again to live together in harmony with the Earth and with one another.

We must listen to the cries of our Earth Mother and her pain, and cry aloud for our sisters and brothers to come together for the first time in history as a true global chorus.

As individuals in isolation we can do little, but in raising our voices together we can restore balance and harmony to the human community and our planetary home.

As a global chorus we can literally save the world.

– John Lundin,
spiritual writer, environmental activist,
author of *The New Mandala: Eastern Wisdom for Western Living*,
written in collaboration with His Holiness the Dalai Lama,
www.JohnLundin.com

PAUL CRUTZEN

May the Anthropocene in future be guided by the collective wisdom of many generations of intelligent humans, through peace and global co-operation, stimulated by Nature's beauty.

Welcome to the Anthropocene!

– Dr. Paul J. Crutzen,
Max Planck Institute for Chemistry, Mainz, Germany,
Nobel Prize in chemistry, 1995

TEMPLE GRANDIN

To solve big problems will require people to work together. Unfortunately, adversity is often required to motivate people to collaborate as a team. When Hurricane Sandy flooded the New York subway system, petty labour squabbles and politics were set aside to get the subway working again so quickly. A certain amount of adversity can have a great motivating effect but an overwhelming adversity may cause people to give up. The subway was repairable and it got fixed, but the earthquake in Haiti was so devastating that the people have not recovered. There are increasing problems with dwindling water supplies, drought and worse weather events. Ways to remedy these problems will range from high technology to simpler back to basics.

High-tech methods that could be developed are economical desalination of seawater and methods for storing electricity from renewable energy sources such as wind. Local low-tech methods such as improved integration of animal and crop agriculture could help insure a steady supply of food. Both high-tech and low-tech developers must work together for this common goal. The world needs both of them.

We need people in the world who do real stuff to improve the world and not just talk and theorize about it. Many policy-makers have no practical experience with the things they make policy about. Their policies have become so abstract that when they are implemented by the people in the field, they may have unintended bad consequences. Policy-makers need to get out of their offices and find out what really is happening.

– Temple Grandin,
professor of animal science at Colorado State University

DAVE TOYCEN

During the conflict in Kosovo, I interviewed a ten-year-old boy named Liridan who had fled with his parents from the conflict to neighbouring Albania. While boarding a farm wagon in his village to escape the invading soldiers, he was struck in the arm by a rifle butt. His arm was broken and over the course of a harrowing three-day journey, Liridan lost consciousness. But in the end, he made it to freedom. Now Liridan and his family were crowded together in a broken-down gymnasium with scores of other refugee families. There was little privacy, a shortage of water and putrid, overcrowded latrines. His mother wept as she described the terror of their ordeal, especially the fear that the soldiers would kill Liridan. As the interview was coming to an end, I noticed a small package of tinfoil in Liridan's good hand. Earlier, one of the church groups had distributed small presents for the children, most of whom owned nothing now except the clothes on their backs. With a child's spontaneity, this traumatized little boy opened his hand, peeled back the foil, broke a section of chocolate into two pieces and offered one to me. I could only nod my expression of appreciation. I felt so small before this selfless act of generosity.

I have hope for our collective future because I have met children like Liridan the world over. I have seen a child's courage reconcile communities, heal deep wounds of conflict and even ignite passionate movements to better serve the most vulnerable among us. Hope is inextricably tied to these children. They don't carry our baggage, they're inquisitive, and they have the capacity to show remarkable gestures of mercy, of care and of affection. They will be the leaders of tomorrow. It's no wonder Jesus remarked, "Let the little children come to me ... for the kingdom of heaven belongs to such as these."

–Dave Toycen,
president and CEO of World Vision Canada

RICK FEDRIZZI

Unless you're doing a little wilderness camping today, you'll find yourself inside of a building. You'll wake up in your home, then stop at the coffee shop for your latte. You'll escort your kids into a school building and then you'll sit down at your desk on a corporate campus or in a skyscraper or in a Main Street storefront. Maybe you have the day off, and you'll head to the mall, or the zoo.

Our buildings and communities define our lives. They are habitat. Shelter. Places for assembly or sanctuary. But they are also our first line of defence in battling climate change and the final piece of a complex puzzle in how we create communities that enhance our lives, not compromise them. The walls around you and the floor beneath your feet, the sidewalks and bike paths that are increasingly linking us together all factor into how we are reimagining our lives and our economy. And the fact that so many of us have undertaken this quest for a sustainable future is what gives me great hope.

But, as someone once said, hope is not a strategy. So together we act. We build green buildings and communities. Energy-efficient, water-efficient, daylight-filled, toxin-and-pollutant-free buildings in walkable communities with access to fresh food and green space, with recycling and composting. It takes all of us working together to fashion these places that protect our planet and nourish our souls. And we're creating more of them every day.

There are hundreds of thousands of people around the world who are undertaking this important work. They are engineers, architects and building facility managers. They are teachers, lawyers, scientists, business owners, manufacturers and writers.

But for reasons unfathomable, not everyone is on board. Our hardest job it seems isn't figuring out how to build green, it's to convince the naysayers that it matters. That it works. That it is a singularly powerful path forward to bringing our world through these times.

Green building is not just about market transformation. It's about human transformation. And we'll get there if we convince everyone to pack up their small tents of special interest and join us in the big tent of collaboration and common purpose. That's how we'll achieve the sustainable future that we owe our children and the generations to come.

—Rick Fedrizzi,
president, CEO and founding chair of the U.S. Green Building Council

EXEQUIEL EZCURRA

My lifelong friend Enriqueta Velarde spends every spring studying seabirds in Isla Rasa, a small flat island in the Gulf of California. Single-handedly, alone in the remote island, she has done that for over thirty years. Through her research, she has restored the health of the island and saved two species, the Elegant Tern and the Heermann's Gull, from almost certain extinction. She is a hero.

Fifteen years ago, analyzing her painstakingly collected data set, we found that when the equatorial currents slow down, marine productivity collapses and the birds cannot find enough sardines to feed their chicks, which die tragically in their own nests. The fact that the speed of ocean currents twelve thousand miles away could predict the fate of a million seabird chicks was for me an epiphany, a sudden revelation of the deep intricate nature of the biosphere. The complex ecological processes that drive life in our planet were much more connected than I had ever realized before. I understood vividly that the Earth has processes that bind all life together, and in the small Isla Rasa we could fathom the pulse of the biosphere.

Since then, my research changed, and so did my view of life. I became much more interested in understanding the enigmatic connections between the land and the sea, and devoted much more of my time and efforts to advancing conservation science; because, how can we allow Nature to be destroyed if we don't even know the impact this destruction will have on the continuity of life on Earth?

–Exequiel Ezcurra,
ecologist with the National Research System of Mexico and
University of California, Riverside

NANCY KNOWLTON

Half-way between Tahiti and Hawaii lie the Southern Line Islands. Too remote to be a commercially viable destination, and too small or harsh to support self-sustaining human settlements on land, they teem below the surface of the waves with sharks, snappers and turtles swimming amongst a profusion of living coral. To go there, as I did recently, is to travel back in time, to a planet only lightly touched by people. Yes, the water is both warmer and more acidic, but these communities still thrive because they are protected from the day-to-day traumas of habitat demolition, rapacious harvesting and sickening pollution. The message is simple – it is not, yet, too late.

It can be hard to remember that there is still hope for this damaged but far from dead planet that we share with millions of other life forms. In years past, my husband and I, jokingly referred to as Drs. Doom and Gloom, trained our students, future doctors of the planet, to write ever more refined obituaries of Nature. Yet human medicine, despite the fact that in the end there is always an obituary, is underpinned by hope.

And so began a search for ocean success stories.

In fact, there are many, and not just in wealthy countries with resources to spare. Yet, most conservation practitioners we met initially seemed unaware that progress was being made. We were once even told that a day-long program focused on ocean success stories would be impossible to fill. But that is changing.

Most success stories begin with one or a few individuals unwilling to take "No" for an answer. They energize others to band together to establish protected areas, manage resources sustainably, restore devastated seascapes and reduce the flow of damaging chemicals into the ocean. Some use the power of art to inspire action. In the end, these efforts promote not just healthy oceans, but also human well-being.

Conservation successes make compelling stories because they are centred on people rather than tables or graphs. They need to be told, so that success can breed more success. So when someone asks you if there is hope, share this African proverb: "If you think you are too small to make a difference, you haven't spent the night with a mosquito."

– Nancy Knowlton,
Sant Chair in Marine Science at National Museum of Natural History (USA)

LEE GERDES

Trauma is not individually experienced today. In fact, horrendous trauma is shared with millions of people worldwide as soon as it happens. Whether experienced personally, vicariously though a close friend, or even experienced remotely via a news report – every trauma adds a drop of stress to our system. Our brains are reservoirs for trauma. In a world more connected, more immediate and more open than ever, the downpour of trauma into our brains is torrential.

The full impact of trauma on brain function is only beginning to be understood. The traumatized brain slips into patterns of overactivation. Even after the traumatic incident has passed, the brain can remain in these overactivated patterns. The brain overactivation may manifest as "striking out" or "running away," if the trauma has been collected in the fight–flight or sympathetic response mechanism of the brain. Or the overactivation may manifest as "freezing in despair" if the trauma has been collected in the parasympathetic response mechanism of the brain. Trauma overactivation may happen suddenly or it may accumulate over time – drop by drop, little by little. We each seem uniquely limited in our capacity to withstand trauma. Yet, where trauma is most severe, most persistent and most widespread, all people in a community experience the brain overactivation. Community fear, war and/or political chaos is the likely result.

Humanity needs help to release both the individual and the collective effects of trauma. Such a process is based on individuals recovering balance and harmony in brain patterns. Diets built more on plant-based foods, together with exercise, quiet times, communing with Nature, and most importantly, a means to directly balance seriously overactivated brains, will enable humanity to evolve beyond the chaos produced from trauma.

Nothing in the world, I feel, is more important for the survival of humanity. As the leader of Brain State Technologies I am dedicated to finding a solution to mitigate trauma in an affordable manner for a significant part of humanity.

–Lee Gerdes,
author of *Limitless You: The Infinite Possibilities of a Balanced Brain*,
founder and CEO of Brain State Technologies
www.brainstatetech.com

MOH HARDIN

How we move forward cannot depend on one spiritual tradition, economy, or political system, but rather should depend on who we feel we are, both personally and socially. What is the nature of humans and society? In this light, human nature is the most important global issue.

— *SHAMBHALA PRINCIPLE,* SAKYONG MIPHAM

We live in a time of tremendous doubt about the goodness of human nature, and with good reason. Acts of cruelty and random violence make big news weekly. We are bombarded by bad. From a bigger point of view, however, these are relatively random acts that exist in a sea of goodness – human society. With all its flaws, human society could not exist and flourish on Earth if its nature had not been basically good from the beginning: caring, with the ability to communicate and co-operate with each other. When a baby is born, their very survival depends on human goodness. This goodness is more basic than good versus bad.

We can reconnect with this basic goodness by reflecting on our own humanity, our human experience, right now. Slow down, soften and touch our aliveness. Appreciate that we can see, hear sounds, smell, taste and touch our world. Awaken to our humanity. It's simple and profound. It doesn't matter what you believe or don't believe, being human is our common experience. Slow down, soften and touch.

Because human nature is basically good, I think that humanity has a very good chance to find its way through our current crises. But it is not guaranteed. We can help create the conditions we need to survive on this planet now, in this "every" moment, by awakening to our humanity.

What would this look like? It would look like the *Global Chorus*. It would look like what so many people are already doing: investing creativity, energy, vision and money into innovation and international communication between people. It would look like networks of people aware of themselves and their interconnectivity with everything else, networks of connectivity working together. It would look like a society whose foremost principle is bringing forth the basic goodness of humanity.

–Moh Hardin,
author of *A Little Book of Love: Heart Advice to Bring Happiness to Ourselves and Our World*

MAREN AND JAN ENKELMANN

Why it is more likely to live a happy and fulfilled life after surviving a life-threatening accident than after winning the lottery? In either case you are facing circumstances you hadn't and weren't prepared for. However, those who almost lost their lives are much more likely to reassess what's truly important to them and pour all their energy into it. The lucky winners who should be able to realize all their wildest dreams often lose sight of the essentials as life suddenly gets a lot more complicated.

Is there something to be learned from the way human beings are able to focus their energies when faced with a major crisis?

As the world today is facing countless challenges – climate change, migration, poverty, shrinking natural resources, the banking system – fewer and fewer people seem bothered to even vote or take an active part in society. The issues appear too big and too complex to even contemplate how to come to grips with them.

But in order to tackle the global issues we need people to take on these challenges on a level that's relevant to them and take pride in playing their part. Like the accident survivor gains strength and focus from a profound personal experience, engaging ourselves in matters that we can actively help to improve might just give us the power to change the world.

–Maren Kleinert and Jan Enkelmann,
authors of *Happiness: How the World Keeps Smiling*
www.enkelmann.co.uk

JAMIE HENN

Four years ago, a group of college friends and I helped co-found the international climate campaign 350.org with author and environmentalist Bill McKibben. Our dream was to unite a new type of global campaign to solve the climate crisis – an "open-source" movement that could involve people from Afghanistan to Zimbabwe, no matter their class, gender or religious affiliation.

We decided to name our effort after the number 350 because according to the latest science, 350 parts per million is the safe upper limit of carbon dioxide in the atmosphere (right now, the atmosphere contains over 392 ppm). The figure 350 was a clear line in the sand, a north star that we could only reach if we united as a global community.

On October 24, 2009, our network came together for the first time in a massive, global day of climate action that connected over 5,200 events in 182 countries. CNN called it "the most widespread day of political action in the planet's history." The events ranged from more than 10,000 schoolchildren marching in the streets of Addis Ababa, Ethiopia, to one lone woman holding a 350 banner in Babylon, Iraq. Together, we've gone on to organize more than 15,000 demonstrations worldwide.

Our movement to solve the climate crisis will never have the money of the fossil fuel industry that stands in our way, so we'll have to find a different currency to work in. At 350.org, that currency has been our creativity, spirit and unwavering commitment to a sustainable future. From Afghanistan to Zimbabwe, a movement is beginning to be born.

– Jamie Henn,
co-founder and communications director of 350.org

LAMBERTO ZANNIER

The world has changed dramatically in recent decades. At the same time that traditional threats persist – most prominently poverty and armed conflict – we have seen a re-emergence of dividing lines along ideologies and religions and the rise of new global challenges. Confronting the impact of climate change, managing limited natural resources, addressing population growth and reducing the impact of human activities on wildlife and biodiversity – to name just a few interlinked challenges – are all issues that require global solutions.

Important ethical considerations come to mind. Though we have reached an unprecedented level of development, the benefits of progress are unevenly shared across nations and within states. Environmental and social concerns, coupled with the global financial crisis, have revived calls to make development sustainable and to address growing inequalities in the distribution of wealth and resources.

Today, leadership is needed to look beyond short-term political agendas and address difficult global issues for which no silver bullet exists. As people claim their right to play a role in decisions that affect their future and that of their children, global leaders must meet their expectations by adopting participatory and inclusive processes that ensure their voices are heard.

The Organization for Security and Co-operation in Europe (OSCE) offers a vehicle for finding common ground and a platform for dialogue not only among States but also with civil society, academia and youth. Although our 57 participating states have different perspectives and sometimes conflicting priorities, by engaging constructively in the OSCE, their leaders can demonstrate their readiness to work together to deliver what was promised to their citizens in the Helsinki Final Act in 1975 – peace, security and justice.

The OSCE experience provides a hopeful example of the fruitfulness of political courage. In the midst of the Cold War, leaders of states with profound ideological differences dared to sit together at the same table and engaged in a dialogue to prevent a new war. The same spirit is needed today, leaving zero-sum games aside, in facing urgent challenges that threaten our security and possibly even our survival.

– Lamberto Zannier,
secretary general of the Organization for Security and Co-operation in Europe

SARA ANDERSON

In global health, some issues disproportionally get more attention than others. The attention and the resources that follow are not based strictly on need, severity, or even interventions available. They are based on which health challenges receive the most political will. For example in low-income countries, HIV/AIDS represents 5.7 per cent of the mortality burden and receives 47.2 per cent of the health funding in those countries. All of the other causes of death combined (94.3 per cent) receive 52.8 per cent of the health funding. So one disease, albeit a terrible one, gets almost half of all funding, while all other diseases and health conditions compete for the remainder.

This insightful research is Dr. Jeremy Shiffman's of American University, and it rings true in my work advocating for neglected humanitarian issues. For the last five years, I have been advocating for the forgotten global health crisis of burns. Nearly 11 million people worldwide are burned annually and more women worldwide are severely burned each year than are diagnosed with HIV and TB combined, according to the World Health Organization's estimate.

However, the U.S. government has yet to devote any foreign assistance funding for burn prevention or burn treatment. We are working to change that, with some minor success, because vulnerable people without access to adequate healthcare should not have to suffer disabilities or life-threatening injuries caused by severe burns.

This advocacy work relates to environmental issues in that both are issues Westerns rarely see or have to face the consequences of – yet. Even for me, who travels to the developing world often, it is hard to grasp a world with limited resources, with half of the population still using open fires for cooking, heating and lighting – when abundance surrounds my daily life.

But I remain hopeful. The political will to combat environmental degradation has been building for years. Although naysayers remain, many are working in their small ways to make a difference, whether it be recycling, consuming less or investing in new eco-friendly technologies. The solution lies in making those small ways expand exponentially to make dramatic and sustainable changes that will allow the next generations to flourish as we have.

– Sara E. Anderson,
chief advocacy officer of ReSurge International

DON GAYTON

Here in North America, we revel in unlimited and nearly free access to energy and automobiles. Right from the 1950s, it has been a rollicking fun trip.

Without realizing it, we became addicted; people, business, governments, society. But the initial high has now worn off, and our petroleum drug of choice is getting expensive. A grim list of unpleasant side effects are kicking in. Who knew that cars and their fossil fuels could melt glaciers, ruin cities and change climates?

Getting off drugs is profoundly difficult, but at least the individual user is surrounded by an un-addicted population. With petroleum, we are all junkies. Our governments and businesses pimp the addiction. We now fracture the Earth, scrape buried tar sands and weld enormous injectable pipelines to support our habit. We happily deal our drug to other countries. The refineries are tucked away, and the actual product is cleverly hidden. We don't ever see or touch or feel the actual substance, only the side effects. A climate is sacrificed on the altar of a massively selfish consumption quest, one which delivers less satisfaction with each coming day. As nations we are drug-addicted teenagers, willing to throw our planet away for the sake of that momentary energy rush. We kill agriculture to build soulless suburbs and then perform high-speed commutes through carbon-enhanced air in 300-horse gas pigs on endless high-maintenance asphalt ribbons to clog cities with dead parkades and angry gridlock.

Who can stand and acknowledge this?

Who can stand at all?

—Don Gayton,
ecologist, author of *Man Facing West, Interwoven Wild* and *Kokanee*
www.dongayton.ca

TANYA HA

For me, it started with the gentle kicks of my unborn child. I had always loved Nature and had an interest in environmental issues, but the birth of my child extended this into my very soul. Suddenly, the vague, nebulous Future became her Future. I also found a new connection to the millions of other mothers in the world, the overwhelming majority of whom I will never meet. But I know they're there, with the same love for their children.

I am one of the lucky ones to be born in Australia, with its high quality of life. Today we live in such a specialized and complicated world; it's all too easy to disconnect from the consequences of our choices. We don't necessarily live near the land that grew our food, see the labour conditions of factories that make our gadgets, or breathe the air polluted by power plants. But other mothers and fathers, and brothers and sisters do; their children breathe that polluted air.

John F. Kennedy once said, "Our most basic common link is that we all inhabit this planet. We all breathe the same air. We all cherish our children's future. And we are all mortal." I remember this in my work teaching greener living to householders. The people I work with don't always understand "carbon sequestration" or "environmental flows," but they do understand fresh air, family and love.

I have choices that many other mothers in the world don't have. We need to have the courage and compassion to make better choices and remember those who have so few. If you live and if you love, you have enough reasons to look after the planet. Our shared future depends on it.

– Tanya Ha,
environmentalist, author, television presenter,
science journalist, sustainable living advocate
www.TanyaHa.com

WES JACKSON

A friend and colleague of mine, the late Chuck Washburn, once said to me in a phone conversation:

"If we don't get sustainability in agriculture first, it is not going to happen."

I can't accurately recount all of Chuck's elaboration, but he did say at one point:

"Agriculture ultimately has a discipline standing behind it. The material sector, the industrial sector has no discipline to call on."

With industrial agriculture, featuring high fossil-fuel-based inputs, the role of the discipline is weak. When thinking about sustainable agriculture, on the other hand, the role of that discipline is strong. What is that discipline? It is the very broad discipline of ecology/evolutionary biology with the modern molecular synthesis.

With annual grains (responsible for 70 per cent of the calories we consume and grown on 70 per cent of the agricultural acreage) the opportunity for those processes of the wild, such as we find on prairies, to exist are greatly reduced. But with perennial grains on the horizon, we can imagine those processes being brought to the farm, making the promises of sustainability in agriculture within reach and by extension into the other sectors of society which currently has no discipline to draw upon.

– Wes Jackson,
president of The Land Institute

FRANK ROTERING

Humankind does have hope, but it is the limited hope of salvaging what remains of the biosphere, and it will require effective action rooted in *historical imagination* and *political courage*. With imagination we can envision a sustainable world beyond capitalism and socialism. With courage we will acknowledge that environmental reforms have failed, that time is running out, and that the only remaining choice is between revolutionary change and ecological catastrophe.

My proposed movement, contractionism, is a response to this reality. Its central tenet is that the core component of capitalism, which generates the system's remorseless expansion, must be immediately replaced. For this purpose I have developed an economic framework called the Economics of Needs and Limits, or ENL. The application of ENL's principles will result in the rapid contraction of the world's bloated economies while satisfying human needs within natural limits.

The unavoidable consequence of this replacement is that capitalism will be historically superseded, a momentous shift that will be fiercely resisted by those in power. This is why contractionism is a revolutionary movement – one that seeks to replace the current ruling class with a group dedicated to sustainable well-being. Such revolutions are particularly necessary in the rich capitalist countries. Their economies are causing the most severe environmental degradation, and must therefore be curtailed with the greatest urgency.

Social turmoil is not a valid argument against revolution because turmoil is now inevitable. In the absence of contractionary revolutions, escalating environmental degradation will cause social chaos as people – especially the poor – face increasing hunger and flee from the rising seas and unbearable heat. We are again faced with only one choice: between revolutionary disruption and a chance to solve the crisis, and non-revolutionary disruption and the certainty of ecological collapse.

The critical need today is for talented leaders to step forward and initiate these movements. An important strategy will be to redefine popular interests: to shift the focus from short-term consumption to long-term well-being. A crucial consideration will be to include conservatives as well as progressives. Business and justice, after all, are both impossible on a dead planet.

– Frank Rotering,
independent economic and political thinker,
author of *The Economics of Needs and Limits* and *Contractionary Revolution*
needsandlimits.org

DOUG MCKENZIE-MOHR

Humanity *will* make the transition to a sustainable future. Nature bats last and, ultimately, will dictate that we fully embrace sustainability. While we have no choice regarding whether we make this transition, we do have a choice regarding how *gracefully* we do so.

The grace with which we make this transition will be largely determined by how we envision the future. At present, we are rudderless. We have no compelling, broadly understood visions of a sustainable future. Without such foresight, how do we mobilize seven billion to work in concert? Without a clear understanding of what is to be gained, how do we build broad support for the difficult choices that need to be made? These shared visions must be both inspirational and collective in their origin. They must also clearly articulate a pathway from here to there.

Just as our collective actions presently undermine the world's ecosystems, collective action catalyzed by shared purpose can heal not only the Earth, but also humanity. Who hasn't been heartbroken by the gulf between what we know to be possible and what humanity has settled for? Acting with shared purpose can embolden the human spirit to expect and strive for more.

We can story our present circumstances as dire and intractable, and in so doing ensure the very future that we hope to avoid. Or, we can story our circumstances as dire but surmountable, and in so doing mobilize the very actions that sustainability requires. How we story this inevitable transition will in large part determine the grace with which we make it.

– Doug McKenzie-Mohr, PhD,
environmental psychologist,
author of *Fostering Sustainable Behaviour*

CLAIRE BOUCHER, AKA "GRIMES"

I don't know if we'll be able to reverse the damage we've already done, but I do believe we can slow it significantly. I think there are two key hurdles that, if overcome, will have a domino effect with regards to solving our environmental problems. First is education, and particularly the education of women globally. Our growing population is a huge problem and women who are educated have less children and are better equipped to care for them.

I also think a broader "environmental education" initiative could yield a lot of positive change. When I was on tour in Asia, many countries had radio commercials encouraging people to unplug lights at night to reduce electricity use. Cities like Singapore and Jakarta would be very dark at night (despite being massive cities) due to people turning off all the lights in their closed businesses. I feel like this kind of government-funded public education is crucial and effective. There was very noticeable pollution in Asia, but there was also a more concerted effort to stop it than I have ever seen elsewhere, and a far more acute public understanding of the dangers of pollution.

The other key issue is lobbying. I think the only way we can save our planet is if there is a complete ban of all lobbying or industry involvement in government decisions. Canada, for example, is completely run by the oil industry and no matter how many people show up and protest, pipelines are always approved, fracking is always approved. This is one of the largest issues facing the world today. Governments need to recognize this, and stop giving dangerous industries control over their policies.

–Claire Boucher, aka "Grimes,"
producer, singer, songwriter, director, painter, writer

DAVID SUZUKI

When asked what the chances are that humanity will survive to the end of this century, Sir Martin Rees, Royal Astronomer in the UK replied, "Fifty fifty!" James Lovelock, who named the web of life on Earth "Gaia," predicts billions of people will die in this century, reducing global population to 10 per cent, while Australian eco-philosopher Clive Hamilton's book *Requiem for a Species* is about our demise.

The eco-crisis of the 21st century is not going to be solved by "ten easy ways" or even a hundred. Despite decades of warnings by top scientists that we are heading along a very destructive path, countries around the world continue the drive for endless economic growth that is undermining the life support systems of the planet.

All I have left is hope, hope that is based on the fact that we don't know enough even to say it is too late to turn things around, but it is very, very late.

– David Suzuki,
scientist, broadcaster, environmental activist

STEVEN ROCKEFELLER

The students sitting in a circle outdoors were looking dejected when the flap of wings startled them. A raven landed in their midst. "Hey," he croaked, "put that UN report on the state of the world away and listen up. The last thing anyone, including all the birds, needs right now is for you to fall into a state of despair."

"The damage industrial societies have done to the beauty and biodiversity of Earth is a terrible tragedy. Humankind is a frightening predator out of control," blurted a young woman.

"Only part of the story," responded the raven. "It is humanity's destiny to become the mind of Earth's biosphere, to create a global civilization that is culturally diverse, just, sustainable and peaceful, and to celebrate the sacredness of life."

"A fine vision," said another student, "but how is it possible to transform industrial-technological society?"

"Don't lose faith in the creative potential of human intelligence and the basic goodness of the human heart when liberated from ignorance and fear," said the bird. "The advance of education, science and participatory democracy is the way forward. Adaptation to climate change will be difficult, but the building of clean energy economies that maximize reuse and recycling and dramatically reduce waste is underway. Innovative leaders are also finding the path to sustainability and the eradication of poverty by creating vibrant, resilient, local communities well integrated with their bioregions."

"Will people develop the sense of shared responsibility and courage to make the hard choices and necessary sacrifices to safeguard the environment?"

"Excellent question. You have inspiring spiritual traditions that emphasize being more, not having more, with a focus on right relationship with oneself, other persons, the larger living world and the mystery of being, the sacred source of the universe. Humanity is beginning to awaken from its anthropocentric delusions. The natural world is not just a collection of resources for human exploitation. Earth's biosphere is a community of life and you are interdependent members of it. Your democracy must evolve into more of a biocracy and implement the global ethic of respect and care for the greater community of life already widely supported in civil society. A new sense of global interdependence and universal responsibility is emerging in the consciousness of millions of women and men."

"There is hope then?"

"There is hope only if you go out and join those brave and visionary women and men who are striving to be their best and build a better world." With that, the raven took two hops and flew away.

—Steven C. Rockefeller,
professor emeritus of religion at Middlebury College, Vermont, USA

JOHN VLAHIDES

I've travelled the world, known princes and stars, yet the wisest words I've ever heard spoken came not from a statesman or celebrity, but from a humble mystic yogi in San Francisco, who told me, "The best thing any of us can do is to sweeten the psychic atmosphere." Our hope lies in the pursuit of spiritual values. We must expand our consciousness. *Excelsior!* To find the way forward, go within: meditate.

– John A. Vlahides,
travel writer, California television personality

SHIN-ICHIRO TERAYAMA

I was a physicist and suffered from cancer in 1984. I transformed, and have been free of metastasized kidney cancer for more than 25 years. I tell the story of the recovery from cancer with cello-playing, confessing how I loved my cancer instead of fighting it. I changed to a vegetarian "macrobiotic" diet, drinking selected good mineral water, and most importantly, I watched the sunrise every day in the morning. It was in front of the morning sun that I made an exciting discovery. I found I was becoming very positive, very relaxed, and healing energy was entering my heart chakra, first through my heart and then to all seven chakras. I began to practise cello again after a long absence. These things were done harmoniously by my intuition and not by instruction.

I call myself a "holistic management consultant" because I approach the healing of the person, company, community and system through holistic means ... as a whole. My work is educating people with loving wisdom, using the tools of subtle energy and energy medicine.

And so, in turn, for healing our Earth and ourselves, here is the prayer that I offer you today:

Now it is the very precious time for us human beings

to pray for the future of the Earth.

This is the prayer without wishes.

We should also pray for us with love.

This love is unconditional love.

We also pray for us within to our inside.

It is also the time for us to transform by ourselves.

Pray for us with love.

Love, Shin

– Shin-ichiro Terayama,
president of Shin-Terayama Office Co. Ltd.,
fellow of the Findhorn Foundation,
vice-president of Japan Weller-Than-Well Society,
author of *My Cancer Disappeared: A Document of the Natural Healing of Cancer*
www.shin-terayama.jp/en

BELVIE ROOKS

On a recent early morning walk, I found myself stopping frequently and marvelling at the majesty and beauty of the San Francisco Bay. As I stopped, I noticed a young white crane nearby. Half an hour later, I noticed, what I thought was, the same white crane. Curious, I decided to be sure. I walked quickly ahead and stopped suddenly. A few seconds, my new friend arrived and perched on a nearby bench.

I stood silently for a moment and looked around and realized there were no other cranes in sight. Ironically, a couple of days earlier, I had seen a 50-year-old photograph of this same estuary in which there appeared to be hundreds of cranes – a whole community of cranes.

I was now conscious of the noisy freeway nearby; the profusion of overhead electrical wires; and the danger signs warming about a recent sewage spill. None of this would have existed 50 years ago.

I eased slowly onto the bench next to my new friend and closed my eyes. I had, of course, seen all of this many times before, but now, I was seeing it as if for the first time from my small companion's perspective. From *that* perspective, of habitat destruction, the surrounding view was a heartbreaking one.

I slowly opened my eyes and my small friend was not only still there but her head was cocked slightly to one side observing me intently. Our eyes locked and it was as if she spoke directly to the very depths of my soul, "Now that you know, will you remember to tell *my* story too?"

What was hopeful about the encounter, for me, was that I was fully present to the message being delivered.

Thank you for showing up and I promise to remember!

– Belvie Rooks,
educator; co-founder of Growing a Global Heart

PETER BEVAN-BAKER

When I was young I didn't think much about the meaning of my life; I was more concerned with learning and growing. I stopped growing physically some time ago, but the learning has continued; I am still growing intellectually and spiritually.

Humanity was, until recently, an insignificant species on a vast and empty planet. For thousands of generations we stumbled around the Earth in small groups learning some useful survival tricks and evolving some valuable traits – like opposable thumbs and big brains. Our impact on the planet back then was minimal. Then we grew, and we grew, and we grew until we now fill almost every corner of the planet, and our sheer size and power threaten to overwhelm Earth's support systems. It is time for humanity to replace our physical growth with intellectual and spiritual development.

I believe we who are alive today are the most blessed generation ever. We are about to oversee that shift – replacing the central goal of getting bigger through economic expansion – to getting better

through spiritual awakening. It is time for us to collectively start thinking about the meaning of our existence here on this beautiful planet.

I know we have the capabilities – never before has there been a species more suited to long-term success; we should effortlessly master living on the Earth. All we need is the will to embrace the wonderful possibilities of being human; recognizing that true fulfillment has to do with relationships, and contentment with spiritual maturity, and that neither has anything to do with material possessions. Our happiness is related to things that are utterly sustainable – friendship, art, spirituality. We can live on this planet in far less consumptive and destructive ways, and find meaning and contentment – indeed it is the only way to discover how to be so.

There is a time for expansion and there is a time for maturation. We are done with the former and about to enter the latter. It will be a time of humanity reaching its true potential. It is time to grow up, and my unwavering belief says that we are ready.

– Peter Bevan Baker,
Green Party candidate in Prince Edward Island, Canada

PAUL STAMETS

We are fully engaged in 6x – the sixth greatest extinction of life on this planet known thus far. There are an estimated 8.3 million species on Earth. We are losing nearly 30,000 species per year and may lose ~3,000,000 over the next century. Unlike previous celestial cataclysms, however, this extinction is uniquely caused by an organism – *Us*.

Loss of biodiversity directly threatens our environmental health. Fungi and algae first marched onto land around a billion years ago. Some 300 million years later, "higher life forms" surged onto land, made possible by a holy union between the roots of plants and fungi.

Then, ~250 million years ago and again ~65 million years ago, two great extinction level cataclysms impacted the biosphere. The Earth was shrouded in dust, sunlight was cut off, the majority of plants and animals died ... and fungi inherited the Earth. Those organisms pairing with fungi (whose mycelial networks do not need light) had better chances for survival.

With the passing of each generation of life, fungi built lenses of soils by decomposing the deceased, creating the foundation of the food webs for descendants.

The lessons of evolution have repeatedly shown that alliances with fungi can help us survive. Putting into practice ecologically rational myco-remedies can help make the course change needed to prevent 6x.

Myco Practices for Protecting our Biospheres:

1. Mushroom cultivation centers should be located in every community for recycling debris and reinvented as environmental healing arts centers. Link all of these centers ("I.A.M.S" – "Institutes of Applied Mycology") through www.fungi.net.

2. Grow mushrooms and mycelium as fungal foods for people and livestock.

3. Use the leftover mycelium from growing mushrooms, to filter water of pathogens (such as *E. coli*, cholera and listeria), phosphates, fertilizers, endocrine disruptors, heavy metals and petroleum-based toxins.

4. Use mycelium and commensal bacteria for biofuels, enzymes, mycoattractants and medicines.

5. Integrate fungal platforms for Permaculture, no-till farming, forestry and aquaculture practices.

6. Grow mycelial mats that service bees by providing essential myconutrients, enhancing bees' host defences of immunity to prevent colony collapse disorder (CCD).

We must muster the courage to chart a new course. The solutions are literally underneath our feet. Please find more information in what is below.

– Paul Stamets,
author of *Mycelium Running: How Mushrooms Can Help Save the World*,
Growing Gourmet and Medicinal Mushrooms, Psilocybin Mushrooms of the World,
speaker at TED 2008 and TEDMED 2011,
founder and managing director of Fungi Perfecti LLC
www.fungi.com

SEPTEMBER

ALEXIA LANE

How can we save the world? First we must ask ourselves if we willing to pay more for energy and water. Democratic governments recognize that their tenure would be short-lived if they insisted that oil and gas companies, for example, show minimal profits in order to reduce the cost of home utilities. Lack of profit from large companies, associated job losses, and rising unemployment would result in mobilization of voters to oust the government that restricted company profits.

However, if consumers accepted paying more for water, electricity and natural gas, governments would be free to impose restrictions not on company profits, but on company practices.

If consumers are prepared to pay more for water, electricity and natural gas, governments are in a position to mandate "cost-prohibitive" extraction technologies and to force the oil and gas industry, for example, to respond accordingly. Waterless methods to extract unconventional fossil fuels exist, but are rarely used due to the high cost associated with the technologies when compared with using essentially free fresh water. Costly technology ultimately translates into higher costs for us as consumers. If we are willing to pay more for our water and energy needs, the conservation effects would be twofold. Firstly, there would be greater impetus to conserve water and energy resources on a home-to-home basis. Secondly, industry would be forced to leave water resources intact, while continuing to surge forward in fossil fuel extraction.

If we are not prepared to pay more for water, electricity and natural gas, we will continue on the current path of destruction using primarily freshwater-intensive extraction methods such as hydraulic fracturing (fracking), because that is the less expensive solution, the one that keeps our water and natural gas bills at their current rates. The extent and intensity with which wells are being fracked across the globe is ever increasing despite known adverse environmental and public health effects. Moreover, fracking permanently removes water from the hydrologic cycle, a phenomenon that cannot be undone.

All the water that will ever be on Earth is here today. How much are you willing to pay for that?

– Alexia Lane,
Water Lane Consulting,
author of *On Fracking*

PAUL POLMAN

If we are to overcome the enormous social and environmental challenges which face us – and I believe we can – then we will have to work differently in future. We will have to work in big partnerships where governments, business and civil society organizations collaborate together.

As a member of the UN Secretary General's High Level Panel on the post-2015 Development Agenda I became convinced that we could "put an end to extreme poverty" whilst at the same time safeguarding the planet for future generations. Central to the achievement of this goal was the idea of a "Partnership for Development" – grounded in a new spirit of solidarity and realized through a compact of commitments.

This is not a pipe dream. A number of such multi-stakeholder partnerships are already in place and delivering results at global scale. The GAVI Alliance is on track to immunize 243 million children against killer diseases in 73 of the world's poorest countries. The Scaling Up Nutrition initiative has brought together multinational food companies, governments and NGOs in 43 countries to address malnutrition.

In the environmental area Unilever and the U.S. government have created the Tropical Forest Alliance. The goal of this partnership is to eliminate tropical deforestation from the supply chains of commodities like palm oil and soy. The Alliance now includes the governments of Indonesia, Norway, UK, the Netherlands and Liberia; dozens of NGOs as well as over 400 companies whose combined revenues exceed $3-trillion. Good progress is being made. If we succeed we will have overcome an issue which accounts for over 17 per cent of all greenhouse gases – more than the entire transportation sector.

In the years to come we will see many more such partnerships. Their energy will be fuelled by an irresistible demand for change from the young. Their call will be heeded by a new generation of business leaders who understand that the economic case for sustainable development is overwhelmingly strong.

I am convinced that we can forge a pathway that will deliver a better future for all – one where prosperity and environmental sustainability walk hand in hand.

– Paul Polman,
CEO of Unilever

ROBERT J. BIRGENEAU

The most significant social crisis facing our world today is the ever-widening gap between the rich and the poor. Three billion of the world's seven billion people live on less than $2 per day, with the most acute poverty occurring in South East Asia and sub-Saharan Africa. In India, one of the world's most-rapidly developing countries, 380 million of its 1.2 billion people still struggle on less than $1 a day.

The Arab Spring uprisings have illustrated that people will not be shut out of the world's growing wealth. Even in Western countries, the increasing wealth gap has sparked recent violent demonstrations in the U.K. and other parts of Europe.

These are complex problems to which there is no simple solution. In 1959, British scientist and novelist, C.P. Snow, in his famous lecture "The Two Cultures and the Scientific Revolution," saw that the growing inequality separating the rich from the poor worldwide would lead to social turmoil. He believed that science and technology could solve the disparity and make the world prosperous and secure but that the different cultures of humanists and scientists would hinder scientific progress.

Although science and technology have made incredible strides in the last half-century, we have not solved the problem of abating global poverty through technological solutions. We need to understand why the gap between rich and poor is growing.

Education that values and unites the "two cultures" must be the answer. This education must be broadly accessible, not just reserved for the privileged few. Solving the world's most challenging problems requires the attention of many academic disciplines coming together to seek solutions. Multidisciplinary, collaborative approaches across the physical and biological sciences, mathematics, engineering, social sciences, arts and humanities and the professions, hold the promise of enhancing our contributions to a better world.

– Robert J. Birgeneau,
chancellor of University of California, Berkeley

SEPTEMBER 4

FATIMA JIBRELL

I live in a small village called Durduri, on the coast of the Puntland State of Somalia, where life evades international conscience. My coastal village is the epicenter for illegal and extractive charcoal production from very scarce acacia trees; something which largely escapes media attention. Unemployment and scarce livelihood opportunities afflict our young men, leaving them vulnerable to the lure of piracy, charcoal burning and chewing Mira. At the same time, foreign nations are looting Somalia's waters through illegal fishing and trawling, while foreign navies patrolling those same waters often deny Somali youth access to fishing as a local livelihood opportunity to which they are fundamentally entitled.

What is happening in my village and across Somalia demonstrates the fractured relationship between local and global. Humanity is united by a common cause – to preserve *our* planet and empower *our* people – and yet I see a world that shrugs off its responsibilities and works against its people. But I also see a world that is waking up.

Grassroots efforts have shown that environmental degradation can be reversed, and that livelihood opportunities can be created. Relentless commitment is however required from all parties, from local communities to national governments through to world bodies such as NATO and the UN. People from around the globe must think about the impact of their actions, and like-minded individuals must come together with a shared vision and commitment to do things differently.

We still have a long, long way to go, but I am not without hope.

— Fatima Jibrell,
women's rights and environmental protection advocate,
founder and senior advisor of Adeso African Development Solutions (formerly Horn Relief),
founder of Sun Fire Cooking
www.adesoafrica.org
www.sunfirecooking.com

MUSTAFA ABU SWAY

The relationship with the environment should be based on companionship. In the Islamic worldview, every component in the environment is a Sign pointing in the direction of God. When members of the environment go extinct, it simply means that we are treading on a path with less Signs, leading to a spiritual vacuum, and endangering our very existence.

Yet, there is hope!

The Prophet Muhammad (upon him be peace) prohibited polluting the water sources, and the path of people. He also encouraged his followers to continuously plant fruitful saplings under the most difficult situations, even under apocalyptic conditions, he said:

> If one of you had a sapling [of a palm tree] in his hand, and the Hour [of the Day of Judgment] has arrived, and he could [still manage to] plant it, then he should plant it.

If you become aware of an issue, then you should act accordingly. And we are conscientious of the environmental crises, and we are invited to act now.

My understanding of the Islamic worldview is that it is imperative to maintain the natural habitat of all species, and to care for the environment as a whole. We should act responsibly and consume food and other materials in moderation and in a sustainable way. Our survival as humanity is intertwined with the survival of other species. But also we should address economic policies that lead to inequality, which in turn affect the environment negatively.

It is not morally acceptable that our globe has two major groups: one that has plenty, and the other hardly subsists. In addition, one cannot neglect warfare and the resources wasted in this respect. Peace is vital for the environment. I have high hopes in our ability to rise to the environmental challenges, and for this, Muslims and non-Muslim alike need to co-operate and rub shoulders in action-based programs.

–Prof. Dr. Mustafa Abu Sway,
Integral Chair for the Study of Imam Al-Ghazali's Work
at Al-Aqsa Mosque and Al-Quds University, Palestine

DAVID BELL

An old Russian proverb defines a "pessimist" as "an informed optimist." The more one learns about the depth and extent of the challenges facing humankind over the remainder of this century, the easier it is to feel discouraged. The current path of global development appears to be taking us toward environmental and social disaster.

Some years ago, I conducted interviews with dozens of sustainability experts from all parts of the world to prepare a 12-hour radio series entitled "Sustainability: Canadian and Global Views." The people I spoke with were highly "informed" about the challenges ahead, but every one of them believed that we are capable of bending the curve, of steering spaceship Earth toward a more sustainable future.

Is there still room for optimism? That's hard to say. But there is a compelling case for hope. To begin with despair is a very poor motivator. And there is much to be done. So hope is the essential, necessary premise of positive action. It is a crucial diet for anyone who wants to make the world a better place to live for current and future generations. Yet, despite the enormous challenges that lie ahead, a diet of hope is not thin gruel. In essence, sustainability poses an "educational" challenge for humankind. We need to *learn to live differently* on this planet. This will require the emergence and widespread adoption of a culture of sustainability which embeds the values of caring for each other, caring for the Earth and caring about the future.

The good news is that the green shoots of such a culture are already very evident. Millions of individuals and organizations all over the world are passionately committed to addressing sustainability problems. The signs are everywhere, in the education sector, in civil society, in business, in government and in everyday living. New technologies of global communication can facilitate this culture shift toward sustainability.

In the spirit of hope, every one of us can do our part to make a difference for each other, for our planet and for our future. And we can have fun doing it!

– David V.J. Bell, PhD,
professor emeritus and former dean of environmental studies
at York University (Toronto, Canada),
board member of Learning for a Sustainable Future
www.lsf-lst.ca

TONY WHEELER

I've always been a firm believer in the virtues of travel. Of course you are, someone might cynically say, creating Lonely Planet has made you a rich man. Fair enough, travel and tourism may be the world's biggest business, but there are many places in the world where it's the only business. In those countries it's all-important.

Yet travel is so much more than something that puts food on the table and sends the kids to school. It's the way we citizens of the world learn about and communicate with each other, because when we travel we see the world and its peoples in reality, not filtered through some media viewfinder or interpreted by some government spokesperson.

That's really come home to me in recent years when my travels have taken me to a list of places which tend to be on government travel advisories in the "don't go there" category. I've been to Iraq and Afghanistan, not as some embedded journalist, but as an ordinary independent tourist. I've travelled around North Korea, Congo DRC, Haiti and Libya. I've been able to compare Saudi Arabia (the weirdest country I've ever been to, after North Korea) with Iran (a far from perfect country, but far friendlier and more democratic than Saudi Arabia). Most recently I travelled through Pakistan and observed the impact on that country from the world's two major powers. One was sending in road builders to help keep the challenging Karakoram Highway open. The other was sending in drones to kill people. Guess which one was more popular?

– Tony Wheeler,
co-founder of Lonely Planet

TRUDIE STYLER

Do we want to be the generation that destroyed ourselves?

Rainforests once covered 14 per cent of the Earth's land surface. Now they only cover 6 per cent. When they've been decimated to the tipping point, there will be no way back. We will face such extreme weather conditions that our planet will no longer support human life. What will it take for us to stop hiding from these terrible truths?

Well, there is a way out of this mess. But we have to face the truth, and we have to embrace change. We can't leave it to the next governments, and the next generation. It's time to take the responsibility – not by 2020, not by 2050, but now – to cut carbon emissions decisively and urgently. Deforestation accounts for around 20 per cent of the world's carbon emissions. Simply halting deforestation would be the single fastest and cheapest way to make a significant reduction. So why aren't we doing it?

We're now at a turning point in our short human history. We have a unique opportunity to shift our focus and to change our priorities. We don't have to make a choice between the economy and the environment. A transition to a clean economic system, one that values vital natural systems, one that understands the cost of pollution and waste, will open up huge opportunities. The shift is inevitable. Countries can't stop it. They can only slow it down. And as they do so, they will be left behind. The time when leaders could claim not to understand the implications of the evidence before us is long past.

You will be judged by your children, your grandchildren and all the generations to come. They will ask, "Did you do everything you possibly could to stop climate change?" We're all mothers, fathers, sons, daughters, brothers and sisters: as a planetary family, whatever our differences, we share one world, one fate and one chance.[10]

– Trudie Styler,
actress, producer, creator of the Rainforest Foundation UK

HERMAN DALY

I think the answer depends ultimately on who (or what) we think we are.

1. Are we the blind result of chance who happen to have evolved a bigger more complex brain than other animals, a brain whose merely epiphenomenal consciousness may amuse itself by projecting picture shows inside our cranium, but having no real purpose or independently causative impact on the world other than differential reproduction?

    Or,

2. Are we creatures evolved from the rest of Creation with the purpose of reflecting to some degree the image of God, and therefore capable of distinguishing good from evil, and true from false, and thereby acting responsibly as stewards and caretakers of the Earth?

If we think we are as described in 1 then in my opinion we are already cooked. Indeed, what reason would there be to care, and in what would we place our hope? Nevertheless, 1 is the worldview of "scientific materialism," which is very influential in our modern secular society.

The second view affirms a basis for hope, and for our own adequacy to respond to that hope. Its truth is recognized in many of the world's religions and does not contradict true science. As for the details of a viable and good future society I have argued that a steady-state economy is a necessary condition. But I doubt that it, or any solution, could be achieved unless "we" see ourselves as the people in 2 rather than 1.

– Herman Daly,
professor emeritus in the School of Public Policy at University of Maryland
steadystate.org

RHETT BUTLER

Every year more creatures are added to endangered species lists, oceans rise with atmospheric carbon dioxide levels, and more wild places disappear. Humanity's footprint on the planet is ever larger and deeper. But while it is easy to view these trends with great despair, we would be wrong to abandon hope. Indeed, there are nascent signs that things can change for the better.

In the past 30 years there have been important developments that have laid the groundwork for a new revolution, where services generated by healthy natural ecosystems are recognized and valued. These are services like erosion control, carbon storage, maintenance of the water cycle and the option value afforded by biodiversity.

Recognizing the value of Nature requires us to first understand it. That's already happening – there have been major advances in quantifying Nature's services. For example, we know that pest control services by native birds in Costa Rica are worth $10,000 a year to a small coffee farmer in Costa Rica, while mangroves and coral reefs generate more than $400-million annually for Belize from ecotourism, erosion control and fisheries.

While this is admittedly a very narrow way to view the value of Nature, it's a first step to engaging decision makers and the public.

Engagement is critical if we hope to transform how humanity stewards the planet's resources. The good news is that new tools – ubiquitous mobile phones, social media and free access to virtually limitless amounts of information – enable public participation like never before. We're already seeing the power of targeted participation in the form of protests movements that are transforming commodity supply chains. Due to activist-led campaigns, today it is taboo for soy farmers in the Amazon to chop down rainforests for farms. It will soon be the same for palm oil producers in Malaysia and paper manufacturers in Indonesia.

Change will not come easily, but greater knowledge of Nature's services, combined with participation by an increasingly informed and active populace, will move us toward a world where humans will live in greater balance with the planet's other inhabitants.

– Rhett A. Butler,
author of *Rainforests*,
founder of Mongabay.com

NIKKI STERN

Contemporary culture doesn't always seem to value the idea of hope. No wonder, when conventional wisdom also confuses hope with expectation: if I hope for the best, the best will surely follow. Yet we soon learn the universe doesn't automatically give back what we put out, or we discover a benevolent deity isn't likely to rush to our aid. Disappointed, we might conclude that hope is a waste of time, has no meaning in modern times or, worst of all, is a nasty trickster making promises it has no intention of keeping.

We mustn't let that happen.

The truth is that we humans are overdue for a retooled version of hope that rejects certainty but embraces possibility. We can't know what the future will bring, but we can envision the best possible future and work for it. Hope freed from the constraints of guaranteed outcomes emboldens us, empowers us and gives us purpose. It sparks the imagination and strengthens our resolve. Flexible, nimble and never without a sense of humor, this hope celebrates discovery, applauds adaptability and thrives on creativity.

Feet on the ground and head in the clouds, hope rejoices in the journey, not the destination. It asks, why can't we? It answers, we can.

There will be days when our better selves go into hiding. There will be nights when we yearn for reassurance. Yet hope is available to light the way, no matter where our paths begin or where they end.

–Nikki Stern,
writer, non-profit adviser,
former executive director of Families of September 11,
author of *Hope in Small Doses*
www.hopeinsmalldoses.com

MATTHEW SLEETH

On graphs that predict future trends, CO_2 levels, population growth and species extinction head skyward on asymptotic lines. Glacier depth, ocean stocks and tropical forests run the opposite direction on black diamond slopes.

The cry goes out to do more, step it up, and engineer more efficiently. If only we could find a way to turn our garbage into 100-octane fuel, our problems would be solved.

Maybe instead of trying harder or going faster, we simply need to pause. Our lives have become one long, run-on sentence without a comma, semicolon or period. Musicians say that it is not the notes – but the silences between them – that make music. Without pauses, our lives just become noise.

Since the time of Moses, society has kept a weekly Stop Day. In my lifetime, we have lost that day of rest. Coming to rest one day in seven reminds us that we do not need more wonders in this world; we need more wonderment. Remembering the Sabbath turns us from human doings into human beings.

As Abraham Lincoln said: "As we keep or break the Sabbath day, we nobly save or meanly lose the last best hope by which man arises."

Scientific studies now show that our unrelenting consumption is killing us and killing the planet. To reverse this dire trend, we do not need to do more; we need to do less.

Give it a rest: stop one day in seven.

– Matthew Sleeth, MD,
executive director of Blessed Earth,
author of *24/6*

DAVID GERSHON

Again and again in history some people wake up. They have no ground in the crowd and they move to broader, deeper laws. They carry strange customs with them and demand room for bold and audacious action. The future speaks ruthlessly through them. They change the world.

— RAINER MARIA RILKE

From runaway climate change that threatens the survival of humanity and the many life forms on Earth, to the many starving people and those just eking out an existence at the very edge of survival, to the desperation of our inner-city youth, to our patterns of thought that perpetuate a divided world, our planet is in need of a radical transformation that goes to the very root of our vision as human beings.

What could enable such a fundamental transformation is our innate longing as human beings to create a better world for ourselves and our children. This inherent desire for self-improvement is a key lever for human evolution because there are enormous possibilities to tap into it. But to access this potential requires transformative change leaders capable of calling forth our intrinsic aspiration. This is a learnable skill set and transformationally minded leaders are growing as more people attempt to lead lives driven by meaning and purpose. All the more so among the Millennials.

At the Federal Convention of 1787, after three and a half months of deliberation over a constitution for the new United States, Benjamin Franklin was asked, "Well, doctor, what have we got? A republic or monarchy?" "A republic," replied the doctor, "if you can keep it." The same could be said about our planet. Whether we get to keep it as a viable dwelling place for human habitation and evolution is up to us. To do this we must be able to change the game. Changing the game is not a spectator sport. It requires each of us to play a position on the team, and to play it with all of our heart and soul and mind. It requires nothing less than our very best and highest efforts.

Those of us alive on the planet at this moment in time have a special destiny in its evolution. We are the ones who must reinvent our world to sustain the fragile social experiment of human civilization. This is a momentous responsibility and opportunity. As we accept this responsibility and seize this opportunity, we align our individual purpose with humanity's advancement. We become conscious actors in our planet's great evolutionary adventure. I wish you and all of us Godspeed on this epic journey.

– David Gershon,
co-founder and CEO of Empowerment Institute
www.empowermentinstitute.net

LILLIAN ROSE STEWART

I believe in miracles, I see them everyday where a modern highway meets an unchanged vista, frozen in time. Earth the way it is meant to be ... the way it was in the beginning.

Snow falls gently, the windshield wipers tap a metronome to the clanking of tire chains ringing against the black macadam surface of the highway. It is a violent symphony accompanied by a chorus

© Jack Durst

of strangers from nine sovereign nations, singing out the lyrics. The chatter resonates in languages I cannot speak, nor understand, but I am not disturbed. After twenty years of driving this bus I know that around the bend awaits a miracle. Amber lights flash dance upon the snow, airbrakes blast an awakening for my captive audience. We will make an unscheduled stop.

They gather in awe, these unlikely brethren, as the majestic Sierra Nevada loom in the distance, reflected upon the waters, mighty moraines cloaked in shimmering white sky fall. It is a masterpiece ... but I see only the faces of strangers as they turn to share their joy.

In that fleeting moment as they stand shoulder to shoulder, these kings and ditchdiggers, the colours of their skin are merely hues in a human rainbow. There are no angry words or lines drawn on a map, just the beating of hearts speaking a common language. I smile ... for in that brief and glorious moment there is ... peace on Earth.

I hope ... this moment becomes a memory ... and the memory becomes ... a knowing, a realization of an ancient wisdom ... that all things are bound by the wonder and the beauty of our mother Earth. And I hope they take this knowing with them to their towering penthouses in Dubai, or to a shanty on the banks of an Egyptian river, or to a bustling backstreet market in Hong Kong. A knowing ... that peace on Earth is an attainable thing ... that the beauty and the wonder of a sustained mother Earth is an attainable thing, anywhere, everyday, for all things of this Earth ... if only we choose it.

I hope ... and hope is a new beginning.

– Lillian Rose Stewart,
retired ski bus driver, screenwriter
www.bluemountainskink.com

LENNIE GALLANT

I often close my concerts with a song titled "The Band's Still Playing," which employs the once supposedly unsinkable *Titanic* as metaphor for the good ship Planet Earth. I ask the audience to become part of the ship's orchestra, and have them jubilantly singing the horn parts, while the lyric laments the "rearranging of the deck chairs" and the band's "crying out for our souls." It is meant to be a sardonic piece about the perilous state of the world and our rather complacent attitude; but I feel the point of the song is often missed … perhaps it's too subtle.

We cannot be subtle anymore. The "iceberg" in front of our ship is menacing and ready to rip our hull apart. It will take a tremendous amount of strength and will to turn the wheel and change our course before it's too late. I believe it can be done, but it must happen now.

The old adage "it is always darkest before the dawn" may be a reality in the world today. I sense there are sparks of hope that are just waiting for the right breath of air to fan them into something far greater. I see it on YouTube in simple acts of kindness that go viral, and in humanitarian movements that kids initiate, first thought to be naïve, that end up having powerful results. I see it in people risking their livelihood and reputations to speak a truth about environmental issues, no matter how unpopular it may be. These things give me hope. We are desperate for inspiration, bravery, ingenuity and real leadership.

How do we fan these embers so they turn into a force passionate and strong enough to change our collective behaviour and present heading? I believe it will take a tremendous shift in our thinking that the media, artists, talk show hosts, bartenders, celebrities, writers, taxi drivers, activists, students, teachers … anyone with any kind of audience, must initiate and propagate. We cannot expect it to come from our political leaders, who far too often have actually become followers. We need a radical change in popular culture as to who and what we designate as being truly newsworthy. It's time to seriously celebrate those who make courageous efforts in greentech and science and in re-establishing our connection with the natural world. If we can make *this* the lead story – inspiring, necessary and cool – then I think we just might be blowing our horns for the right reason. "Wake up! Grab the wheel … Iceberg ahead!"

– Lennie Gallant,
songwriter, father

FERNAND PAREAU

From the time I first saw the mountain, there have been many changes. It is now much more dangerous. In recent years, there have been large rock slides, for example, particularly in the west face of the Dru [l'Aiguille du Dru of the Mont Blanc massif in the French Alps]. And the glaciers are shrinking – those of Bossons and the Mer de Glace have lost up to seven metres in thickness per year. They used to descend into the valley. Now, there are two lakes at the bottom of the Mer de Glace! And this decline is everywhere. And faster and faster.

It is we who are responsible for the global warming. It is we who are pollutant.

With the ARSMB (Association pour le Respect du Site du Mont Blanc), we denounced this pollution, and have gained in the knowledge of its components. There is now a regional call to action that is unfolding here, notably with: the involvement of doctors who have reported an increase in certain diseases; changes toward more environmentally friendly heating methods within the municipalities of the Chamonix valley; car-sharing programs that are coming into effect; and an increased number and frequency of trains, in order to encourage commuters to drive less – as the train schedule of Zermatt, Switzerland, is being used as a model example, where there are trains every ten minutes and no cars.

All these measures can be extended and developed even further. But when the air is this polluted, we need even more drastic measures to be put into place. And the ultimate solution for the Chamonix valley will be its classification as a UNESCO World Heritage Site. Preservation of the area in this manner will prohibit the passage of all large transport trucks, will reduce this devastating pollution and environmental impact to the site, and will bring an incentive toward buying local and in-season fruits and vegetables.

If pollution is reduced, the air quality will improve, it will slow global warming and the melting of glaciers will stop. And if we save our mountains, we allow our children to live there! Life is in the beauty of Nature and the mountains, which must be preserved.[11]

– Fernand Pareau,
85-year-old doyen of guides to the peaks of Chamonix (France)

JAN ZWICKY

This obsession with *doing*, with *making* things happen: it's at the root of the problem. Many of us are incapable of sitting still; incapable of listening; incapable of looking and learning in silence. We can't let the world just be itself – we always have to be fixing it, changing it, making it better, improving things. (The way I fuss over my garden!)

Have humans made progress? Let's rephrase. Is global consumer culture an improvement on regional Paleolithic culture? Are the transnational corporations, to whom we've handed over control, improvements on the power structures of Paleolithic societies? As a woman who deeply appreciates the degree of personal freedom afforded me by contemporary North American culture – a degree of freedom unknown to nearly all other women who have lived and died on this planet – I find it hard to say *no*. But there is little doubt that, in planetary terms, *no* is the answer to these questions. There is also little doubt that the planet itself is going to answer them. When it does, many of us will be up against one of the other things that humans are not very good at: letting go.

There is, I believe, no hope that anything like contemporary North American society will exist on the other side of the crash. The car is already spinning out over the cliff. What is left to intelligent, moral beings in such a situation is witness. Down on our knees, then, in grief. Down on our knees in remorse if fear for our own comfort has made us refuse to listen, if we've allowed wealth to insulate us from the truth. Look, now, one last time.

Really look. Open your heart as wide as it will go. Then open your hands.

– Jan Zwicky,
poet, essayist: *Songs for Relinquishing the Earth*,
Wisdom & Metaphor and *Auden as Philosopher: How Poets Think*

ALASTAIR MCINTOSH

The great question of our times is: *what does it mean to be a human being?* Are we just egos, on legs of meat? Here today, gone tomorrow? Obsessed with competition, consumerism and war?

Or is there more to us than that? Are we still in the early days of the unfolding of humanity? Facing the come-what-may of the come-to-pass, but on a pilgrim sojourn?

Sometimes when I feel very alone, doubting and lacking perspective, I go to a still dark place and look to the stars. The last time I was home on the Isle of Lewis I went by the five-thousand-year-old Callanish standing stones. Afterwards I dropped in for a cup of tea with Calum, the minister of the village's Free Church of Scotland.

His Calvinist theology is not quite mine, but we Quakers "seek that of God in all," and it has been my experience to find this pastor's pulse a beat ahead of my own.

"The old people of the island," he said, as I broke a piece of cake, "maintained that there is only one quality in the human heart that the Devil cannot counterfeit. We call it the *miann*. It is a Gaelic word. It means *ardent desire. The ardent desire for God.*"

I do not know Calum well enough to speak for how he understood that desire. But for me, it is about a very flesh-and-blood kind of love. The ground of all that we most truly are, the essence of good things, the fabric of community and the meaning that gives meaning to meaning.

I left Callanish that day sparked by the fire of this *miann*. We can but ask for it inwardly. To raise our eyes. To see life's starry connection. And who knows? To glimpse the opalescent shimmer of love's hope.

– Alastair McIntosh,
author of *Soil and Soul*
and *Hell and High Water: Climate Change, Hope and the Human Condition*

GRANT LAWRENCE

I believe there is hope.

Whenever I speak with skeptics about our global social and climate crisis, I often say this: even if you don't believe that the climate is changing, even if you think global warming is part of some giant hoax left over from the hippie era, look at it this way: pretend the planet is your yard, your property. Do you dump your garbage out of your open kitchen window onto your lawn? Do you toss out your used appliances into your front yard? Is your backyard filled with your last twenty years of computer monitors? Unless you're from Manshiet Nasser, the answer is probably no. You pride yourself on keeping your private property neat and tidy and free of trash and garbage. You probably recycle your newspapers and your bottles and you might even compost.

If we can abide by this simple logic in our attitudes toward the Earth by applying NIMBY thinking ("not in my backyard") to our entire planet, no matter where you stand on climate change or what your stance may be, our planet will be a better place now and for future generations.

Let's treat the rest of the planet just like our own private property. Earth is our home. We need to clean up the mess.

–Grant Lawrence,
radio host of CBC Music

SIMRAN SETHI

To the ancient Greeks, she was hope. Elpis: a spirit bearing flowers, borne out of the actions of the first woman, Pandora.

Pandora was the all-gifted one. Crafted from earth and water, she was Zeus' punishment to mankind, retribution for Prometheus' theft of fire. The gifted beauty let ills spring forth into what had been a perfect world.

The chaos was her doing.

At least that is what we have been told. That curiosity overwhelmed Pandora. She opened a box she had been instructed to keep closed – and evil escaped. Small winged creatures of sickness, plague and bane, calamities that could not be undone. Pandora recovered in time to capture only one spirit: *Elpis*.

This mythology reverberates through the challenges we face today: poverty, environmental degradation, inequality. We opened the box. The crises have taken flight. All that remains is hope.

But if hope was mingling with the evils in that box, she might be one of them – another cause of suffering. Because hope is not action, it is expectation.

Like the ancient Greeks, we question if hope is worth having. We consider keeping her locked away.

Let us revisit the myth of Pandora's box. Because what she actually opened was a vessel – *pithos* – not a box. Smooth and rounded, some called this vessel the womb; others, life. Pandora was our stand-in: wife, mother, householder. And tucked into her earthy vessel were spirits that would only later come to be known as maleficent. Some say the vessel was not full of evils, but necessities – the elements required to sustain a household. And Elpis was seed, bits of grain set aside for planting, the hope for abundance. Hope made manifest through action.

This was Pandora's doing.

Perhaps it was agency – not curiosity – that compelled Pandora to open the vessel. And hope, caught under the lip of the jar, was not imprisoned. Loath to leave us, she stayed. She endured. She is with us still.

Hope is the beginning and the end, the ripe seed that holds the promise of the next planting. We prepare the ground, we nourish and we water. And then, we hope.

– Simran Sethi,
journalist, educator
simransethi.com

RAJENDRA K. PACHAURI

I am optimistic that humanity can find a way past the current global crisis that we face. The challenge of climate change of course is by far the most daunting of all the complex problems that afflict planet Earth, and indeed it would take an enormous amount of determination, enlightenment and possibly lifestyle and behavioural changes to effectively meet this challenge.

The strongest basis for my optimism lies in the fact that we have today a wealth of scientific knowledge by which we can project the impacts of climate change in the future, if human society were to do nothing about this problem. At the same time, we also have knowledge by which we know that mitigation actions to reduce emissions of greenhouse gases can be taken in hand with very modest, and sometimes even with negative costs. Our major effort therefore should be to disseminate knowledge in a balanced and dispassionate manner, so that human society can take decisions which would help us in meeting this challenge for our benefit and for generations yet to come.

Albert Einstein was right when he said that problems cannot be solved with the level of awareness that created them. We have to use scientific knowledge which has been produced in creating widespread awareness, for in that lies the strongest basis for addressing the problems we face.

In summary, therefore, I remain optimistic, and I think we have every reason to be hopeful, even though the path ahead is not going to be without barriers, resistance and difficulties.

–Rajendra K. Pachauri,
chair of the Intergovernmental Panel on Climate Change,
director-general of TERI (The Energy and Resources Institute, New Delhi)

IAN WILLMS

The idea that we need to "save the planet" is entirely ridiculous. The Earth doesn't need us for anything. From formation of its molten core to its multiple ice ages and numerous extinction-level asteroid impacts, our planet has evolved into a nearly perfect, self-correcting system. We'll kill ourselves long before we destroy the Earth.

I have spent the last three years photographing the indigenous communities located in the region of the Canadian oil sands. A couple centuries ago, their ancestors roamed the Athabasca region of northern Alberta, following the caribou herds and living in harmony with their environment. Today, their First Nations bands have been confined to remote reserves where their sources of food and water are so polluted that they now must cope with rising rates of cancer, miscarriages and other serious ailments. As more and more of their hunting territory is strip-mined and drowned beneath with man-made lakes of toxic waste, the prospect of reviving their traditional livelihood is quickly fading away. They are the canary in the coal mine.

For the 2012–13 fiscal year, the Canadian government budgeted $9-million in tax revenue to fund an ad campaign that attempted to convince Canadians and the world of the importance of oil sands developments. The ads trumpeted words like "energy security" and "economic progress" while insisting that environmental protection was a top priority. They also reminded us that the oil sands are worth $1.7-trillion to Canada's GDP over the next 20 years while neglecting to mention that the oil sands industry alone emits more carbon per annum than the entire nation of Turkey. The public will buy the government's line because they're too afraid to face a new and unknown world.

The oil sands are the reason why my country pulled out of the Kyoto Protocol and why my government continues to sabotage the international climate change debate with destructive policies and a noncommittal stance on proposed climate accords. While Canada is not solely responsible for global climate change, our actions contribute to a greater whole. We will not choose to transition to a sustainable existence until that change becomes a necessity. By that time, it will be too late to avoid major loss of human life. Extreme weather patterns have already become the norm and there are climate change refugees all over the globe. A new and unknown world is coming and we must adapt in order to survive.

Beyond simply surviving, we must live. The coming centuries will present us with an opportunity to rebuild our world while considering the hard lessons of today. The greed and inequity that has flung us into this quagmire of systemic destruction must not be carried forward. Our brilliance as a species to create and invent needs only to be focused in the right direction for us to create something that is truly lasting and beautiful. Good luck, everyone.

–Ian Willms,
Boreal Collective

DAVID HOLMGREN

Organized international responses (between nation states) to the current global environmental and social crises are unlikely to be effective or in time, and are more likely to worsen the crises because they will all be designed to maintain growth of the corporation dominated global economy and protect the power of nation states.

Despite the pain and suffering from the ongoing, and likely permanent, contraction of many economies, the explosion of informal household and community economies have the potential to ameliorate the worst impacts of the crises by rebuilding lost local resilience.

I believe the diversity of integrated design strategies and techniques associated with concepts such as Permaculture will be most effective at building household and community economies as the global economy unravels. The diversity of these strategies and techniques promises that at least some will provide pathways for longer-term survival of humanity while the adverse impacts of some strategies will tend to be more local and limited allowing natural systems (especially at the global scale) to stabilize.

Because the future will be more local than global, the critical path is the ongoing development and refinement of effective local designs, while the Internet and other aspects of the failing global systems still have huge potential to allow the viral spread of the most effective and widely applicable designs.

Systems ecology and indigenous wisdom both suggest that in a world of limited resources, the ethics of "care of the Earth," "care of people" and "fair share" will prove more advantageous to local survival than those based on greed and fear, that have been so powerful during a century of unprecedented abundance. To put it crudely, hungry dogs hunt co-operatively and share the results, but given an abundance of food, they fight each other for the spoils.

I have great hope that the diverse local cultures that emerge from the ruins of industrial modernity will be based on these ethics and informed by design principles found in nature. The uncertainty is how much more pain and despoiling are yet to unfold before fear and greed prove maladapted to a world of limits.

– David Holmgren,
co-originator (1978) of the Permaculture design system for sustainable living and land use,
ecological builder, farmer, author, teacher, activist
www.holmgren.com.au

CÉLINE COUSTEAU

Hope serves as a driving force for positive change. This hope inspires us to look to our future and take the necessary steps to ameliorate our lives.

When we talk about protecting our planet it is not just for the sake of the environment, it is for own livelihood as well – for the health of this planet is our own health (lest we feel we can survive on oil, cement, pollution and dwindling natural resources).

But much like a marathon, we should be ready to work, train and believe in our ability to reach our goals. It is in part hope that creates the conviction needed to endure the challenge.

By shifting our thinking, and believing in a global community with a common stake in the future of our species, we can and will make positive socio-environmental change happen. In fact, we have no other choice – our human potential to survive relies on a shift in consciousness and our unified action.

I have hope that we can make that shift happen and that we can act more like a tribe; a community with a common future. We need to believe in this, else we lower our arms in defeat, and that is not an option.

–Céline Cousteau,
multimedia documentarian, socio-environmental advocate,
founder/director of CauseCentric Productions
causecentric.org

STÉPHANE DION

Despite empirical evidence and science's warnings regarding the ever-increasing deterioration of our natural environment, unsustainable economic activity, political wrangling, self-serving practices and just plain negligence keep trumping environmental imperatives.

Most political leaders care about this tragedy. But concretely, they are not accountable to the planet; they are accountable to their jurisdiction. That's why, most of the time, local trumps global, and short term prevails over long term.

Now, assume that we change the rules of the game. Imagine a world where each decision maker, public or private, has to pay the real cost of pollution and where we all know that our partners and competitors have to pay for this cost as well. In such a world, political rulers would still think of their own jurisdiction's welfare first but their decisions would be more mindful of the global commons.

Putting a price on pollution: this is what the overwhelming majority of economists, scientists and environmentalists – and a few foolhardy politicians – have been urging us to do for years. This applies notably to the climate change crisis.

The current UN climate negotiations are stalled; that is the inescapable conclusion of a cool, lucid mind. So let's redirect these negotiations towards achieving a universal harmonized carbon price.

We need a world where pollution is no longer cost-free. We need to switch from self-destructive development to sustainable development. Action on this survival necessity and moral imperative is long overdue; it will require individual commitment, business support and political will.

–The Honourable Stéphane Dion, PC,
Member of Parliament for Saint-Laurent–Cartierville (Montréal),
former Minister of the Environment

SETH GODIN

We're all going to die.

Of course we are. Everyone does.

Not only that, but it's far too late, and the politics are too entrenched to imagine that we'll be able to maintain the status quo as we know it. The ice caps are going to melt, temperatures are going to rise and our lives (and more importantly, the lives of our grandchildren) are going to be dramatically different.

So, does that mean we should give up? Does that mean we should heedlessly burn and destroy and consume, acting as if everything is just fine?

I hope not.

No, this isn't a problem to be fixed the way pottery can be mended or a skinned knee can heal. This is the new normal. But even with that acknowledgement, we must work ceaselessly because we know that all of our efforts will make a difference: they will contribute to ameliorating the problem we caused in the first place.

And mostly, it's a problem to be fixed because humans don't give up. We don't shrug our shoulders, avert our eyes and just watch our offspring live a life that's not nearly what it could be. It's our nature to fight, to improve and to innovate.

I guess I'm asking you to stop looking for the certain solution, stop hoping for the perfect hope, and instead embrace what we've got, which is the task at hand, which is the effort to make a difference.

Because it matters.

− Seth Godin,
author of *The Icarus Deception*
www.sethgodin.com

BRENNA DAVIS

I have an unshakable hope that the Earth will be renewed. My hope lies in the mind and heart of humanity – in the heights of our innovation, and in the depths of our compassion.

Human beings have a passion for innovation. One of the biggest watershed moments in modern history was the invention of the combustion engine, which birthed the industrial revolution. From the development of metallurgy, to the mastery of physics, the creation of the engine required millennia of innovation. An engine is an exquisite example of our ability to innovate, despite the unintended consequences of climate change. Our generation is beginning to apply the same innovative spirit that created the engine to environmental innovation. We are finding ways to reduce our carbon footprint, eliminating toxins from manufacturing and expanding use of renewable energy. We are in an era of astounding environmental innovation across the globe.

Human beings are being called to environmental innovation because of compassion for future generations. We know that we are already experiencing climate change that impacts people worldwide. Even if we stop all emissions today, scientists found that the climate wouldn't return to a state of stasis for at least a century. This scientific finding rings in an era of intergenerational environmental justice. It calls the entire world to unprecedented levels of compassion for human beings whom we will never meet. Compassion for people of the future may seem like a tall order, but compassion has an amazing quality – when we develop compassion for ourselves, we develop compassion for others. It stands to reason, then, that our most important work is to develop compassion for ourselves. When we do, our compassion will overflow into our relationship with the world, including protecting the Earth for those yet to be born.

When our hearts and minds merge, each human being has the innate ability to compassionately innovate for the good of all. This is how the Earth will be renewed for the well-being of future generations. As the Hopi elders generously and wisely stated, we are the ones we have been waiting for.

– Brenna Davis,
environmental scientist, sustainable business expert

CAM MATHER

I have been involved in the environmental movement for 30 years and there has never been more evidence than is available today that we are on the cusp of a human-caused environmental calamity. However, what I have learned from living off the electricity grid for the last 15 years is that there *are* solutions and that you can enjoy a comfortable life while contributing a minimal amount of carbon to the atmosphere.

It all comes down to one simple solution – putting a price on a carbon. Since we know that carbon dioxide is the main driver of climate change, by putting a price on it we can encourage individuals to make smarter choices for how they heat and power their lives. Many of us are used to paying for each bag of trash we send to the landfill, and this is no different.

Technologies do exist to live carbon free. What's missing is the incentive for people to do so. Once carbon is priced properly I believe the marketplace will provide even more ingenious solutions to help people save money while reducing their carbon footprint.

All that's missing today is the political fortitude to do the right thing. What can the average citizen do in the meantime? Live your life as if carbon was extremely expensive and vote Green to send the message to the governing party that the time has come to take tough action on the most important political issue.

The fate of humanity depends on it.

– Cam Mather,
author of *Thriving During Challenging Times: The Energy, Food and Financial Independence Handbook*,
publisher of Aztext Press
www.cammather.com

ADRIA VASIL

We don't need a foggy crystal ball to see the world screeching toward the brink of catastrophe – the early fruits of short-term thinking are popping up everywhere. They're showing up in the persistent toxins in umbilical cords, in the growing rates of mysterious cancers and disease, in vanishing forests and species, in the droughts, floods, fires and storms stirring up with increasing fervour around the globe. The heavy truth is, there are hidden ramifications behind each of our daily actions, choices big and small, on water, wildlife, workers, climate – and the very people that use this stuff – us.

Today my job involves flagging those impacts. The only thing that keeps me from throwing in the towel in total paralysis is knowing this: every positive action sparks an even greater positive reaction. My mother told me when I was young that the globe is essentially a giant domino board – that we can actually transform the world by focusing on changing our little corners of it, setting into motion the forces for transformation from person to person to person.

Okay sure, as a collective, we've been putting the Earth's five a.m. wake-up calls on snooze for a while now, but have no doubt, the Earth will keep smacking us upside the head until we all get with the program.

In my personal crystal ball, I see an emerging world where our throw-away, single-use culture of built-in obsolescence is a thing of the past, everything is recycled in a closed loop in perpetuity. We get our energy from sewage, rotting food and all sorts of surprising sources now going to waste. And green chemistry ensures everything we make, buy and use is as safe as water and mimics Nature's patterns. I believe, ultimately, that we'll realign with the ecosystem we depend on once we realize that the only way to save our own behinds from Nature's wrath is to reconnect and get in tune with Nature's brilliance. Thankfully, millions of souls – scientists, researchers, engineers, farmers, teachers, business folk, moms, dads, are already doing just that.

So, chin up, listen to mom and keep working on your little corner – it holds the key to transforming the entire globe.

– Adria Vasil,
environmental journalist, columnist,
author of the bestselling *Ecoholic* book series

JAMES P. BRUCE

At times, it is difficult not to despair about the future. Current economic and political practices which focus on the short term – a business quarter or a four-year term – ignore future impacts on humans, other species and the environment.

The implications for climate change are most evident. Digging up or pumping out the last drops or chunks of fossil fuels and burning them in gas-guzzling vehicles and inefficient power plants has already begun to leave a legacy. With more water vapour in the warming atmosphere, storms, floods and droughts are causing much suffering and economic damage. But we are seeing only the beginning of this terrible trend.

That is only one of the environmental problems that the present economic practices encourage. Another is the growing concentration of harmful chemicals in our air and water. Some 23,000 of the 80,000 to 100,000 distinct chemical compounds in North American commerce have been identified as chemicals of concern (Health and Environment Canada, 2006). But the endocrine disrupters, pharmaceuticals and many other potentially harmful substances are not removed at sewage treatment plants or in air pollution controls. Governments rarely regulate, and choose supporting short-term profits over their responsibilities to protect health and our common environmental heritage.

Is there any cause for hope? As climate change, chemical pollutant effects and species extinctions become more evident and severe in coming decades, the public will place increasing value on health and on protecting remaining ecosystems. Voters must elect different kinds of politicians, those with concerns for the "Public Trust," and we all must expect more responsible actions by corporations. If we learn well from First Nations' teachings, we will all care more about future generations, and the world our grandchildren and their grandchildren will inherit.

– Dr. J.P. (Jim) Bruce, OC, FRSC,
former assistant deputy minister of Environment Canada,
senior officer of World Meteorological Organization, Geneva

OCTOBER

ROB SISSON

ConservAmerica is an American conservation group of Republicans and conservatives who care about environmental protection. For the past two decades, there has not been a lot of reason to be optimistic that we'll leave behind a sustainable world for future generations.

Today, however, I am extremely optimistic and hopeful for our shared future. We have a moral obligation to lead on major global issues like climate change, clean drinking water and clean air. Ronald Reagan referred to America as "the shining light upon a hill" giving hope to all the world's citizens. A purposeful failure to answer the present environmental challenges would extinguish that beacon.

My political party is the keystone – currently the missing piece in building the national will to tackle these problems. I'm confident that the Republican Party will soon rediscover its great conservation legacy. The demographic landscape in America will force the party to adapt.

Voters under the age of thirty believe environmental protection should be a priority. Hispanic voters, the fastest growing cohort, strongly support climate action. Pro-life voters, always taken for granted by Republican candidates, are now recognizing that sustaining life after birth is equally important to protecting it before birth. Recent polls even demonstrate rank-and-file Republicans support laws protecting the environment.

It is among faith-based voters, the salt of the conservative movement, where I have greatest hope. There are 70 million Catholics in the United States, and I am one of them. The last two popes – John Paul II and Benedict XVI – spoke eloquently and often about caring for creation. Pope Francis has surpassed his predecessors in the ability to reach into the hearts of Catholics around the world. His focus on environmental protection and justice is awakening the slumbering Church. If – when – he issues a call to U.S. Catholics to rise above politics and self-interest to serve God and humanity, American politicians will race to the front of the legion.

In 1984, Ronald Reagan described our mutual obligation:

> *We want to protect and conserve the land on which we live – our countryside, our rivers and mountains, our plains and meadows and forests. This is our patrimony. This is what we leave to our children. And our great moral responsibility is to leave it to them either as we found it or better than we found it.*

Thirty years later, I am brimming with hope that we will heed those words.

– Rob Sisson,
president of ConservAmerica

JENNIFER J. BROWN

When I think about our future as a species, I always look back at our history for perspective. The stone age must have seemed like all there was for a while, and then the bronze age too. And at times, the fossil fuel age we are in feels so entrenched that it is something we cannot change, but of course, it will pass, as all other ages have. Our future will shine with the realization of the promises of solar and wind generated energy; that future is blossoming even now. Alternatives to coal, oil and gas are all around us above ground and will sustain our needs with clean renewable energy. Our future is as bright as the sun.

Looking into our future as a species I see a time when life is respected universally, with the rights of people and animals protected around the world. People will continue to turn away from the barbaric practices of the past, embracing the path of vegetarian and vegan diets for a healthier planet. As the demand for animal products fade, the animals, birds and fish will regain a place of honour in the world of *Homo sapiens*. Their rights will be respected as ours are. We will survive to see a peaceful and natural world, rich in variety.

I have hope, and we have hope, because of the growing awareness among young people who can reach beyond borders as they learn about their world. The Internet and social media continue to connect us to each other in ways that defy nationalism and push us toward a more peaceful planet.

– Jennifer J. Brown, PhD,
author, mother, scientist

RYAN VANDECASTEYEN

I have hope that there is indeed a way past our current global crises.

We've reached a critical point in our collective history; all around the world we're seeing the impacts of our continual need for growth. Governments are favouring big business over the welfare of people and the sustainability of our life systems. Climate change is causing sea levels to rise, increased severity of major weather events and desertification.

Resource use is poisoning our land, air and water. We've entered the only era in the history of our planet where humans are a leading driver of geophysical and ecological change.

Despite how bleak the picture can be at times, I'm empowered by the thought that we've reached a critical turning point, and before us lies an amazing opportunity. It doesn't have to be this way.

Every day I'm inspired and given hope by stories of groups of people all around the world standing up and demanding to be heard, telling us that business as usual is unacceptable, and taking affirmative action to affect real change.

I found myself being a part of one of these kinds of stories of standing up for change, as two colleagues and I set out to kayak the length of the British Columbian coastline to connect and engage citizens with the risks posed by the proposed Enbridge Northern Gateway Pipeline.

I'm lucky to live in a place where these kinds of stories are unfolding in my own backyard, where thousands of people from all walks of life are standing up to say no to dirty energy, to protect the places they call home and one of the last truly wild places on Earth.

Change is messy, and it's not an easy task. For us to survive, we each have to recognize that we all play a role; history is being made right here and now and every one of us is already a part of it. To me the question is, will we be known for our inaction, or for our drive to recognize and act on the world-changing issues with which we're faced?

—Ryan Vandecasteyen,
filmmaker, environmental advocate,
co-creator of The Pipedreams Project
www.thepipedreamsproject.org

NORIE HUDDLE

Yes, we can transform ourselves, all of humanity – and do it very rapidly and enjoyably.

Remember: transformation is not a linear process; it can happen all at once.

To survive and thrive as a species, to heal the Earth and ourselves, we have a big job ahead of us and must come together as never before to support and empower and cheer on one another. How grateful I am for all that you are doing – and how grateful I am for our partnership in the Great Work ahead.

Be connected, be authentic, breathe with awareness, be flexible and open, remember that we're all students and all teachers, find the perfection in the moment, feel and express gratitude, follow your bliss, be kind, inform yourself, grow in your capacity for love and contribution, collaborate wholeheartedly and cheerfully, create beauty.

Thank you so much for doing your part! Together we can do what no one of us can do alone.

Love and Blessings,

– Norie Huddle,
author, public speaker, consultant, artist
www.gardenofparadise.net and www.butterflyblessings.net

One of the 1001 original butterflies drawn for the "Butterfly Countdown to Global Transformation."
The final butterfly, #1001, was drawn on May 19, 2013.

GARY HIRSHBERG

Self-interest. It's our greatest threat and yet also our greatest hope.

Self-interest has led us to ignore our "externalities" – the direct consequences of our economic behaviours that we then leave off our balance sheets and income statements as if they don't exist.

The bad news is that most of these outcomes – toxification, depletion of biodiversity and natural resources, climate change, cancer rates – have worsened. And this may be history's first generation to live shorter lives than their parents.

But therein lies the good news. The very same self-interest that got us into most of these messes is probably the only hope to get ourselves and our planet back to good health. Climate events have displaced millions and cost billions. The President's Cancer Panel reports that 41 per cent of us will be diagnosed with cancers from exposure to chemicals in our foods, air and water. Disappearing pollinators pose serious risks to farmers and food prices. These are not just statistics. We are all being touched. We feel fear, hardship and pain.

And pain will makes us change. Because it is in our self-interest to do so. I have hope because I have seen that ecology is really long-term economics. That healthy soil sequesters carbon and produces higher yields. And biodiversity controls pests better than chemicals. That the cheapest form of healthcare is not getting sick. And food is better when Nature's rules are followed.

When it comes to expediting our evolution, pain is a good catalyst.

–Gary Hirshberg,
co-founder and chairman of Stonyfield Farm,
chair of the Just Label It! campaign
justlabelit.org

DAVID HELWIG

Enduring Prophecy

Geography abandons itself to history;
cities afloat on the fires of the infinite
falter in the elisions of our knowing.

Who will whistle the lovely notes of the bobolink,
the meadows lost? Who will warranty
the exactly certain doom of our gardens?

Beneath the wild leaves of metaphor
wind and grass and ocean shallows
seed futures which will come or not come.

Unease kindles beyond the half-life of certainties.
We try to believe our grandchildren will forgive us
if we bless them and abandon thinking.

The inevitable rises like a great flood.

– David Helwig, CM,
former poet laureate of Prince Edward Island (Canada),
author of over 40 books, including *The Stand-In*, *The Year One* and *The Names of Things*
www.davidhelwig.com

PAUL BECKWITH

Abrupt climate change. It is happening today, big time. We have changed the chemistry of our atmosphere with fossil fuel emissions. Climate system statistics are now different. Rates of change have surpassed tipping points. Extreme weather events are skyrocketing in frequency, intensity and duration. Societal and economic costs are already substantial and are rapidly accelerating. Oceans are acidifying. Global food supplies are threatened. We are still at very early stages. Climate change is just getting warmed up.

Powerful feedbacks have caused enormous Arctic temperature amplification with exponential collapse of sea ice and snow cover. Thawing terrestrial and sub-sea permafrost is releasing ever-increasing amounts of powerful climate-warming methane. Atmospheric circulation patterns without guidance from stable jet streams are water vapour turbocharged from increased evaporation. Regions unlucky in our new climate casino are inundated by torrential rainfall and becoming water-worlds. Or baked from persistent heat waves and drought and fires exploding in size, frequency and severity. Or buried by snow and ice storms. Lives are in turmoil. Infrastructure like houses, roads, train tracks and pipelines are being hammered.

What next? There is no new normal. Far from it.

We have lost our stable familiar climate. Likely permanently. Rates of change greatly exceed anything recorded in paleo-records. By at least 10 to 30 times. Greenland and Antarctic ice caps are melting and calving at unprecedented and accelerating rates. Large chunks will soon slide into the ocean causing tsunamis and abrupt sea level rise, swamping coastlines. We are heading to a much warmer world. Abruptly. Within decades. The transition will be brutal for civilization. Global flora and fauna face a sixth mass extinction.

There is hope. Knowledge of this climate threat is spreading widely to our society that has been brainwashed into inaction by fossil fuel corporations and their subservient governments who maintain the status quo. More and more people see trees dying in their backyards. Devastation to their houses, roads and cities from extreme weather events is awakening them to the grave dangers. Soon a threshold will be crossed and a tipping point reached in human behaviour. A wisdom reached on the reality of the risks that we face. And finally global concerted action. To slash emissions and embrace renewable energies. And change our ways. And retool our economies and reset our priorities. And not take our life on this planet for granted.

– Paul Beckwith,
part-time professor of climatology/meteorology at University of Ottawa (Canada)

CLARE DELANEY

We live on the most perfect planet. Our "pale blue dot" to quote Carl Sagan. It is perfectly positioned in space to give us everything we need to sustain diverse life. Similar perfection is hard to find.

Despite this, we extract, transport and burn fossil fuels at an unprecedented rate. We don't account for the external costs (pollution and its associated health problems, disposal and waste) that go into producing energy, products and "growth" as we currently define it. Our centralized food production system doesn't consider the environmental cost of chemical fertilizers, pesticides, animal welfare and habitat destruction.

Collective suicide is not factored into annual profit reports.

Large corporations are by no means the only problem. We know that we must reduce carbon emissions if we are to avoid catastrophic climate change. Yet the biggest emitters – China, USA, Russia, India, Japan – will not meet those requirements. Japan will actually *increase* emissions, as will Australia and Canada.

Most countries are run by politicians who are frequently tied to and dependent on corporate capitalism. By necessity, politicians think short-term (the next election). A decision that is good for the planet but may cost them votes, is political suicide.

And then there's the general populace. You and me. We're concerned with jobs and money. We also think short-term. Sure, save the planet, but don't inconvenience me or make me pay more.

Rampant capitalism, powerful corporations, politicians dependent on votes, and a predominantly uncaring population. It's a deadly combination. Said Albert Einstein bluntly: "We shall require a substantially new manner of thinking if mankind is to survive."

Even with so many passionately showing us the error of our ways, do we have sufficient commitment to make the necessary radical changes to save our beautiful – and fragile – pale blue dot?

Are we "fiddling while Rome burns"?

It's time to recognize that dramatic change is, quite simply, essential for our survival.

We have a small window of opportunity to mend our ways before it is too late.

Join the global chorus for action.

Because the alternative – the destruction of our perfect planet, our dot in infinity – is just too final to contemplate.

– Clare Delaney,
environmentalist, sustainable living writer, speaker,
founder of EcoFriendlyLink
www.EcoFriendlyLink.com

DAVID R. BOYD

I'm an optimistic environmentalist. That's not an oxymoron. Over the past fifty years we've witnessed an extraordinary transformation of human legal systems, values and behaviour. Hundreds of international environmental treaties. Thousands of new environmental laws. The emergence of a new human right – to live in a healthy environment – now endorsed by 90 per cent of the world's nations. This right is protected in over 100 constitutions, indicating it is among our most deeply cherished values and aspirations.

Some environmental laws are like hibernating polar bears, not yet active, but many are already fulfilling their goals. Safe drinking water has been extended to billions of people around the world. CFCs and other chemicals threatening to destroy the Earth's protective ozone layer have been virtually eliminated. The most deadly persistent organic pollutants are globally banned. Endangered species including grey whales, bald eagles and sea otters recovered from the brink of extinction. Levels of some air pollutants are down 90 per cent.

Humanity still faces monumental environmental challenges. But our track record of successes provides a powerful elixir of hope. We can reboot society to flourish on 100 per cent renewable energy from sun, wind and water. We can create a circular economy without waste and pollution. We can grow delicious and nutritious food locally. We can build bright, green cities where everyone lives within a five-minute walk of green spaces – parks, community gardens and orchards. Walking, cycling and public transit will be more convenient and economical than driving. Buildings will produce more energy than they consume. From Vancouver to Stockholm, these visions are becoming reality.

Western cultures are recovering the indigenous wisdom that we depend on Nature for health, well-being and prosperity. We must treat this wonderful planet, our home, with the respect and reverence it richly deserves. Within the geologically infinitesimal span of one or two generations – ours and our children's – we can ensure a cleaner, greener, healthier and happier future for all of Earth's inhabitants.

– David R. Boyd, PhD,
author, environmental lawyer, professor,
co-chair of Vancouver's Greenest City Action Team

GEORGE MU'AMMAR

How do we discuss "change"? "Did the dinosaurs evolve or die out?" Both and neither; the problem is only linguistic. "People who love this country can change it" has more meanings and implications than words. Language appears inappropriate for defining, analyzing and solving problems that go beyond individual daily personal life. We are language animals, genetically built for communication. But we do talk too much, giving ourselves unjustified praise, often lies, to satisfy our justice-seeking sentiments, or those of the conqueror within us. Language distorts and misrepresents reality, even nullifying efforts of entire communities. Years of manipulation using language produced societies that can be driven to consensus by religious/political leaders but, regardless of centuries of scientific advancements are incapable of agreeing upon solutions to problems that are easily observed and quantified by individuals.

Today we realize that global social and environmental problems are relentlessly advancing uncontrollably because of financial and political drivers. Commodities are incorrectly priced, discounting the real cost of the social/environmental impact their production caused. Incorrect measures of human success, defined in previous eras were based upon religious fantasies or military ideals with no regard for the bigger picture drawn by human accomplishments. We must start today defining standards for equilibrated globalized pricing of our industrial production based on the real cost to the planet, and more importantly (but less urgently) redefining the meaning of "success" by giving individuals the ethical background and support to define their moral compass and their goals in compatibility with those of their community and society, if necessary by calling upon the human need for religion and justice.

Human knowledge is adept at saving the global situation, requiring extensive and prolonged efforts on behalf of us all, with the only reward being the awareness of not having damaged Mother Nature as our predecessors had. Our consumption/disposal of food and non-food commodities must change based on new ideals to which our industrial practices must adapt, driven mostly by adjusted pricing. Our energy production/consumption must be redesigned and our demand for military hardware must cease, outlawed. Obtaining this in a democratic world requires not only increased global awareness but also a correct metering of our actions and ambitions and those of our communities, guided by scientific strategy and not political blurb.

– George Mu'Ammar,
spatial analyst for the Food Security Analysis Service,
Vulnerability Analysis and Mapping, UN World Food Programme; hobbyist beekeeper

ANITA STEWART

If humankind is to survive, let us rekindle the extraordinary spirit that built our respective nations. Let's learn and honour the fact that farmers and plumbers and cooks are as important to society as lawyers and politicians and pundits. Let's cook, eat and preserve the harvest together, sharing our knowledge generously. Let's embrace one another's happiness as our own.

These dreams are indeed achievable. As Jesuit thinker Thomas Merton wrote, "We are already one. But we imagine that we are not. And what we have to recover is our original unity. What we have to be is what we are."

– Anita Stewart,
culinary activist, food and travel journalist,
founder of Food Day Canada
fooddaycanada.ca

MARY EVELYN TUCKER

More than ever before in human history we are facing a moment of immense historical consequence. Our planet has evolved over four and a half billion years. It has brought forth complex and beautiful life forms. We are latecomers to the Earth community. Our planetary presence and our technological powers are causing the climate to change, species to go extinct and ecosystems to be diminished. We have an immense challenge before us.

In over two hundred thousand years of our presence on this blue-green planet we have never been asked to renew the face of the Earth. That is what we are being asked to do now. To renew our wetlands and restore our woodlands. To re-inhabit cities and countryside in a sustaining way. To participate in healthy cycles of carbon and nitrogen. To become a life-enhancing species on a life-giving planet. This is no small task.

The possibility that is held forth for us as humans in renewing the face of the Earth is to become worthy of our name *Homo sapiens sapiens*. Perhaps we had to be named twice, sapiens, so we could reflect on what our gift of self-reflection would mean over time. We have to earn the name of wisdom.

To do that we will need to draw in the powers which have helped to shape our universe and Earth. As Thomas Berry suggested, this immense journey may be a source of great strength as we align our efforts with the unfolding universe:

> *If the dynamics of the universe from the beginning shaped the course of the heavens, lighted the sun, and formed the Earth, if this same dynamism brought forth the continents and seas and atmosphere, if it awakened life in the primordial cell and then brought into being the unnumbered variety of living beings, and finally brought us into being and guided us safely through the turbulent centuries, there is reason to believe that this same guiding process is precisely what has awakened in us our present understanding of ourselves and our relation to this stupendous process. Sensitized to such guidance from the very structure and functioning of the universe, we can have confidence in the future that awaits the human venture.*
>
> — *THE DREAM OF THE EARTH*[20]

– Dr. Mary Evelyn Tucker,
founder of the Forum on Religion and Ecology at Yale University

JOHN POMEROY

We are in a very dangerous time in history due to rapidly rising greenhouse gas concentrations and other impacts of our growing population. Climate warming means that we are now starting to see exactly how loss of cold melts snow, permafrost, sea ice and glaciers and how intensification of the hydrological cycle results in severe storms, floods and droughts. This involves irreversible thermodynamics and complex ecohydrological regime changes which take time to manifest themselves and are often unanticipated. Changes to water are focused and magnified downstream in river basins and are inordinately directed to rivers, lakes, ponds, wetlands and floodplains where key ecosystems and our main communities reside.

I have found humanity's response to the degradation of climate, ecosystems and water to be discouraging – we almost always respond and correct our behaviour only after a disaster and rarely with foresight. And then we try to forget about it. I fear that we will only begin to reduce our greenhouse gas emissions after repeated catastrophes have limited our ability and will to emit. It is virtually certain that we will see more extreme climate, ecosystem and water problems before the effects of declining emissions on climate become apparent. But there will be no return to "normal." The responses to climate forcing will alter the Earth dramatically and irrevocably and require all the adaptation that humanity can tolerate.

Though unrecognizable in many instances, this will still be our home. Our clever species and many others will survive – intrinsically refigured by the trauma of change. Through this we must ensure that decency, diplomacy, integrity and our natural creative, hopeful spirit survive as we contend with irreversible thermodynamics and ecohydrological change.

–Professor John Pomeroy,
Canada Research Chair in Water Resources and Climate Change,
director of the Centre for Hydrology at the University of Saskatchewan

ROSS JACKSON

I believe the greatest threat to our survival is the way we have organized our international economic/political structures. For example, the rules of the World Trade Organization work fine for corporations – especially the largest multinationals – but are particularly perverse in the way they penalize any country or company that tries to take the leadership in developing more environmentally friendly technologies. This is because the WTO rules do not permit a country to impose tariffs on foreign products produced with a lower environmental standard. In fact, a country cannot even demand to know how an imported product was produced. This one rule is, in my opinion, the greatest single barrier to a sustainable future.

The dismal record of the EU's CO_2 emissions quotas is a perfect example. The intention was fine, but there is no way to protect European companies that develop friendlier, but more costly technologies, because they will be undercut by foreign competitors.

The result is that quota prices are too low to have any effect. If they were high enough to be effective, the EU's corporations would scream and threaten to leave the EU (many have already done so). The difficulties of reform are further compounded by the fact that the people in charge of the WTO/IMF/World Bank are the very ones who benefit from the current system.

In *Occupy World Street*, I outline what I call a "breakaway strategy" that I believe has a chance of succeeding. It requires a few small countries to unite in forming an embryonic new organization giving the highest priority to sustainability and human rights – rather than economic growth – and then invite others to join. The strategy requires that civil society around the world subsequently unites in support of the breakaway states.

I believe that this is our best chance for survival. All it really needs is a single visionary leader to step forward and follow Mahatma Gandhi's advice: be the change you want to see in the world.

– Ross Jackson,
co-founder/chair of the Gaia Trust Foundation (Denmark),
co-founder/funder of the Global Ecovillage Network and Gaia Education,
author of *Occupy World Street: A Global Roadmap for Radical Economic and Political Reform*
www.gaia.org

SUSIE MATTHIAS

I say "yes": that we as humanity can survive the current, and future, environmental and social crises.

But our global social issues cannot even begin to be solved if we as a people do not better ourselves toward being able to treat all others as equals – regardless of race, religion, colour or creed. As a person with a disability, I have met people of all kinds who have assisted me at times, and I see a lot of them with kindness once given a chance.

With regards to the environmental crisis, as a human race, we once had to rely on each other and the environment in order to survive. But over a period of time, we have become more selfish and self-centred. We have become greedy and less caring about how we treat the environment, taking all of the Earth's resources without replenishing them.

Everything comes down to respect: if we accept others' differences, and if we maintain the same respectful attitude toward our environment, then I feel that we all have an opportunity to survive and thrive.

–Theresa Helen "Susie" Matthias,
mouth painting artist, Mouth and Foot Painting Artists of Canada

DON MCKAY

Let me point to a pair of benefits of the environmental crisis – paradoxical benefits, to be sure – but apparent just the same in the remarkable shifts we can observe in the general mindset regarding the environment. One is the new-found sense of its *losability* – the awareness that natural elements we took for granted (e.g., dependable sea levels, seasonal regularity, arable land) are subject to radical, perhaps catastrophic, change. Losability leads us to value what we've got when – to adapt Joni Mitchell – it's not *quite* gone, much as we do when a friend or relative contracts a serious illness. It's a sad irony that astonishment and attachment increase when that black frame settles around a species, a landscape or a place.

The second, related shift in our thinking could be called a sense of *membership*. As the truths of ecology gather and gain acceptance (a long process, it has to be admitted, given that it's a 19th-century idea) our idea of ourselves shifts from the notion of the Master Species at the summit of a hierarchical order to that of a member of a system that works as a vast web of interdependencies. Membership in the natural world has already brought us fresh insights into its intricacies, its amazing symbioses and networks of communication. Of course, membership includes the recognition that we have often damaged and destroyed parts of the ecological web, and put its very existence – at least in its current life-enhancing form – in jeopardy.

As the official name for our epoch becomes accepted as the Anthropocene, we will implicitly acknowledge the role of *anthropos* – us – in altering the planet's systems sufficiently that a geological record will be left. Simultaneously, we will position ourselves as inhabitants of deep time rather than a shallow, human-centred history. Membership and losability: these gifts will mean that, to whatever extent we are able to mitigate the disaster, we will have earned back some capacity to grieve, rather than numbly suffering the ravages of environmental degradation. They mean that when we say "we," the collective pronoun will resonate beyond the bounds of the much celebrated human saga into remote reaches of our temporal and spatial dwelling. Perhaps, to draw upon one of the most eloquent human arts, we may be privileged to perish as characters in tragedy rather than farce.

–Don McKay, CM,
Canadian poet, editor, educator

TAMI SIMON

What matters most is our motivation. If we orient ourselves towards a motivation that is based on an awakened heart, then whatever the outcome of our efforts, we can rest in the assurance that we have done our very best as human beings and as a species.

So what does it mean be motivated by an awakened heart? To me, it means aligning ourselves with the good of the whole, with the deep heart that feels our interconnection with all of life, the sensitive heart that breathes with and is in communion with the flow of life itself. When we drop into this deep, pulsing heart, a heart that is not defended in any way but is acutely sensitive to the relational field and the needs of the moment, there is a natural desire to be of benefit and to serve the good of the whole. Can we continually return to this true heart and reconnect with our deepest motivation to serve all beings, again and again and again?

If so, we become a living heart-fire of love and justice in the world. This heart-fire is contagious; others will catch it when they hear our warm voice or touch our sensitive hands or see our kind face. We become an indestructible human torch of goodness. This is not an idea but something that needs to be deeply felt and embodied. If we can embody this motivation in our life and in our moment-to-moment actions, then we can join together and creatively solve whatever environmental or social problems we face.

The fire of the human heart can never be extinguished. It burns brightly in the face of any and every challenge. The open, tender, creative human heart is our best refuge and hope.

– Tami Simon,
founder and publisher of Sounds True

DAVID KAHANE

My work involves convening citizens to deliberate about climate change and climate policy. Whatever life and political perspectives people bring to the table, they hear each other, dig deeply into their own priorities and values, and grapple together with tough choices. They show the collective wisdom and care that humans can generate, person to person.

Are these human capacities enough to deal with global environmental and social crises? I don't know. I often doubt it. Our political, economic and cultural systems tend to cut us off from the effects of our actions, insulate us from the suffering of other beings, and lead us to pursue short-term rewards even when these compromise what we care about most deeply. These systems churn along, seemingly relentless.

I'm interested in what happens if we give up hope as well as the reactivity and despair that are its flip side. What happens if we act with fearlessness and integrity and compassion – not because we're convinced these can turn the tide, but simply because they reflect who we are and aspire to be?

We can do this as a personal practice: cultivating a sense of our own basic goodness, the goodness of others, and of human society. Being as present as we can to our bodies, our emotions, our interactions, the phenomenal world. Passionately connecting with our everyday lives: eating, dressing, gardening, cooking, washing dishes, walking, working. Recognizing our tendencies to dissociate and to dull out, and shifting these.

We can do this in our social and political lives too: weaving relationships and projects that reflect real human interconnection and mutual concern, that wear away our habits of fear and aggression, that draw upon our deepest intelligence to cease harming and support healing.

Will these shifts create the conditions necessary for human survival and the survival of other species? My questions back: how would we know, and why does it matter? At worst, the relationships and structures and personal capacities that we build will increase our courage and resilience as the world slides toward catastrophe. At worst, we will tap into some real human dignity and joy in the time we have left.

–David Kahane,
professor of political science at University of Alberta,
director of Alberta Climate Dialogue

DEBRA PRINZING

It feels daunting to think one person can change things in this world. That is when I turn from the macro to the micro and focus on individual action. A single gesture takes on meaning far greater than me, my family, my block, my neighbourhood, my city. When that gesture is frequently repeated, its impact is exponential.

I have always turned to flowers, those growing in my garden and in the fields of my flower farmer friends.

The symbolic gesture of giving flowers has been practised for generations. Flowers appear in history, in literature, in every culture and in every land. Gathering flowers as a show of affection or a celebratory display is no small thing. It is a timeless, universal practice.

Flowers connect humans with Nature and heighten our awareness of the seasons. They root us to our place on the planet. Our senses see, smell, touch (and even hear and taste) botanical beauty. This is a truth understood by all humans.

I do believe that flowers parallel food. We don't often eat petals and buds, but they feed us nonetheless. The spiritual sustenance of flowers has caused me to think more intentionally about how I consume them. I have been inspired to start the Slow Flowers movement, a conscious practice of sourcing flowers grown close to me rather than ones shipped to me from afar. When I choose local flowers, I am preserving farmland, ensuring economic development in rural areas and keeping farm jobs viable.

As an advocate for those who grow flowers enjoyed by so many, I believe it's important to remember the human toil required to plant, cultivate and harvest those blooms. I find hope in honouring the flower farmer, hearing his or her story and acknowledging the farmer's role in bringing beauty into our lives. By making a simple connection between flower and farmer we humanize an entire industry, one that has previously been so disconnected from us. It is perhaps more *indirectly* rather than directly world changing, and yet, it is the act I know makes a difference far beyond the vase on my dining table.

–Debra Prinzing,
author, speaker, designer,
founder of Slowflowers.com

ADAM RAVETCH

I know there is much concern about the environment and our natural world. I, myself, have seen much change over the last two decades in the Arctic. But even as the planet shifts and changes, I can't help to stop, if only for a moment, to admire what we have.

I feel fortunate to be part of an amazing generation of wildlife documentarians that have made an incredible contribution to how the world views Nature.

And in the last 50 years, a select group of cinematographers working in some of the world's most inhospitable places on our planet are responsible for a phenomenal natural history archive of how we see and understand our planet today.

So what is its value as we move forward? What purpose does it serve? How does this remarkable effort help us, if at all, as we head into a future of uncertainty?

As our population grows and expands, the amount of natural lands will most likely reduce, and the consumption of our natural resources will increase, which will put more pressure on all living things. As a society, we will be faced with huge decisions just to ensure our own survival on this planet. And for wildlife, future generations will have to decide which animals to protect and which to let go.

But for these future leaders, they are lucky to not be alone. At their fingertips will be a rich and detailed natural history archive; a chamber of wise consults to support them – voices of the passionate caretakers of wildlife, whose determination and single-minded focus produced imagery that gave us all a better understanding and knowledge of the amazing wild life of our planet. It is truly inspirational, and will hopefully inform our future citizens to allow them to realize that what is really unique and important about this planet is LIFE itself!

Today, there are more cameras and cinematographers in the wild then ever before, and I for one am encouraged about the future, knowing that the world is watching!

– Adam Ravetch,
wildlife cinematographer and filmmaker,
National Geographic's *Arctic Tale*, Disneynature's *Earth*, IMAX's *To the Arctic*
and Arctic Bear Productions' *Ice Bear 3D*

ANNETTE SALIKEN

To survive on this planet, I believe humanity needs a framework for decision-making that guides us toward innovation and prosperity, without burdening future generations and threatening our existence. I envision an "endurance framework" comprised of thoughtful questions carefully designed to lead us to better choices. These self-queries would prioritize our economic, environmental and social needs to help us make decisions that reflect what is most important to us as a society.

This endurance framework would apply to everyday choices in households, companies and governments. For example, at home we might ask, will my decision have a positive or negative impact on the financial, environmental and social well-being of my family? How will it affect these same needs of my children and grand children? What will be the affect on my neighbours? For businesses, since they typically have a mandate to maximize shareholder wealth, we as shareholders should demand them to use an endurance framework with questions forming a more balanced mandate, such as: how will this decision help our firm meet its greenhouse gas emission reduction targets? How will it affect the social well-being of our employees, their families and the community? For governments, the endurance framework could be used in the development of laws requiring them to address each of the questions as part of their legislative process: how will this resolution impact the economic, ecological and social well-being of our citizens? Will it compromise these same needs of future generations? What effect will it have on our global community, including other countries, their people, and other species?

If society can make the paradigm shift from traditional money-first thinking to an endurance framework for decision-making, then I believe we can create the conditions necessary to survive on this planet. This does not mean we should stop seeking economic growth or sacrifice our creature comforts; rather, it means we need to refocus on a more balanced, sustainable decision-making process. I believe we can work together successfully in this way to ensure the endurance and well-being of humanity on this planet for this generation and those to come.

– Annette Saliken,
author of *Cocktail Party Guide to Global Warming* and
Cocktail Party Guide to Green Energy

ROBERT SANDFORD

Beyond population growth and its unanticipated effects, the greatest threat humanity presently faces is a changing planetary climate. With warming mean global temperatures, our planet's atmosphere holds more water vapour and becomes more turbulent. Extreme weather events are becoming more common everywhere. Droughts are becoming longer, deeper and more frequent, and intense rainfalls are causing extraordinary damage and great human suffering around the world.

People everywhere want to know whether we can turn these problems around while they are still more or less linear and incremental, before the world begins to change all at once. Others worry about hope for their children. They want to know if there is hope for the unborn, which is to say intergenerational hope.

Hopelessness emerges directly from helplessness. Much current hopelessness comes from the recognition that our political systems are not designed and structured in such a way that would easily allow them to be capable of addressing issues of this magnitude. The scales are all wrong. While political systems are designed to function within limited, often competing, jurisdictions over timeframes of four or five years, the problems we have created for ourselves span generations and encompass not just nations but the entire globe. Many don't believe it is possible to rescue our political systems from the influence of vested economic and ideological interests and the self-referential focus of party politics in time to prevent collapse of important elements of the Earth system.

So where do we go now? Firstly, it is important to realize that a storm is coming. This is not the time to throw up our hands in helpless despair. The sky is not falling and the world is not coming to an end. But the problems we face are real and substantial, so we need to act decisively. If we are to adapt, we cannot permit ourselves to be made to feel helpless. If there was ever a time in history that demanded personal courage, inspired citizenship and thoughtful and persistent leadership action, it is now.

– Robert Sandford,
EPCOR Chair of the Canadian Partnership Initiative
in support of the United Nations "Water for Life" Decade

GARY SNYDER

I am tired of seeing optimistic hopeful and largely predictable ideas being put forth by very nice people over and over again when no one is asking the hard question of what might work. We need a hands-on, gritty, on-the-ground, post-liberal, post-humanist, post-utopian push into that territory.

—Gary Snyder,
poet, essayist, lecturer, environmental activist

HEATHER EATON

Can we get past this crisis? Yes we can. Perhaps we will. The crucial changes require new visions, actions, politics, economics, ethics and so much more. How to do this? There are many ways. This path I walk has three aspects:

1. A substantial knowledge of the dynamics and processes of the universe and of Earth. This changes everything.

2. We, as humans, navigate life within stories, worldviews, or social visions.

3. We need a new vision that empowers and inspires responses to complex global, social and ecological issues.

When we become aware of the wild, ingenious, creative and evolutionary processes of this gorgeous and extraordinary Earth, we experience wonder, awe and even reverence. We see the depth of continuity between the Earth processes and ourselves. Earth is our home, and our source. We are a process of the Earth, a self-conscious element of the Earth's crust. We live on a thin layer of culture over a vast expanse of nature.

Our stories and visions about what is real, important and vital are too narrow, inadequate and incomplete. So is our response to the current crisis. The relationship between vision and action is crucial to understand. If we contemplate the resourcefulness of the Earth, and that we emerged from and are animated by these great processes, we are inspired and energized. Such awareness leads to a profound spiritual and ethical awakening, and insightful political actions.

We need a spiritual vision that teaches us how to be present to the Earth, on Earth's terms. Spiritualities are teachers of consciousness, and are as intimate and as vital as breath. They arouse desires, a zest for life and the ability to feel awe and wonder. Spiritualities encourage inner depth, strengthen courage and inspire reverence in the face of the immensity and elegance of existence. Developing a spiritual consciousness is often described as moving from death to life, from illusion to enlightenment, from confinement to liberation.

We need vision to see our way forward, and for this we need to awaken to Earth.

– Dr. Heather Eaton,
professor at St. Paul University (Ottawa, Canada),
co-founder of Canadian Forum on Religion and Ecology

MATTHEW R. FOSTER

The people and the planet have many dire problems. We must accept that there is only one key with which to effectively tackle these problems. We have given the scientists, corporations, politicians and the UN the opportunity to resolve the global social–ecological crisis; now it is the people's turn to step directly into the process in a more effective way.

From the Rio Earth Summit of 1992 until now, we've seen little meaningful progress. We must ultimately react more quickly and resolutely.

We know the issues; we have unlimited knowledge accumulated in several million NGO databases; we have the means and know-how to communicate globally; we know the power of social media.

We are fragmented and all trying to be heard in our various political systems, which unfortunately are highly influenced by powerful international market forces and unreceptive to our concerns. It is indeed a bad situation in which the whole world shares, but it is not hopeless. Collectively we can propose and significantly influence meaningful changes if we can simply get organized into a cohesive, worldwide movement. Here's how we could begin:

❖ Develop a social media site dedicated solely to social–environmental issues.

❖ Incorporate multi-language capabilities to communicate with the world.

❖ Categorize all social–ecological issues into manageable groups (to a maximum of 26).

❖ Prioritize the issues in each category through debate and consensus and put them into a 20- to 25-year plan.

❖ Use the new site, and/or allied sites, to put the issues to the world's people for approval in a logical format with a consistent approach (i.e., one issue in each category every two weeks enables the addressing of 26 separate issues per year).

❖ Forward the duly considered petition, with the names of the signatories, concurrently to the legislatures of all nations, as this is a crucial worldwide emergency that affects everything.

❖ Require every category unreservedly to have equal weight and equal opportunity to put its particular issues to the public for debate and consideration each year in its turn.

❖ Accept that time is our unforgiving enemy.

–Matthew R. Foster,
retired engineer, online environmental campaigner
stopstopstop.org

PEMA CHÖDRÖN

We have the capacity to wake up and live consciously, but, you may have noticed, we also have a strong inclination to stay asleep. It's as if we are always at a crossroad, continuously choosing which way to go. Moment by moment we can choose to go toward further clarity and happiness or toward confusion and pain.

Taking this leap involves making a commitment to ourselves and to the Earth itself – making a commitment to let go of old grudges; to not avoid people and situations and emotions that make us feel uneasy; to not cling to our fears, our closed-mindedness, our hardheartedness, our hesitation. Now is the time to develop trust in our basic goodness and the basic goodness of our sisters and brothers on this Earth, a time to develop confidence in our ability to drop our old ways of staying stuck and to choose wisely.

Our personal attempts to live humanely in this world are never wasted. Choosing to cultivate love rather than anger just might be what it takes to save this planet from extinction.[12]

–Pema Chödrön,
Tibetan Buddhist teacher and author

SILVER DONALD CAMERON

I'm breathing hard in the thin air. Gazing at Taktshang Goemba, "The Tiger's Nest."

A magnificent Buddhist monastery. Gold, white, burgundy. Hanging on a cliff-face in Bhutan. Across a deep gorge from me.

I'm 72 years old. Yesterday: New Delhi, elevation 233 m. Today: 3120 m. I've climbed 700 m from the Paro Valley floor, far below. Grinning Bhutanese kids scamper past in flip-flops. I climb ten steps. Stop. Breathe.

Buddhists think about breathing. Buddhists believe in the unity of the world.

I believe it too. Breathing unites us.

Air is 1 per cent argon. David Suzuki quotes the astronomer Harlow Shapley, who calculates that a single breath contains 30,000,000,000,000,000,000 argon atoms. Argon is inert. It isn't absorbed; it doesn't change. I breathe it out; you breathe it in.

Breathing connects us to all life on Earth, through all of time. I breathe what the dinosaurs breathed, what my seventh-generation descendants will breathe. Each breath of mine includes 400,000 argon atoms that Gandhi breathed. In the Himalayas, half of my oxygen comes from plankton in the sea.

And breath is only one bridge between organisms. Through our digestion, our skin, our voices, our thoughts, the cycle of birth and death, we continuously collaborate with the world around us. As Alan Watts wrote, "We do not 'come into' this world. We come out of it, as leaves from a tree." Or a breath from a body.

We *are* the world around us.

This is the most important fact of all. Contemporary science knows it. All great wisdom traditions know it. Industrial society blinds us to it. We must strive to see, and to know who we really are. If we act with humility and reverence, the world may yet find us worth keeping.

– Silver Donald Cameron,
author; current host and executive producer of TheGreenInterview.com

LISA BENDALL

People are often disheartened by the glut of bad news in the world. Every time you turn on the TV, they complain, miserable things are reported.

My comeback: it wouldn't be news unless it was extraordinary. What rarely makes headlines is the everyday goodness that happens so frequently we can almost forget how special it is: the snow shovelled for a neighbour, for example, or the donated groceries or the compliment that was made on an outfit or the seat that was offered or the door that was held.

Acts of generosity are rampant, pervasive in our world. That's because the human species evolved to be kind. It's simple logistics: in a society of compassion, we are more likely to survive and reproduce, passing along these genes for niceness. In fact, there's increasing and exciting scientific evidence for our biological drive to connect with and help others.

Will we one day ruin ourselves and each other? See, that would go against our nature. Our genetics, I'd like to think, will save us well before the end.

I remain optimistic.

–Lisa Bendall,
freelance writer, blogger,
www.50gooddeeds.com

STEPHEN HAWKING

As we stand at the brink of a second nuclear age and a period of unprecedented climate change, scientists have a special responsibility, once again, to inform the public and to advise leaders about the perils that humanity faces. As scientists, we understand the dangers of nuclear weapons and their devastating effects, and we are learning how human activities and technologies are affecting climate systems in ways that may forever change life on Earth. As citizens of the world, we have a duty to share that knowledge, and to alert the public to the unnecessary risks that we live with every day. We foresee great peril if governments and societies do not take action now to render nuclear weapons obsolete and to prevent further climate change.

...

We are entering an increasingly dangerous period of our history. Our population and our use of the finite resources of planet Earth are growing exponentially, along with our technical ability to change the environment for good or ill. But our genetic code still carries the selfish and aggressive instincts that were of survival advantage in the past. It will be difficult enough to avoid disaster in the next hundred years, let alone the next thousand or million. Our only chance of long-term survival is not to remain lurking on planet Earth, but to spread out into space.

There are so many questions still to answer.[13]

–Stephen Hawking,
emeritus Lucasian Professor of Mathematics at the University of Cambridge,
author of *A Brief History of Time*

ANNA WARWICK SEARS

All our names are writ in water. From floods to droughts, from canal building to wetland draining, to the simple act of fetching with gourd or bucket, water has marked the rise and fall of people and civilizations. Is the water fresh or salty? Clean, or polluted with chemicals and disease? There is nothing more essential to life. Water forms the blood in our veins and – through plants – gives us food to eat and air to breathe. Water binds us together, as humans and with all other species, as shared inhabitants of our watery planet. This bond is the link to our future.

In the developed world, we take water for granted. I can walk to the sink and fill my cup, hot or cold, on demand. The asphalt shingles on my roof keep out rain and snow. But the water gods of mythology were capricious. Climate change is reminding us that water has vast power – as tides flow into city streets, and deep droughts dry up crops. Access to water has also been used as a weapon of control, by colonial powers and warlords. Water can be merciless as well as kind.

Yet, in water also lies our hope. Water is so powerful, it can even transcend politics. And in a world that has never had so much knowledge and communication, it brings people to the table – politicians and diplomats, farmers, fishermen and school teachers. The wave of changes we must make – to our laws, cities and irrigation systems – to accommodate new weather patterns and a swell of population, are changes that relate to water and aquatic systems. We can't ignore our collective dependence or influence on it. We fail or thrive based on our relationship to water.

– Anna Warwick Sears,
writer, speaker, Executive Director of the Okanagan Basin Water Board

ALEX SHOUMATOFF

The latest studies are not encouraging: we are too selfish to make the sacrifices necessary to turn around global warming. Species and languages and the last tribal subsistence cultures are disappearing at ever-accelerating rates, and their ecosystems as well. Extreme weather events are more common and intense. More and more people are living in cities and having little or no contact with the natural world, spending their lives indoors staring at screens, prisoners of gizmos. The modern world, the whole world, it seems, is disintegrating economically, ecologically and ethically. There are way too many of us. We have been too fruitful and multiplied too much and consumed too many of the fowls of the air and the fishes in the sea and there is no health in us, or in the Earth which we are laying waste to.

Our only hope – and there is always hope, even in the face of this, the greatest challenge we've ever faced to our continued collective viability – is to devise a completely new system of governance, a new way of doing business on and with the planet, based not on getting as much as you can for yourself but on the premise that every living thing has the right to be here and a role to play. The remaining animistic societies, with their deep understanding of the kinship of all life, have much to teach us: to widen our circle of caring to embrace the cosmos, and all our brothers and sisters, human and non. We are the Walrus. Every living thing is a "person." So does Buddhism. The planet needs more female nurturing energy to heal from and counteract all the run-amok male resource-gathering energy. If millions of us come together to forge this new empathetic civilization – there are thousands of ways to help the cause – maybe we can get out of this. It will be very interesting to see if we can make this adaptation, if the forces of good can prevail. They will have the instinct to survive on their side, and nothing is more powerful. Except the course of nature.

– Alex Shoumatoff,
contributing editor to *Vanity Fair*,
editor of DispatchesFromtheVanishingWorld.com

NOVEMBER

ANGELA SUN

I am not a scientist or writer, nor am I anything special. I am just a sum of my experiences and I have been very lucky to be able to have had some extraordinary ones. One of the biggest life lessons I have learned was in creating my documentary *Plastic Paradise: The Great Pacific Garbage Patch*. It's been an eight-year journey now to tell, through the lens of an independent voice, the tale of plastic pollution in our oceans and how it has and will continue to affect our lives. I tend to get asked why I keep continuing on this journey through all the hardships and strife of pre/post production, to maxing out credit cards/financial worries, to sleepless nights organizing outreach and screenings and responding to emails, etc. I've seen many of my friends and colleagues and even interviewees in the film get married and start families while this project has been all-encompassing of my personal life, at times leaving me feeling utterly alone and lost.

But my overall hope comes from those special moments during post-screening panel discussions, Q&As and conferences where kids ask questions and demand answers in such an inquisitive and curious way, and with such an innocent twinkle in their eyes, that they give me great encouragement for a brighter future. Because it is our duty to protect that future of theirs. I have encountered so many passionate, excited, invigorated audiences who have restored my faith in humanity because they demand transparency and change. Ordinary citizens doing extraordinary things coming together for a common shared purpose to discuss, learn, innovate and implement ideas and solutions.

It will take legislation in a global context, producer responsibility (companies that create plastics), nurturing the scientific community toward eco-friendly innovations, and consumer responsibility for us to progress. On the smallest scale, could you imagine if each one of us refused disposable plastics and reused and consumed less?

It would be glorious.

– Angela Sun,
documentary filmmaker, television journalist, sportscaster,
member of the Ocean Defender Advisory Board
www.plasticparadisemovie.com

JAMES D'SILVA

On my Yoga journey I have found myself constantly drawn to the teachings of compassion, charity and service to others, embodied in Mahatma Gandhi – my greatest hero.

Time after time I look to Bapuji, who inspired people to non-violent resistance. This slight man was above all a humanitarian who understood that with freedom comes responsibility – something we seem to have forgotten today.

In our search for individual identity we find ourselves choosing uncompromising acquisition, equating wealth with happiness.

The time has now come to ask ourselves whether this is the right choice. In the very first teaching on Yoga it is said,

There are two paths....
One leads outward and the other inward.
You can walk the way outward that leads
to pleasure
Or the way inward that leads to grace ...
Both of these paths lie before each person
eternally.
It is the way of things.
— KATHA UPANISHAD

Responsible change begins with each of us. Every individual needs to find time for introspection before we can make choices that will change us and everything around us. Unless we are ready to look to ourselves for change, we cannot expect change in others. Spending time in meditation, developing an asana practice and being of service allows us to see the universe as a whole and to develop our significant part in it. These practices do not take a lot of time out of our daily lives – and they bring only joy.

It is time to make change happen – change that like Gandhiji's will echo through humanity and time. Like him we have to start living the change. Each of us, in our own small way, walking our own path, will make the difference.

May yours be an inspirational journey. May you find the joy of meditation – the world is yours to change.

Namaskaram

– James D'Silva,
yoga instructor, DVD fitness instructor, Garuda Pilates Studio and Clinic
www.thegaruda.net

GREGOR BARNUM

Who would we (humanity) be if contradiction was seen as art and the beauty of our ontological quest? There is beauty in so many differing cognitions, feelings, actions.

Of course, if Love is Love, wherever would Love not be?

–Gregor Barnum (1952–2012),
first director of corporate consciousness at Seventh Generation Inc.

SALLY ARMSTRONG

The Earth is shifting. Women's issues are in a hot light that is illuminating changes to the economy, conflict, culture and religion. The evidence is all over the place – from zones of conflict to the United Nations, from banking institutions to political offices and even the water cooler.

The news is this: women are the way forward. From Kabul and Cairo to Cape Town and New York, women are issuing a clarion call for change. And this time the power brokers are listening. Economist Jeffrey Sachs, of Millennium Development Goals fame, claims the status of women is directly related to the economy: where one is flourishing, so is the other; where one's in the ditch, so is the other.

The coming changes are based on the notion that financially, the world can no longer afford to keep half of its population oppressed.

Supporters are jumping onto this bandwagon like born-again believers in the power of women.

The thugs in the lives of these women who got away with denying the girls an education, refusing to let the women go to work; the rapists and warlords who saw them as pawns or worse, something to barter, are on notice now. The last frontier for women is having control over their own bodies. They're are on the doorstep of change, a change that will alter the world's economies, health status and level of conflict. The state of the world's women will never be the same.

– Sally Armstrong,
journalist and human rights activist

RICARDO ROZZI AND FRANCISCA MASSARDO

At the southern end of the Americas, a group of artists, philosophers, scientists, members of the Yahgan indigenous community, teachers, students, naval officers and government authorities created the Omora Ethnobotanical Park, and developed a methodological approach – Field Environmental Philosophy (FEP) – to integrate ecological sciences and ethics.

One of FEP's applications is "Ecotourism with a Hand-Lens," which has invited researchers, decision-makers and the general public to appreciate the aesthetic, economic, ecological and ethical values of the Miniature Forests of Cape Horn, a metaphoric expression to highlight the biodiversity hotspot of lichens, mosses and other bryophytes found in southwestern South America.

For global society, "Ecotourism with a Hand-Lens" not only amplifies the view of mosses and other small organisms, but it also offers a lens that broadens our mental, perceptual and affective images about Nature and our relationships with Nature. Science teaches us that mosses, humans and all living beings share the common vital pulse of cellular respiration, growth and reproduction. If the southern "biocultural ethical hand-lens" could help global society to listen to the breathing of the mosses, to the calls of the birds, to the waves of the oceans, and to the many human languages that perceive the mosses, the birds, the oceans and other beings understood and respected as co-inhabitants – as sisters and brothers, rather than as mere natural resources; if global society could recover the capacity to listen to the multiple human and non-human voices of the community of co-inhabitants with whom we share our daily lives, at local or distant habitats, then hope would be present with us in a global chorus. Individual self-absorption will be understood as an idiocy that needs to be corrected.

A biocultural ethic will promote an integral life and a harmonic co-inhabitation that requires listening, respecting and understanding the beauty, the truth and the value of each of the human and the other-than-human voices of the life chorus.

Photo by Adam M. Wilson

— Ricardo Rozzi, PhD,
philosopher, ecologist, professor,
director of the Sub-Antarctic Biocultural Conservation Program in the Institute of Ecology and Biodiversity
at University of Magallanes (Chile) and University of North Texas (USA)

— Francisca Massardo, PhD,
plant physiologist, conservation biologist, professor,
director of the Institute of Ecology and Biodiversity at University of Magallanes,
director of Omora Ethnobotanical Park (Chile)

ZACK METCALFE

I have to believe we will succeed in saving ourselves. As a young man in a struggling world, I have everything to lose by succumbing to apathy or despair. I have yet to find my place in life, to fall in love, to become a father or to change my own corner of the world for the better. As my grandfather likes to say: "Whether you think you can, or you think you can't, you're probably right."

I believe the solutions to our problems are subtle. It isn't necessarily about driving electric cars and shutting down coal plants. These are only signs of the cure, not the cure itself.

First, we need to put a greater emphasis on scientific literacy in the public. People need a healthy understanding of how the world works, through science. This makes them resistant to the pseudo-science, anti-science, junk science (take your pick) that plagues the world today, making people question whether or not climate change even exists! When we see through the clouds of nonsense to the real, frightening and approaching truth, it will be a resounding call to arms.

Second, we need to expand our borders of empathy, not only to one another but to the natural world and the animals we share it with. We need to acknowledge their right to land, their right to water, their right to exist and their right to prosper.

With these broad changes in place, we will stop robbing the oceans of fish faster than they can repopulate. We will fall short of deforestation, for fear of ruining the land for ourselves and our animal cousins. Profit margins from multinationals will mean nothing when compared to the free services offered by the natural world, and to the affection we rightfully have for it. There are a thousand solutions to every problem you could pose, environmental and social. We need the knowledge to see those solutions, make sound decisions on a global scale and have a moral compass to guide our steps.

Can we do it? Yes.

Do I have hope? I have no other choice.

– Zack Metcalfe,
author, journalist

JULIA BUTTERFLY HILL

Everywhere we look today, our world and our planet are in deep and profound crisis. Our human family, with such wealth of opportunity and resources, seems determined to make the worst possible choices for our collective well-being. Even the most "conscious" among us are making choices every day that cause harm to the planet and all its beings and life support systems.

When I look at the problems we face, I recognize that every single issue is merely a symptom. ALL issues are symptoms of the Disease of Disconnect. When we are disconnected from our intricate interdependency with the Earth, we make choices that destroy it without realizing how we destroy ourselves and future generations in the process. When we are disconnected from people and animals, we make choices that cause harm and suffering without even realizing it or thinking about it.

I was born a highly sensitive person. I feel pain and suffering of others, of everything, on a very, very deep level. To be "awake" in the world today is to be open to pain and grief. To see what is possible for our species – without adding one more piece of technology – just with what we already have available to us, and the reality of the gap between what is possible and how we behave, breaks my heart, overwhelms me and makes me process a lot of grief and then rage.

I tell people all the time, "I am probably the world's biggest cynic. I just don't happen to let that stop me." The reality is that INACTION is as much a part of shaping and co-creating our world as the actions of others! We don't have a crystal ball to tell us if we have what it takes to turn our *Titanic* away from the iceberg. And although much of what I see in the world today makes me feel like most of us are running around rearranging the deck chairs and arguing about the best spot for the view, what I do know is that the only thing I can control in this wild uncertainty of life is how I choose to show up for it. So, I do my best to not let my cynicism stop me from showing up each day with a heart committed to learning, growing, caring and serving with all that I can.

"Hope" and "hopelessness" or "cynicism" are each made up. We make them up. They are not true or fact. They are thoughts and feelings and we are 100 per cent responsible for them. No matter if you are someone who has hope or does not have hope, what I know makes a difference right here, right now is how boldly, courageously and fiercely we are committed to bringing the consciousness of love to our own choices and to the world around us. If we somehow make it around the iceberg, it will be because enough people answered the call to put love into action. If we do not make it around the iceberg, at least our lives would have been used to bring more loving awareness into the world. And for me that is something worth living for.

– Julia Butterfly Hill,
artist, activist, author

DAVID ANDERSON

Research in recent years has provided marginal improvement in our knowledge of climate change, but no change to the policy imperative. The need to move to reduce greenhouse gas emissions remains as the overarching challenge for humankind.

It is discouraging that in the 21 years since the 1992 Rio Conference, no successful international framework has been established to guide the globe to a more sustainable future. It is equally discouraging that so few serious national efforts to curb greenhouse gas emissions have been undertaken.

Is there hope for humankind? Perhaps, but the experience of the 21 years since Rio have shaken previous optimism in this regard.

The annual gatherings of the international community to discuss climate change since Rio, the Conferences of the Parties, is unhappy proof of this.

The record is dismal. Nations seem incapable of putting short-term national considerations aside and determining a collective approach to a collective problem.

The hope for humankind may paradoxically lie in the increasing number and severity of the problems that climate change is generating. As past experience makes clear, a threat in the future may be discounted as hypothetical, but turning a blind eye is more difficult when that threat materializes as a challenge to be confronted, perhaps as an extreme weather event, or, in Northwestern North America, as a weather-induced kill of tens of thousands of square kilometres of pine forests.

Optimism for the future of humanity may be justified. But for that optimism to be rooted in realism, Nature must set the stage. That, unfortunately, is taking time. And time is not on our side.

– The Honourable David Anderson, PC, OC,
Canadian Minister of Environment, 1999–2004

MARILYN WARING

The future requires more than hope.

It requires commitment and resilient defiance in the face of all the patriarchy wishes to hurl at us and destroy for personal wealth and political, religious and military gain.

They want us immobilized with fear and they want us to give up.

So the first act of creative feminist politics is to refuse to comply with their agenda, to defy their corrupt and destructive ideologies and to act to change our world with ideas and creative alternative practices that have at their heart the dignity of all peoples, and the care, nurturing and return to health of our beautiful ecosystem.

–Marilyn Waring,
feminist, author of *Counting for Nothing/If Women Counted*,
professor of public policy at AUT University (Auckland, New Zealand)

COLIN BEAVAN

The Buddha always refused to speak about unanswerable questions like whether there is life after death. He said trying to answer such questions is like a man who has been shot with a poison arrow who, instead of removing the arrow, insists on finding out who shot the arrow, who made it and how long it is. The most profound question in life, the Buddha believed, is not *What happens when I die?* but, just in this moment, *How shall I live? What is my function?*

Asking if there is hope for humanity is a little like asking one of Buddha's unanswerable questions. If you are walking down the sidewalk and a car runs over a child, what do you do? Do you stop and ask, is there hope for this child? The question itself distracts you from doing what is important. You must run and help the child.

Now, at this moment in history, our world is like the child. You must help it! Me too. We all must. Don't get distracted!

This sounds like a terrible responsibility but it is actually a wonderful opportunity. The world has so many problems that it needs all our special skills and talents. It needs scientists and economists and singers and musicians and children and Christians and Hindus and people of every type. What makes this such a wonderful moment is that, with so much trouble, each of us can make a difference.

So don't waste time asking if there is hope for this world. Rather, what can you do right now – as the amazingly special and uniquely talented person you are – to pull out the poison arrow, to save the child on the sidewalk, to help this suffering world? The question is not whether the world has hope. The question is, how do I give this world hope? Or more simply, how can I help?

– Colin Beavan,
speaker, consultant, activist, human,
author/star of the book and film No Impact Man,
director of the No Impact Project
www.colinbeavan.com

BARB STEGEMANN

In 2006, my best friend, Trevor Greene, was wounded while serving as a captain of the Canadian Forces in Afghanistan. While taking part in a village shura (peaceful meeting) on water and healthcare distribution, he was struck in the head by a 16-year-old boy. He had a long recovery, and while I was visiting him in the hospital, Trevor inspired me to write and self-publish *The 7 Virtues of a Philosopher Queen,* a motivational book for women that I had long dreamed of writing. I promised Trevor that I would carry on his mission: I would find a way to support Afghanistan.

When I read an article about a man named Abdullah Arsala, the owner of Gulestan Essential Oils distillery in Jalalabad, Afghanistan, it made me realize that perfume could be the way. Arsala was trying to stop local farmers from growing opium poppies, and was instead encouraging them to produce orange blossom and rose – which are perfect for fragrances. So after some investigation, I was able to get in contact with Abdullah Arsala and promptly purchased $2,000 worth of orange blossom oil on my credit card.

To date, I have invested $120,000 in Afghanistan by purchasing essential oils through the company I have founded, The 7 Virtues Beauty Inc. Our slogan is "Make Perfume, Not War." Make anything instead of war.

We source essential oils for our fragrances from our supplier, who provides seasonal employment for his tribe and community. Every time we purchase legal essential oils from Afghanistan, we are doing our part to provide alternatives to the illegal poppy crop (which also causes instability in our own communities). We have grown, and through the matchmaking of our partners we found our supplier in Haiti, who needs buyers for his products in order to rebuild his community. The Vetiver oil of Haiti is considered the best in the world!

I am not a brave soldier, nor am I a world leader, but I set out to empower women to harness the huge buying power they possess to address issues of war and poverty. Our goal is to encourage other businesses to do trade with business people in Afghanistan, Haiti, the Middle East and other nations experiencing strife, as a part of the solution to building peace.

–Barb Stegemann,
founder of The 7 Virtues Beauty Inc.,
author of *The 7 Virtues of a Philosopher Queen*
www.the7virtues.com

JOEL MAKOWER

Hope for the planet is everywhere, in thousands of ideas, projects, campaigns and organizations. There is no shortage of ideas, passion or commitment. There is no shortage of enabling technologies, inspiring examples or solution sets. We know the questions. We have the answers.

What we lack is a vision – a compelling vision of "what happens if we get things right." It's funny to think about. We have no shortage of visions of what failure looks like: of environmental destruction and the loss of community and security, of food shortages and "resource wars." We've heard plenty about rising oceans and spreading disease vectors, and the loss of topsoil that will make it difficult, if not impossible, to feed nine billion empty bellies.

But we don't have a vision of success – a story being told by leaders in business, politics and popular culture about the happy path: the opportunities to harness sustainability to create healthy individuals, communities and economies. To ensure abundant energy, water and food. And the well-being that comes from a world in balance.

What is that compelling story? Who should be telling it? How can it become the irresistible vision of what's possible?

We need a new story and lots of new storytellers.

– Joel Makower,
chairman and executive editor of GreenBiz Group,
author of *Strategies for the Green Economy*

JULIA MIRANDA LONDOÑO

Colombia is a singular region of planet Earth because of the predominance of contrasts. On the one hand, it holds a huge amount of biodiversity and natural resources, but on the other hand, basic needs for thousands of people are still not covered. As a matter of fact, there is poverty, represented as hunger, and lack of education, health and good housing. States are making big efforts to develop their countries and enhance life quality of their citizens, facing at the same time in some cases political and institutional instability, which makes governability of their territories something difficult to achieve.

Nonetheless, in the middle of this critical reality, states, economic sectors, environmental NGOs but mainly, organized local communities, have been working hard in order to accomplish the conservation of ecosystems which provide invaluable environmental services. This job has been serious, consistent and persistent, and it has had as its ultimate goal the effective conservation of protected areas – as well as sustainable production with environmentally friendly technologies – in those areas where water resources, forests and fauna along with traditional knowledge are of main importance. Furthermore, partnerships between the public sector, communities and the private sector have been fundamental in order to arouse the attention of all society sectors that value natural richness and that are claiming for more environmental sensitivity, which results in clearer laws and stronger public institutions that could enforce policies and rules.

I believe that this model could work if it is strictly implemented. If the so-wanted economic growth is achieved, mixed with well-being for humans, based on the respect and value of natural resources of countries, and if enough areas of well managed ecosystems are left that could keep providing their goods and services, a better and more balanced planet will be possible. A planet with a real future!

– Julia Miranda Londoño,
General Director of Parques Nacionales Naturales de Colombia (Colombian National Parks Authority),
UIC-WCPA Regional Vice-chair for South America

SWAMI AMBIKANANDA SARASWATI

Whenever I think of our present or future, Thomas Merton's warning that we "live in a time when the technological ending of the world will be legal," echoes through my mind. This is our crisis: we have created the means and the institutions to end billions of years of life. We were not here at the beginning of life on this planet, but we threaten to be the cause of its end.

Hope for our future cannot therefore be found in our awesome technology or any of our grand institutions.

Our only hope now lies in the transformation of human consciousness.

This new consciousness refuses the call to be exploiters and competitors. It calls us instead to walk humbly with each other offering sustenance and dignity.

To invite it we must do the work that makes changes in ourselves possible, including standing together peacefully against interests that seek to divide and destroy. In this togetherness we must continually remind each other that we ourselves are the art of life: we are the canvas, the painter and the brush. The future is not independent of us, it is not made by blind forces that we can barely name – it is being created by each of us. If there is to be a painting of the future, it is one we are colouring now.

While finding hope in scientists like Nobel Prize-winning geneticist Paul Nurse, who reminds us that all life is more closely related to us than we ever thought, to inspire my own transformation I turn to the very first teaching of Yoga as a practice, which was given in the Katha Upanishad by the God of Death, Yama:

> *The Self is the ultimate reality ...*
> *Who sees this Self,*
> *Sees it resting in the hearts of all.*

– Swami Ambikananda Saraswati,
founder of the Traditional Yoga Association and
The Mukti Project

ROBERT BRINGHURST

Humans have lived on the Earth for more than 100,000 years. For 99.9 per cent of that time, we as a species did only modest damage to the self-repairing fabric of our planet. We may even have contributed to its beauty nearly as much as we took away. Then we acquired industrial power, with no concomitant increase in wisdom. Then we robbed the bank of fossil fuel and began to burn the house down, dancing to the flames.

Individuals, when they've committed atrocious mistakes, often reflect and change their ways. Societies can change their behaviour too, though less deliberately and consciously than persons. Societies are essentially creatures of habit, feeble-minded and short-sighted. They have appetites and customs, assumptions and beliefs, but they don't see visions or cultivate ideas. Species are more unconscious still. They change through genetic rather than cultural adaptation, turning into different species as they go.

Can we reverse the damage we've done to the global envelope? Very unlikely. Maybe the Earth itself can do so, over a space of a few million years. Will we as a species still be here? Hugely improbable. Will we adapt to the changes facing the Earth in the meantime? Might we, in other words, leave evolutionary descendants? Some species probably will; we are unlikely to be among them. Bacteria, archaea and protozoa, which mutate much faster than we can, will have the advantage. From that foundation, new species as complex as whales, herons and elephants may arise. If we are lucky, then, distant cousins of ours may walk, fly and swim here again, in a world that might be as sweet as the one we destroyed.

– Robert Bringhurst,
poet, philosopher, linguist, translator, typographer,
author of, among many others, *A Story as Sharp as a Knife*, *The Tree of Meaning: Thirteen Talks*,
Everywhere Being Is Dancing, *The Elements of Typographic Style*,
The Surface of Meaning: Books and Book Design in Canada

NANCY ELLEN ABRAMS

If you've ever wondered why humans work pretty well as individuals but humanity seems so reliably dysfunctional, you may not have considered this possibility: that the universe we assume we're living in is not the one we're actually in. For centuries people have extrapolated from the way things work in the solar system to how they must work in the universe. But on very large scales, cosmologists have discovered, the rules change. Most of the universe is two mysterious, invisible things: "dark matter" and "dark energy," which don't behave like anything we've experienced on Earth.

Why does this matter? "The universe" is not just the big stuff – it includes *all* size scales, including Earth, its oceans, animals, bacteria, atoms and elementary particles. The universe integrates it all, so how the universe operates is relevant to our world. Cosmological concepts may help us re-envision humanly large scale and long-term problems like climate change.

We were taught that Earth is an average planet of an average star in possibly endless space, but Earth is actually an extraordinary planet in a wildly dynamic universe. Our idiosyncratic solar system travels up and down like a carousel horse, orbiting the center of our galaxy, the Milky Way. The galaxy rotates like a pinwheel inside a vast halo of whizzing dark matter, while all the distant galaxies are being carried away ever faster by dark energy. The "Double Dark" theory offers revolutionary ideas that as metaphors can help us reframe politics, economics and even what is sacred.

Even more marvellously, we now have the first origin story ever told that's supported by scientific evidence, and it's equally true for everyone on Earth. Throughout history a shared origin story was what united a culture. If our poets, artists and scholars, as well as scientists, help present this new origin story in ways everyone, including children, can appreciate, we could have not only smarter thinking but a bond that connects humanity worldwide. Our descendants could live comfortably on this jewel of a planet for *millions more generations*. For more information, see new-universe.org.

– Nancy Ellen Abrams,
philosopher of science, lawyer specializing in scientific controversies,
co-author with Joel R. Primack of *The View from the Center of the Universe* and
The New Universe and the Human Future
viewfromthecenter.com, new-universe.org

CARMEN MILLS

I have had it with people shit-talking my species.

Listen up: humans are no more greedy or evil than any other critter. Just like dogs or whales or paramecia or tomato plants, we just want to be happy. We are motivated by whatever will keep us warm, well-fed and laid. Particularly laid, because above all, we want to perpetuate our precious DNA. To this end, like all animals, we will tend to feed and breed until our population reaches carrying capacity. At which point, we execute a dramatic mass die-off, and the cycle begins again.

We're not more worthy of survival than any other beast, but neither are we execrable slime who "deserve" to be wiped from the planet. In spite of our careless behaviour, we mean well, and even when we act just as crudely as our fellow carbon-based life forms, heaping insults on poor *Homo sapiens* will not help to address the perilous global situation.

We hairless primates are unique among animals in this: we have the capacity to act for the greater good, even if such actions might be painful or inconvenient. We have somehow managed to develop these huge frontal lobes, and in the face of the next great wave of extinction, we might just be able to use them to override self-destructive animal behaviour. We are starting to reject the ancient biological imperative to care only about our own blood and tribe. That's a new thing. We are shutting down nuclear plants, feeding hungry strangers and deciding to take a pass on procreation. You won't see dogs or amoebas doing that.

We are very clever critters. I figure, if we were smart enough to get ourselves into this mess, then we might be smart enough to get us out of it. What are the odds? Who knows? The odds of a fish crawling out of the ocean were pretty slim too. But there is no time to be wasted in working out the numbers – we either do something, or we do nothing. The Doing Something camp is where the most fun people seem to be hanging out. So I say, let's shake off the ashes of species self-loathing and get our collective ass in gear. It is time to stand by our species.

– Carmen Mills,
graphic designer/event manager for Emerald City Communications,
bikeshevik, community organizer, writer,
co-facilitator of Young Urban Zen in Vancouver (Canada),
freelance mischief-maker
www.BicycleBuddha.org

RONALD WRIGHT

Societies behave much like individuals. They resist reform with denial and delusion, often thinking the answer to their problems is more of the same only better. The most widespread delusion of our times is that "progress," in the sense of technological inventiveness and growth, will save us – when unbridled progress is exactly what has brought us to the fix we're in now.

History and archaeology show us that societies seldom change their self-destructive ways until circumstances force them to do so. By then it is often too late. Yet there have been times and places where humans managed to think ahead for their long-term good. Several small-scale societies – among them the Tahitians, the Inuit and the hunter-gatherers of the Kalahari – learned to keep their numbers and demands within their ecological means.

A few much larger societies, notably the ancient Egyptians and Peruvians, also learned to respect natural limits, by ceasing to build on farmland. In modern times the European Union, for all its flaws, is probably the boldest effort to learn from past mistakes. It took two World Wars – one should have been enough – but in the end true progress was made by the formation of this unique multinational association of erstwhile foes, which has grown from six countries to nearly thirty. Long may it last.

Our world is overcrowded, inequality is worse than in pre-Revolutionary France, and natural systems are buckling under the weight of our demand. But I have not written off the human ability to change. Giving in to despair is always a self-fulfilling prophecy. Now is our last chance to get the future right.

– Ronald Wright,
novelist, historian, author of *A Scientific Romance* and
A Short History of Progress, on which Martin Scorsese's *Surviving Progress* is based

JAKOB VON UEXKULL

I am convinced that we will be able to overcome the challenges of our time if we address the interlinked crisis with interlinked solutions. The exceptional opportunity which lies in times of crisis is that big changes can be easier than small steps, as only they are seen as adequate and thus able to inspire and mobilize.

There are many historical examples of such changes growing rapidly from small beginnings. We are often told we cannot change our world – or human nature. Yet both are changed all the time. New norms, technologies and lifestyles spread across continents. Public attitudes shift. Culture is not static, but adapts and evolves continually, as does human consciousness.

Across the world we share key values. We want to hand over a healthy planet to our children. We want to be co-creators of our future. We are not powerless victims of unstoppable forces. We can create a different human story of global citizenship, empowering us to deliver sustainable well-being for all without exceeding planetary limits.

We need political frameworks to be changed, as ultimately there is no faster way to make change happen than through binding legislation. With the best laws and right policy incentives we can mobilize human inventiveness and entrepreneurship for human development and a healthy planet. Building public support for coherent policy action – and assisting policy-makers in implementing it – is the indispensable meta-initiative to ensure that our efforts to promote human development, human rights and peace and security are not squandered.

– Jakob von Uexkull,
founder of the Right Livelihood Awards and World Future Council

JENNIFER BAICHWAL

Colorado River Delta, by Ed Burtynsky

I am frequently surprised and humbled by the optimism of those who live closest to the ground in the struggle for social and environmental justice, and by the relative resilience of Nature. When these two forces come together, I am filled with hope.

I just finished a film called *Watermark* about

human interaction with, and impact upon, water around the world. We were in ten different countries and witnessed a myriad of human relationships with that primal natural force, crucial to life. One of the most affected places we visited was the Colorado River Delta. It used to be two million acres of lush wetland habitat, and is now a desert. Las Vegas, Phoenix, Los Angeles, the Imperial Valley, with its agriculture that many of us depend upon – these barren places have been terraformed by, and exist because of, water from the Colorado. So much is taken in the U.S. – 14 dams worth – that the mighty river limps across the border into Mexico and dies. Most of the time, since the 1960s, no river water reaches the ocean.

But in 1977, some (not much) agricultural wastewater from Arizona was accidentally released back into the Delta, creating a desert lake now called La Ciénega de Santa Clara. Almost overnight, the landscape transformed. Plants and birds and fish returned, and this small amount of inadvertent runoff made the area a flourishing estuary habitat again. It has been tended by Juan Butron, his family and the community of Ejido Johnson for the past 35 years, and in 1993 was designated a biosphere reserve. The area has provided an indispensable living model for water activists like the Sonoran Institute in their ongoing daily work with local residents to restore the delta.

Optimism + resilience = hope.

– Jennifer Baichwal,
documentary filmmaker

Ciénega de Santa Clara, by Po Camberos

BRAD RABIEY

I grew up on a third-generation family farm. We always had and still keep an amazing garden. Despite our high latitude in Canada, every summer we enjoy cucumbers, tomatoes, corn, peas, beans, pumpkins, carrots and more. We build the garden soil with planting rotations and my Dad would never even think about spraying the weeds that pop up on it. Yet prior to the farm's transition to me, my parents used fertilizer and pesticides to produce crops like wheat on the bulk of our farmland; grains that ultimately become food for other people. That inconsistency started to bother me many years ago. So, when it came time for the farm to be transitioned to my generation, I dug my heels in to ensure the farm would be certified organic before I took it over; because I only want to grow food I'd actually eat myself or proudly serve to my own family.

That is my story and I tell it everywhere I can, including on this page, because it makes people consider how they can live consistently. It encourages people to examine how their decisions impact the broader world; whether it is where their clothing is made or how they travel to work each day. My story is not a fear-mongering tale, because when we say the sky is falling and it does not do so, in a way that impacts the audience directly; the next day, or even the next year, we become trapped in another parable about a boy crying wolf.

So what should we do to gain trust of the majority and steer society away from the proverbial cliff on issues that are not often instantaneously perceived? We need to teach compassion and empathy. We need to get people to realize that what they do has a ripple effect around the world and generationally, whether through the fabric of society or the warming waters in our oceans. In other words, that we are all eating from the same garden.

—Brad Rabiey,
co-founder of @TheCarbonFarmer,
restoring his family's farm in Canada (and others around the world) with more trees
www.thecarbonfarmer.ca

LOU LEONARD

From Hollywood to Bollywood, there are so many ways to escape; to the past – with kings and thrones – or the future – where we fight or fall in love with our computers. But is there really a more exciting time to live than right now?

As a human family we have never been wealthier, healthier or safer. We have tools our grandmothers could never have imagined. We are a planet of super-heroes, strong and ready.

We face threats, yes, but we see them: our scientists, heroes by any measure, already have discovered the invisible climate pollution seeping into our life support systems. We know that our current path puts at risk our coastal cities, our food production and half the species on planet Earth.

And already we have begun the amazing process of changing our entire way of living, beginning what David Korten calls *The Great Turning*. We are moving away from deadly coal, gas and oil toward clean power generated on our own roofs. We already have invented all of the technologies needed for this transformation.

But we are running out of time. Decisions we make – about energy, forests and agriculture – over the next decade will shape the world's future, forever.

So why haven't more people made this great turning part of their life's work? Two words: Fear and Doubt. Fear says don't even look at this exciting yet scary moment; don't accept that this is the most important time in human history. And a creeping, sinister Doubt whispers that we really can't make a difference.

And this makes me hopeful for our future, because the villains Fear and Doubt are within our power to vanquish. We can find the quiet courage to stay with the truth for just a moment without turning away and then surprisingly discover energy to act. We can realize that the turn toward this safer, more beautiful future already has begun. And we can see the growing chorus standing alongside us.

So don't be silent, talk to your friends, hold your leaders accountable. Start small, but then stretch yourself to do more. You're not alone, but you are oh so important.

– Lou Leonard,
vice-president for climate change, World Wildlife Fund
www.worldwildlife.org

ANNA GUSTAFSON

Is there hope for planet Earth? Yes, and hope provides the energy that fuels action. In our current global situation, each of us contributing locally *in our own way* can reverberate across the world. From my region, the west coast of Canada, I can offer up a prime example of what gives me hope.

Dr. Tom Reimchen, a biologist at the University of Victoria, asked a simple question: "Why are trees closest to streams bigger?" Using his curiosity and determination he discovered a surprising answer to this question. In essence, he and his team found that the wild Pacific salmon, along with its predators, scavengers and insects, are a nitrogen delivery system from the Pacific

Ghost Salmon, Reimchen's Data – At the Crossroads, by Anna Gustafson

Ocean to the Rocky Mountains. Their work, *Salmon/Forest Project*, demonstrates why protecting individual species also helps to protect entire ecosystems.

Tom both gave me hope and inspired me as a visual artist. With his permission, I combined his current scientific research with archival images to create my ongoing project *Ghost Salmon*, which has been seen by many people.

Though it began locally, this research continues to grow in scope. Pacific salmon inhabit and enrich the North Pacific Rim, from Japan, Korea, China, Russia, Alaska, BC, Washington, Oregon and California. There is also the possibility that nitrogen is delivered in a similar way in other ecosystems throughout our planet. For example, hilsa are a fish of the Indian subcontinent that also live in saltwater, returning 1,200 miles inland to spawn and enrich life on land.

Some of our unique human behaviours such as curiosity, passion, determination and ambition have brought us to this critical and dangerous point in history; but with the crucial addition of inspired leadership, knowledge and co-operation, they can bring us to a place of hope which then energizes action. *Ghost Salmon* and *Salmon/Forest Project* are examples of how answering a local question furthers global understanding, which is necessary for a more sustainable world.

It is my sincere hope that you are finding your own ways to contribute locally for planet Earth in the desperate times that we face.

– Anna Gustafson,
visual artist, Salt Spring Island, BC (Canada)
anna-gustafson.com

MATHIS WACKERNAGEL

Humanity's resource hunger and ecosystem exploitation exceed what planet Earth can sustain. Now the greatest challenge is how to live within our ecological means. But it is also our greatest opportunity.

Fortunately, we have the tools at our disposal to measure both our demand on and the availability of Nature. Now the question is, do we have the courage to calibrate our policies to align with the facts? Or will we do as many have done in the past – address the dilemma of limited resources with brutality, while leaving large segments of humanity in the dust?

Learning to live within the means of one Earth will require the best in human spirit and planning. The promise is a far more stable and peaceful global community.

We can succeed and I want to, because if we don't, everyone will lose.

– Mathis Wackernagel, PhD,
president of the Global Footprint Network

JOSIE MARAN

When I think about why we should have hope for the planet (and everyone on it), I think about the miracles that happen every day because people don't lose hope.

Big miracles, like Rosa Parks changing race relations in the U.S. forever by refusing to sit at the back of the bus, or Barack Obama becoming the first black President with his "Hope" campaign – which couldn't have happened if Rosa Parks hadn't done what she did all those years before.

Or smaller miracles, like my grandma having breast cancer and keeping her hope alive so that now, at age 85, she's still playing tennis every day.

Our society and our world is just a conglomeration of individual people, and if each of us keeps that kind of hope in our hearts, I'm sure that, together and separately, we'll do the right thing and save the planet.

– Josie Maran,
chief eco officer for Josie Maran Cosmetics

RICK HANSEN

At the age of 15, when I sustained my spinal cord injury, I learned a very valuable life lesson: with support, courage and sheer determination, anything is possible. Since then, I have lived my life with purpose, holding fast to the belief that we all have the ability to make a difference and leave a positive impression on the world. The challenge, however – for every individual on the planet – is in making that choice to live life with meaning, deciding every single day to do something that will make a difference. This could be something as simple as being kind to others or engaging in community, fundraising for a cause or picking up garbage off the beach. It's the accumulation of those little gestures of respect and humanity towards other people, and our Earth, that I believe will move us forward towards a world that is healthier and more inclusive.

For as long as I can remember, I have had a passion for the outdoors, resulting in personal volunteerism and leadership in environmental conservation. My love of the wilderness has fuelled a deep respect for the environment and the ecosystem that feeds our planet. As I look to the future, I believe the next generation of youth are going to play a vital role in the conservation and sustainability of our Earth. I believe that through education and understanding, we can inspire the values of gratitude and appreciation for the beauty and abundance of our planet, and that the young people of today will become the leaders of tomorrow who promote and encourage their peers to nurture our planet and ensure the survival of all species.

We all have hope – this is what makes us human and gives us the courage to make this world a better place. You can make a difference, simply by starting here and answering the following question: what is the cause that passionately calls for your help? Because when each of us chooses to change one small thing, together we can do anything.

– Rick Hansen, CC, OBC,
Difference Maker, spinal cord injury advocate, Canadian paralympian

HEATHER A.E. PINNOCK

The Caribbean region is comprised of some two dozen territories, most of which are small island developing states that are very vulnerable to the effects of climate change. The tropical nations of the region are inherently climate sensitive, with our lives and livelihoods inextricably connected to our environment. A groundbreaking study published in October 2013 identified the Caribbean region as being on the frontlines to suffer the effects of climate change with worst case scenarios placing cities in the region among the first on the planet to reach the global warming tipping point by 2023. The social, economic and environmental implications are staggering: extreme heat, coastal erosion, vector-borne disease, drought, flood and more intense storms are some of the key concerns. These can and will affect everything from personal comfort, natural habitats and physical infrastructure to the agriculture, marine and tourism industries on which we rely.

The only way to overcome these crises and thrive is a radical change in behaviour – for individuals and communities to live more sustainably, for better national and regional management of natural resources and for a global reduction in greenhouse gas emissions and other unsustainable development practices. Though the Caribbean region accounts for less than 2 per cent of global greenhouse gas emissions, we recognize and appreciate that every bit of responsible behaviour counts as we bear the brunt of some of their effects on the planet's climate.

It is clear that we must do more than hope, we must act ... and now. While we work to adapt, develop social and physical resilience and even find ways to thrive in a deteriorating environment, it is also critical that we raise our voices to join if not lead the chorus to effect global change. We can and will continue to find, develop and implement the sustainable development practices and grow the green economies critical not only to our survival but also for our long-term prosperity.

−Heather A.E. Pinnock,
Caribbean sustainability advocate, green builder, project manager,
director of Hill 60 Bump Ltd.
www.hill60bump.com

CHRISTINA PIRELLO

Can humanity save itself from itself?

For me, the salvation of our planet and modern society begins, and ends, with our food. We can clearly see that our modern food choices have destroyed any delusions that food has no impact on our health and the welfare of our planet. Entire societies are plagued by preventable diseases that are driven by our lifestyles. Our planet groans under the weight of our healthcare costs, our trash, the by-products of the way we produce food ... and the actual weight of humanity itself.

If we look at our collective health and that of our planet, we must despair. But a groundswell of conscious people are seeing the light, making changes and demanding better quality food to feed our families, our children, our future.

Reclaiming our food begins with reclaiming the meal. When we gather around the hearth, the table, we cultivate the skills we need to create a compassionate community ... from communication and sharing to social justice; the tools we need to preserve our very humanity are in the kitchen and are carried to the table.

The ecology of what we eat has an impact on our personal health and the health of our fragile planet. Choosing whole, unprocessed, seasonal foods sustainably produced can change the world. That may sound simplistic, but it's simple truth ... and can feed the world, creating a different humanity than what we see.

Imagine a world of healthy, compassionate humans working together to reverse the damage done by multinational corporations and special interests. Imagine life lived on a planet that is vibrant and healthy. Simply stated, we worry about the environment around us, but consider this. Our internal environment, the state of our internal health reflects the world we have created. If we were to eat foods fit for human consumption and "clean up" our internal environment, we would not tolerate the chaos and pollution around us ... and the world would change ... because we changed it.

As it always has, the future begins in the kitchen, with humans cooking real food and gathering around the table creating real communities.

– Christina Pirello,
Emmy Award-winning host of the U.S. national public television series *Christina Cooks*,
bestselling author, health activist

RICHARD ZURAWSKI

There was a time when I was younger that I could say with confidence that the emergence of rational thought was set to usher in a new era of prosperity and a golden age of reason. It was time when scientists were generally respected, and some were even revered. But in the past two decades, the rise of religions, consumerism, self-interest and media complicity have eroded and marginalized science and its twin pillars of knowledge and rational thought. Everywhere, the attack on science and scientists is returning us to the dark ages, where scientists and science are vilified and persecuted. Is this hyperbole?

In our schools, fundamentalists insist on including "creationism," masked in its new-age nomenclature of "intelligent design," as a viable alternative to the science of evolution. Parents are eschewing inoculations that have saved countless lives over the years and are placing their entire faith in practices such as homeopathy, which is leading to an inevitable resurgence in childhood diseases. Vested interests such as

the tobacco lobby have succeeded, with their vast financial reserves, in flooding the media with pseudo and distorted science, creating a method of doubt in science and scientific enquiry that is creeping throughout our society. Our universities are under financial assault as they are forced to become pawns of industry. And the massive, incalculable assault on the environment though the twin devils of population explosion and consumerism is just beginning to unfold.

In light of these almost overwhelming challenges, it is hard to be anything but a pessimist. Yet it seems that when the light is the dimmest, when the road ahead is darkest and almost totally obscured, humanity rises to reveal its best. Somehow the best, the brightest and the greatest come to the fore and give us a renewal and strength to mitigate the worst. It has happened time and time again, and it is my profound hope and wish that out of the potential disaster, reason and sanity will triumph.

– Richard Zurawski, BSc, MA (Research), PhD candidate, author, lecturer, radio talk show host, meteorologist, documentary filmmaker

LYNN HASSELBERGER

The environmental and social crises are complex and at times our circumstances can feel impossible to turn around. There's discourse about how to resolve our problems and even heated controversy over what crises are real. Pile on our political, economic and religious differences, sprinkled with language barriers, and you've got chaos.

How do we get past this? It will take Herculean strength, but the answer is simple. We need to toss aside our differences and concede that we're all human. Each and every one of us needs clean water, clean air, safe food and shelter; and these basic needs are human rights regardless of race, social status or religious belief. That has to be our foundation for moving forward.

Now we have to take that a step further – while the world is comprised of different countries, one country's actions impacts all others in some way. We need to be accountable to one another because we're all connected and, ultimately, share the same air and water. Nothing should stop the global community from collaborating and agreeing upon incentives for corporations and entire countries that develop technologies and practices that protect our environment (i.e., clean energy, sustainable farming, educational tools for developing countries, water retention and purification). There should also be globally enforceable consequences for corporations and countries that harm the environment in any way. Why can't we integrate this into our international human rights law?

It has to start with individuals. You and me. Thanks to the Internet, we have an instant global community. We can initiate these conversations and influence others one by one to join this redefined humanitarian movement. Our survival and that of all species left on this Earth depends on it.

If we put humanity first, there is hope.

−Lynn Hasselberger,
concerned mom, environmental advocate,
founder of www.myEARTH360.com,
writer at www.lynnhasselberger.com,
contributor to the *Green Divas Radio Show*, Be You Media, *elephant* journal

DECEMBER

YASMIN RASYID

We already have the basic know-how and the technology to address current global environmental and social crises. We have so many amazing technological advancements but we use them more for selfish and self-destructing reasons. What is missing is the political will and the pressure from all parts of civil society to ensure proper governance and enforcement on the ground. Today we seem to be having too many meetings, talking too much, with minimal actions on the ground. This has got to change. We need more people to walk the talk. Technocracy is getting in the way of any efforts to work on building a sustainable planet.

Many of us have hope, but that's not enough. Hope needs to be translated into real, tangible actions on the ground, and many of us are still not changing ourselves for the better – be it in the way we live sustainably or the way we utilize resources. Sitting around and hoping doesn't do justice to the environment; we need to rise to the occasion, even if it's something small like working with your neighbours to solve trash issues, or educating children about sustainable living in schools, or even starting with changing the way you manage your home. I believe if we can all collectively pick one thing we can change for the better today, we can make more visible differences to the planet.

Every day, the human race hopes for something, but hoping does not help solve any problems around us. Doing something will change more parameters.

– Yasmin Rasyid,
founder and president of EcoKnights,
chair of Malaysian Environmental NGOs (MENGO) 2013/2014

STEPHEN GARDINER

Seven billion people stranded on a small planet face a big problem. Nothing stands in the way of their confronting this problem but themselves. Yet the challenge is extreme: the problem is genuinely global, profoundly intergenerational, and current institutions and theories are poorly placed to cope. Worse, the position of the most affluent is ethically compromised: they face strong temptations to continue to take modest benefits now while passing severe and possibly catastrophic costs to the future, and especially to the less advantaged and other species. This global environmental tragedy constitutes a "perfect moral storm." Climate change is a paradigm example.

The perfect moral storm is a severe challenge, and so far we are not doing very well. Yet succumbing to the storm is not inevitable. The dominant institutions of the age – markets and standard election cycles – may be good at highlighting short-term, narrowly economic motivations and bad at capturing concerns for distant people, future generations and Nature. Still, this does not mean that we do not have such concerns, or that they cannot be made operative in policy. In my view, we do and we can. Confronting the storm will require extraordinary courage, imagination, creativity and fortitude. It will take a great generation to try, and an even greater one to succeed. Yet we can be that generation.

We must.

– Stephen M. Gardiner,
Ben Rabinowitz Endowed Professor of the Human Dimensions
of the Environment, University of Washington,
author of *A Perfect Moral Storm*

MAE MOORE

We will not know if we can turn around the destructive path we are on until the time arrives when we have accomplished it.

To get there, we must protect the last remaining wild places on Earth from resource extraction and we must live by a new model that values health and happiness over economic profit. Each and every person in the First World must recognize with gratitude (and not a sense of entitlement) that her/his lifestyle comes at a cost to the environment, to the Third World and to the planet, and must take steps to shift this. We need to move away from being rabid consumers and realize that there is nothing more important than clean water, clean air and fertile soil.

Our population is too large to be supported by our planet. We have disrupted entire ecosystems under the guise of progress. We cannot keep doing this. People are awakening to one climate crisis after another. Our time is running out to effect change.

Do I have hope? I answer that question with no, I do not have hope, as hope is too passive an election. I will, however, live my life with the lightest footprint possible and I will work toward actively redirecting our collision course, through education, through public governmental lobbying against fossil fuel, through growing food organically for my family and community and through protecting our environment for other species at risk – through civil disobedience if called for.

—Mae Moore,
Canadian musician, artist, organic farmer, activist

ALLANA BELTRAN

All crises, personal and global, lead to change. The current crises have arisen in culmination of past attempts to avoid our humanity by escaping into materialism. Hope for our future requires a shift in human consciousness.

Sustainable cultures throughout history have one major characteristic that is largely missing from the current dominant forms of governance: a spirituality that sees the divinity in all things and surrenders to it. Without a sense of spirituality we seek fulfillment and identity in temporal material objects and power. These illusions we have been pursuing are now crumbling at our feet – witnessed through the destruction of society and the environment. Realizing this, I believe many people will reconnect to their spiritual self by praying in surrender to their personal divinity for help. I feel this shift has already started.

In the breakdown and disillusionment of materialism, the active power of love and compassion will be enabled to arise from our innate nature. We will feel reverence for the interconnectedness of all life and subsequently act to protect it. In our stewardship of the Earth, true fulfillment will arise in the hearts of humankind.

I believe it is because of these crises and the consequential changes that our collective consciousness can shift to a higher state of being. I believe we may well be as never before, walking into a time of global oneness in which we will experience everything – rivers, oceans, birds, animals, humans, mountains, forests, all life – as an interconnected part of our own self.

– Allana Beltran,
Australian artivist

MATTHEW WILBURN KING

Although evolution has backed us into a corner when it comes to existential threats such as climate change, it also offers us a way out. Climate change poses real challenges for current and future generations. The failure of traditional human governance institutions to come to grips with climate change – to perceive the threat, formulate a coherent and flexible response and then enact it with vigor and discipline – is all too plain.

Cultural evolution makes it possible to create the necessary changes for survival despite our inherent biological traits that favor short-term interest over our long-term welfare. The survival and evolution of cultures rely on the inheritance of learned behaviors that can be transmitted and that change over time. Evolutionary history has also equipped us for long-term planning and action. We can imagine and predict multiple, complex outcomes and act accordingly in the present to achieve desired outcomes in the future. This human capacity is nearly two million years old.

Although evolutionary theory shows that we care most about our genetic relatives, culturally we have embodied and acted upon concerns that extend beyond family to others and to times beyond our own lifespans. Governments have traditionally performed this role, but they have not been effective. Fortunately, we are now seeing the emergence of a kind of governance that departs from the centralized, top-down structures we have so far relied upon to solve problems. Networked systems of governance are a shift toward a more self-organizing approach that brings together dispersed individuals from the state, civil society and private sectors that have a shared interest. Each acts independently yet remains connected through exchanging information, planning for future events and co-operating as is useful.

Networked governance is the type of social evolutionary development or adaptation that will make it possible for us to counter our inherent biases so that we can begin to reorder our lives in a way that moves us toward a more sustainable future. We can help drive their evolution by exploring ways they might be replicated at varying scales to share lessons learned and encourage adoption of good governance practices. Networked systems of governance are currently the most versatile, agile and adaptive systems available to meet the challenges ahead of us. The task now is to identify and strengthen these new systems as they are emerging.

– Matthew Wilburn King, PhD,
social entrepreneur, consultant, adviser, researcher, philanthropist,
founder and president/chairman of Living GREEN Foundation
www.livinggreenfoundation.org

KRISTIN MCGEE

Of course I think humanity can find a way past the current global environmental and social crises. I believe in our ability to adapt and to create solutions to our problems. I think more and more people are coming together in a communal way through yoga and other forms of movement, creativity and expression, through meditation, arts, music, theatre and healthy food. I believe the more we come together and find communities in our neighbourhoods, cities, states and countries, we can affect change and grow towards a more positive environment and way of living.

We are a global community and the amazing technology that we have today allows us to communicate with everyone all over the world. Through education, communication and social movements, we can create whatever we need to make sure we as a species – as well as all species – can thrive on this planet.

I have always seen the glass as not only half full, but overflowing with potential and infinite opportunities. I don't even think we are in a crisis, just in a place where we need to discover what isn't working for US (all of us, from the birds to the bees to the trees!) so that we can move towards something that will sustain us in a healthier, more positive way.

YES, we can do it!

–Kristin McGee,
celebrity yoga/Pilates instructor and trainer

MARTHA "PATI" RUIZ CORZO

We have postponed addressing the planet's emergencies beyond the limits of its forces; this emergency demands a wave of action. Society must walk in the direction of being more self-sufficient and frugal, and above all, turn its eyes to Nature and our close relationship with Her.

We must embrace the values of service and the common good, where generosity and love are the drivers. And since all that glitters is not gold, it would be best to leave this life having provided service and creativity rather than any debt generated by ambition and the destructive control of our system and the marketing of life on Earth.

The re-evolution towards a society in kinship with the biosphere means to embrace the simple life, accept the challenge to see who can live with the least and be healthier, not compete, cause minimum impact, dedicate our personal gifts to work and commit our emotion to the beauty and wisdom of creation.

So, cheers to the humans who recognize the Earth as their Mother and who relearn the purpose of having life and the capacity to act and construct futures with hope.

–Martha "Pati" Ruiz Corzo,
co-founder and director of Grupo Ecológico Sierra Gorda IAP,
UNEP Champion of the Earth,
National Geographic Conservation Leader
www.sierragorda.net

MARK Z. JACOBSON

We believe it is technically and economically feasible to transform the world's all-purpose energy infrastructure (for electricity, transportation, heating/cooling, industry) into one powered by wind, water and sunlight (wws) within 20–40 years.

The primary limitations are social and political, not technical or economic.

The limitations can be overcome by education of the public and policy-makers and demonstration of the health, climate and reliability benefits of clean energy technologies.

Ongoing efforts on large-scale conversion plans are discussed at www.stanford.edu/group/efmh/jacobson/Articles/I/susenergy2030.html.

– Mark Z. Jacobson,
professor of civil and environmental engineering and
director of the Atmosphere/Energy program at Stanford University (USA)

GRETCHEN BLEILER

Now more than ever, there is a feeling we are living in a world that has spun out of balance. It seems the principles of force and effort are dominant in our society on all levels, and because we are all connected, it is this exact model that is not working and that has taken us to this place of global environmental and social crises. I think we are getting close to the point where we as a collective are so disturbed with what we have created that we say "we won't take this any longer." But right now there is already change brewing. And I believe one perfect example of this change is Marianne Williamson's Sister Giant, which is a movement to start a new conversation, a "politics of the heart" (sistergiant.com/sistergiant/creating-a-culture-of-peace).

Movements like Sister Giant are what we need to bring the qualities of masculine and feminine back into alignment in our world. There is always a masculine face and a feminine face to every energy and these two faces depend on one another to thrive. But we've been living in a world where the goal-oriented, assertive and individualistic qualities of the masculine have dominated the intuitive, non-differentiating, joining qualities of the feminine. So in order for this world to truly prosper individually and collectively we need our feminine energy to step into its full power again with the masculine.

Once we as a people have brought balance back into our society through the balance and union of the masculine and feminine, we will naturally find balance with Nature again as well. Instead of fighting against Nature as we have done for so long now, we will start to learn from and work with her. As Deepak Chopra and David Simon have written in their book *The Seven Spiritual Laws of Yoga*, "Nature's intelligence functions with effortless ease. If you look at the ebb and flow of the tides, the blossoming of a flower, or the movement of the stars, you do not see Nature straining." We can echo Nature's intelligence to live and create a new world of effortless ease, balance and rhythm.

And that is where it seems we are standing just on the cusp of potential.

−Gretchen Bleiler,
environmental activist, U.S. professional half-pipe snowboarder,
Olympic Silver Medallist, four-time X Games Gold Medallist
www.gretchenbleiler.com

PAULA KAHUMBU

I wake up at two a.m. and my mind is racing. I don't have the answer to the question posed to me yesterday: "What are we going to do to stop this?" My caller was referring to the five rhinos slaughtered over the weekend, part of the ongoing epidemic of rhino and elephant poaching.

Experience teaches us that extraordinary leadership can create a tipping point to turn around public views and drive unlikely actions. In 1989, Kenya burned 12 tons of ivory in what remains the most iconic conservation message of all time. It was a risky, dangerous plan: that ivory was worth millions of dollars. But Richard Leakey and President Daniel Arap Moi did it anyway. The world celebrated and the consumers of ivory felt the shame. That year, the world banned the international trade in ivory and over the next 20 years, elephant populations recovered. Now the problem is back – only it's much much worse – and we are really at risk of losing all our elephants and rhinos in a matter of decades.

I believe it will take extraordinary creativity to achieve understanding amongst consumers and poachers so that people comprehend what is at stake if elephants and rhinos go extinct. Most Africans are poor and yet we are proud people. Our continent is recognized the world over for her diversity in people and wildlife, which are housed in astounding beauty. People say that their lifelong dream is to go on safari to Africa. They experience a connection to the land of the origin of humanity. At the rate things are going, we stand to lose it all. Africa's wildlife belongs to the world and we Africans are beginning to realize our obligation to humanity to help fulfill this human dream of seeing the herds of the Serengeti, the scarps of the Rift Valley, the snow on the equator.

We have the capacity to change – we just need courage to uphold sacred values of fairness, transparency, honesty and accountability. We can do this, and develop our economies by using the tools of this technological age of connectedness.

– Paula Kahumbu,
CEO of *WildlifeDirect* blogging platform
and a voice for conservation leadership in Africa

LLEWELLYN VAUGHAN-LEE

How can we heal and transform our ravaged ecosystem, our dying world? How can we become free from the soulless monster of materialism and its child, consumerism, and instead create a civilization that values all of creation, one that supports the interdependent web of life of which we are a part? First, there is a need to recognize that beneath this outer ecocide another tragedy is being enacted, as devastating as it is unreported: our forgetfulness of the sacred nature of creation. Our culture regards the Earth as a resource to be exploited, not as something sacred to be revered. And without this central spiritual awareness, which was at the foundation of almost all previous cultures, our world becomes increasingly out of balance.

We need to return to a simple awareness of the sacredness of the Earth and all of life. Then we can reconnect with the real nature of the Earth as a sacred being, what indigenous peoples know as the Mother who sustains us, both physically and spiritually. There are many ways to make this connection – for example, being aware of the sacred nature of the food we eat, or holding the Earth as a living being in our hearts and prayers, feeling our love for the Earth. Through simple means we can bring the sacred back into our daily life, and so help to heal the split between spirit and matter and restore the balance in our world.

Recognizing the Earth as a living, spiritual being with a soul as well as a body, we will find that she can regenerate, come alive in a new way – no longer a resource to be used, but full of wonder and sacred meaning. Listening to her deep wisdom we will find ways to work together that sustain all of life, that care for the soul as well as the soil. This is the future that is waiting for us, full of all the magical possibilities of creation as well as the mystery and joy of the sacred.

–Llewellyn Vaughan-Lee, PhD,
Sufi teacher, author of *Spiritual Ecology: The Cry of the Earth*
www.goldensufi.org, www.spiritualecology.org

KITTY VAN DER HEIJDEN

Sustainable development means balancing the economic, social and environmental pillars of development. If you ask an economist to review progress since the Earth summit in 1992, chances are that she or he will boast about tremendous growth, particularly in the Asian tigers and African lions. Ask that same question to a development practitioner, and he or she will highlight the great strides in reducing hunger, child and maternal mortality. But important MDGs, such as gender equality, lag behind, and inequality is rising between countries and within countries. Now ask that question of an environmentalist. Chances are she or he will look at you bewildered. Progress? PROGRESS? Almost all indicators indicate a worsening trend: loss of biodiversity, deforestation, pollution, climate change, ocean acidification, resources scarcity. In statistical jargon they call such curves a "hockey stick," with a gradual change at the outset, then fast acceleration upward.

As humankind, we are in that fast lane now. We are speeding towards a cliff of ecological destruction. That hockey stick will hit us hard – all of us. But it will hit the poor and young most of all. We are the first generation that, rather than sacrificing ourselves for our children's future, are sacrificing our children's future for ourselves.

The upbeat note is that we are not just part of the problem, we are also part of the solution. We can change. Take climate change. We can end global deforestation. We can beat the glum statistic that 30 per cent of food produced is lost or wasted, squandering resources such as water and land, and needlessly producing GHG emissions. We can achieve major emission reductions if consumers worldwide abide by the WHO advice regarding animal protein intake. We could reduce GHG emissions by 10 per cent if we would simply phase out environmentally perverse subsidies on fossil fuels.

Of course we can do it. It is a matter of choice.

As CEOs and corporate employees, we decide what and how to produce.

As consumers, we decide what products to use.

As shareholders and constituents casting our votes, we decide what policies and politics to refuse.

We are *all* in a position to lead change. Take charge.

– Kitty van der Heijden,
Special Envoy for Sustainability and Development, Ministry of Foreign Affairs, Netherlands

RAFFI CAVOUKIAN

In every age, love is redefined. In our time, this will be in terms of what we do to restore our children's stolen future. With climate change, the greatest threat on Earth, the global family needs a survival shift in awareness.

> *Losing my future is not like losing an election or a few points on the stock market ... You grownups say you love us. But I challenge you, please, make your actions reflect your words.*
> — SEVERN CULLIS-SUZUKI,
> AGE 12 (RIO, 1992)

Every society's treasure is its young, its promise to a better world. Yet an uncaring, bottom-line commerce that ignores social and planetary costs is wreaking havoc. No spiritual tradition condones this abuse of Creation and her young. The remedy is an integrated vision I call Child Honouring, one that simultaneously respects Earth and Child.

We can't overlook what's known about the Child – humanity's foremost learning system. Being human is not neutral: infants must learn to feel their loving nature or flounder. Failure is not an option; it scars lifetimes.

Creating the conditions that honour infants' formative needs is the most practical way to shape humane and sustainable cultures, ones that grow mature, resourceful, compassionate individuals. That's why Child Honouring is a universal ethic to enrich life for generations.

Fast forward a Copernican shift in consciousness: from the "childism" prejudice of societies centred on adults to a child-honouring world in which the early-years ecology benefits all. For our survival, Godspeed a new peacemaking economy, a "bionomy" to revive "global chi."

Each of us can be a change-maker. Shun ideology. Embrace radical inquiry. Empower your inner 8-year-old to free your heart's most generous impulses. Live along your highest spiritual values. Honour the young.

In the Child, the human face of ecology, we find our reflection and infinite potential. The well-tended garden yearns to yield riches.

−Raffi Cavoukian, CM, OBC,
singer, author, ecology advocate,
founder of the Centre for Child Honouring

CHRISTY MORGAN

The easiest way to make the greatest impact on the environment is through our diet.

Agriculture and factory farms create more greenhouse gases than the transportation industry. Also, our desire for quick, packaged food and produce that is not seasonal to our region creates a heavy drain on our precious resources. Use your dollars more wisely by choosing whole foods over packaged, organic over conventional and local over transported. These choices are more healthful in the long run for you and your family.

Visit your local farmers market to see what's in season during the year. You may discover some new and exciting vegetables you've never tried before! The most important thing we can do for our health and the health of the planet is to eat a diet rich in natural, whole foods. Eat foods in all the colours of the rainbow. Kale, lettuce and celery for green; carrots, yams and oranges for orange; eggplant for purple; cabbage, strawberries and apples for red; pineapple, squash and grains for yellow; grapefruit for pink; beans for brown; cauliflower, daikon and tofu for white. Fruits and vegetables that are beautifully coloured are rich in antioxidant elements that protect us from free radicals and make our health soar.

Start by adding in the good stuff and then crowd out the things that aren't serving your greater good. A balanced, whole food, plant-based diet can give you the energy you need to make your body, mind and spirit happy as well as nourish the planet!

–Christy Morgan,
vegan chef, educator,
author of *Blissful Bites: Vegan Meals That Nourish Mind, Body and Planet*

DAVID JEWITT

Some historical perspective: up until 500 years ago you, as a citizen, would understand the world through the words of an authority figure. It could be a king or an emperor, or perhaps a religious leader in charge of a rigid system of permissible thoughts, questions and actions. Your authority figure would lack any real understanding of the world, but he (it was almost always a "he") would point to the writings of the ancients, perhaps to Aristotle, to Confucius or to something in the Bible, as the ultimate basis of his authority. Nobody could see the world clearly under those circumstances.

Since then most authoritarian political and religious systems have cracked, allowing our two great inventions of modern science and practical democracy to blossom. The all-wise leader is replaced by the idea that truth can best be found through insightful observation accompanied by critical reasoning and free thought. The world still has religion, and a few fading dictatorships persist, but there is no serious doubt that science and democracy are transcendent.

So, 500 years ago I would have doubted our chances for the future, but today I am extremely optimistic. For the first time in recorded history, our eyes are open to the world, giving us enormous power both to appreciate its beauty and to identify and address its problems. We have never been more perceptive, more powerful or more capable. We have never been better placed to determine our own future on this planet than we are now.

– David Jewitt,
professor of astronomy at University of California, Los Angeles

ATOSSA SOLTANI

We stand at the crossroads of history, where our collective actions over the next decade will determine the fate of humanity for the next millennia. At present, we are crossing many tipping points and face multiple crises, the most alarming being global climate chaos. I believe we have no choice but to change course to ensure that future generations will inherit a livable world.

Many indigenous peoples hold as their aspiration to be "good ancestors" to future generations. I believe that if we are to survive, this must now become our collective aspiration. To have lasting change, we need to reshape our values and worldviews. Growing numbers of us realize the dire need for rapid systemic change. However, the majority continue living in a business as usual mindset, in what could be called collective denial.

Indigenous peoples represent only 4 per cent of the world's population, but their territories hold 80 per cent of the Earth's biodiversity. From these guardians we can learn how to hold all life sacred and live in greater balance with Nature.

The ecosystems of the planet that produce our oxygen, water, rainfall and soils are key to our survival. Safeguarding and restoring the planet's remaining forests, mangroves, coral reefs and other productive ecosystems is a critical priority. And dismantling global corporate economic domination and bringing back responsive government is a prerequisite. We can bring the world to embrace local traditional food systems, decentralize energy production, cut overall resource consumption, phase out fossil fuels, overhaul our transportation systems and improve the condition of women and the poor to stabilize our population.

We have the knowledge, the understanding, the creativity and the technology to act in time. The people who understand this urgency need to step into leadership and make it their life's work to transform and recreate our world. There is the analogy of when the U.S. was on the eve of the Second World War and called on its citizenry to join the war effort and the majority did, helping the U.S. significantly retool its economy in under a year. That's what we need now. All hands on deck!

– Atossa Soltani,
founder and executive director of Amazon Watch

JONATHON BUTTON

Within every individual there is a need to give and contribute to the greater of humankind. We all want to make a difference. The main hurdle is that most of us don't know where to start. Through education, society can further understand what the biggest issues are. Through understanding these problems, individuals can break them down into smaller obstacles which can be attacked.

With Life Out of the Box, we have been on an evolving adventure throughout Third World countries searching for these issues and understanding the source of them. What we have found is that many of those in need simply lack the tools to further develop into the person they want to become, which would lead them to further contributing to society and helping humanity. Without knowledge, it is impossible for the world to understand the problems, which results in a lack of action.

Life Out of the Box is dedicated to inspiring people to get out there, explore the world, learn and then take action towards making a difference. It is easy to think out of the box, but the key is making it happen and actually living your Life Out of the Box to make the world a better place for all. Thoughts and ideas are a necessary step towards accomplishing the goal, but they are nothing without actually taking the steps towards making them a reality.

I have great faith in the future. As the world is becoming more connected through social media, the understanding of the world becomes more clear and enables individuals to recognize the needs that must be addressed in order to ensure our existence. Through this new awareness, we can reflect on our actions and understand how they are currently contributing in a positive or negative way to the globe. Life is great. It should never be taken for granted and together we must contribute towards ensuring that all living species can experience this precious gift.

– Jonathon Button,
co-founder of Life Out of the Box
www.lifeoutofthebox.com

MAUDE BARLOW

With all my heart I believe that hope is a moral imperative. I could not do my work otherwise.

However, if truth be told, there are days when it is hard to hold on to this place of hope. A friend says she is numbed by "apocalypse fatigue." Not me. Every new study on Arctic melting, species extinction and water depletion invades my soul.

Is there a way past the current crisis? Yes, there is. But it lies on a different path from the dominant economic and development model of our time. Growth, deregulation, privatization, free markets, more stuff travelling farther with fewer barriers – that is the dominant political narrative currently driving most governments, the big-business community and global institutions. It is killing the planet and disenfranchising billions.

An important recent study found that the global trade in food is consuming the bulk of the world's water heritage and depleting groundwater far faster than it can be replenished. One American environmentalist said that unlimited growth has the same DNA as the cancer cell. It has to turn on its host to survive. Now we are being told that unless we place a price on Nature and bring it into the market economy, it will not survive.

The way forward lies with an alternative narrative. Instead of seeing Nature as a "resource" for our convenience, pleasure and profit, we need to see it as a living ecosystem from which all life springs, and adapt our lives and laws to those of the natural world. That means challenging the growth imperative and moving to more local economies of scale. It means recognizing that Nature has rights too. Conservation, preservation, biological diversity, co-operation, local sustainable food production, fair trade, economic justice, public trust: these are the hallmarks of the path forward.

Bolivia's President Evo Morales says the goal must be to live well, not to live better than others.

Listen to the Earth. Listen to the ancient peoples. The answers lie there.

– Maude Barlow,
national chair of the Council of Canadians,
chair of Washington-based Food and Water Watch,
author of *Blue Covenant: The Global Water Crisis and The Coming Battle for the Right to Water* and *Blue Future: Protecting Water for People and the Planet Forever*

DAVID BUCKLAND

It is perhaps unsurprising that it has been the scientists reporting the evidence of global warming who have become the most passionate in calling for society to urgently change its course.

However, this urgency isn't being communicated successfully enough to provoke the real change needed in our global societies to reduce greenhouse gas emissions and mitigate climate change. The resistance to cultural change is baffling in the face of extreme weather events and other disturbances across our planet. Anthropogenic climate change threatens us all with an uncertain physical, social and economic future, so why are we not engaged in sorting out our future? Perhaps cultural approaches can succeed where the hard facts of science have failed.

The international Cape Farewell project, now in its 11th year, aims to do just that. It embeds artists, writers, architects, musicians and filmmakers with climate scientists as they measure and evaluate planetary changes at the Earth's known climate change "hotspots." So far, we have made seven expeditions into the Arctic aboard the 100-year-old Norwegian schooner *Noorderlicht* (Northern Lights), one expedition to the Andes and the Amazon and one to the Scottish Western Isles. Each of these journeys has enabled the diverse expedition team to examine how anthropogenic activity is affecting our habitat.

When I set up Cape Farewell in 2001, the aim was to create a different language of climate change with which to engage the public. Over 140 arts-based practitioners have taken part in these voyages, openly engaging with more than 45 scientists, creating artworks, exhibitions, books and films that have toured worldwide. This international effort, including people from China to Mexico, has brought distinctly different cultural sensibilities to the story of climate change's causes and impacts.

The overriding memory of each of the voyagers engaged in these adventures is more akin to having fun than experiencing suffering. Climate change is truly a cultural challenge; it affects all of us and we all need to become part of the solution. But perhaps we should approach it more in the spirit of an expedition that encompasses the optimism of moving forward. As Marshall McLuhan put it, "Spaceship Earth doesn't carry passengers, only crew."[14]

– David Buckland,
founder and director of Cape Farewell
www.capefarewell.com

MAGGIE PADLEWSKA

Is there hope for the future? I am sure I'm not the first to say that this question is as complex as it sounds simple. I've pondered it over the years, only to find my thoughts drifting in directions as varied as the research, articles and books we read, the experiences we encounter, the things we witness and the richness of stories, views and perspectives of the people we meet throughout our journeys. I'm a one-woman-band, frequently travelling solo to meet people the world doesn't often get to hear about or the communities that are not actively engaged in the global dialogue that is thriving online ... and it is often through those people that I learn the most.

Our world is, without a doubt, facing countless and serious crises, from threats against global cultures to irreversible environmental damage. The communities I meet with are familiar with these things, mainly because they are often the ones directly affected by the negative effects of foreign policies, multinational trade deals and the intensifying extraction and depletion of natural resources. Yet many remain silenced, misunderstood and dismissed as the uneducated poor.

This, in my modest opinion, is where the world fails.

Human rights and environmental considerations have become secondary to the ambitions of the wealthy elite and policy-makers. Communities are being displaced from traditional lands to make way for exclusive development projects, the natural landscape is being contaminated, cultures are being threatened by globalization, and traditional wisdom is overlooked by the ideologies of the self-righteous.

We are at a crucial juncture, a moment with enough evidence to establish two clear options. The first, to continue along a destructive path driven by political or corporate greed, or second, to pause and rethink what it truly means to be human and the kind of life and behaviours that would sustain a healthy global community and planet for generations to come.

Is there hope for the future? Yes, IF the world recognizes the devastating consequences of its current trajectory and redirects its behaviours to truly reflect a commitment to a healthy future – not focused on cleaning up the messes that would be created, but on preventing them from happening in the first place by learning from those who have been living that way for centuries.

–Malgorzata "Maggie" Padlewska,
video-journalist, founder of One Year One World
www.oneyearoneworld.com

ELIZABETH LINDSEY

There's no greater power economically, politically or socially that can compare to the power that lies within each of us.

The problem is we've forgotten who we are.

In an era of technological advancement, we're bloated with information yet starved for such wisdom. Malnourished and overwhelmed, millions lead lives of "quiet desperation." Connected 24/7, loneliness is at an all-time high.

What to do?

"When the veil of forgetfulness is lifted," my native Hawaiian elders said, "and people remember that within them is a spark of the Divine, strife will cease."

The world doesn't need us to save it. The world needs us to save ourselves. It doesn't need our anxiety and fear. It needs our clarity and courage.

Once we understand that what exists outside of us is a reflection of what stirs within, then and only then, will we be able to make a difference in the world. Until then, we offer Humanity nothing more than a pale imitation of who we might have been. And none of us is here for that.

No one else will see the world through your eyes or express it as only you can.

Imagine if a small woman in India thought that caring for the poor and the dying was too much trouble. We might never have been inspired by a nun named Theresa.

This is the Power of One ... one person's willingness to be transformed. By changing ourselves, we change the world.

–Elizabeth Kapu'uwailani Lindsey, PhD,
humanitarian and the first Polynesian Explorer in the history of the National Geographic Society

EDUARD MÜLLER

In spite of great individual intelligence, humans have failed to achieve collective intelligence. Our western development style, brought upon most of the people on Earth, willingly or not, has come with intellectual reductionism, globalization of markets and monetization of cultures and nature. Competition is at the core whilst co-operation and solidarity are left behind. Current global challenges require solutions with major investments and structural reform where governments, private sector and society as a whole must act beyond self-interest, making decisions considering global interdependence and well-being. It is now clear that solutions won't come from governments, global meetings or corporate responsibility alone. Civil society, meaning each individual through collective action, must change, based on ethical values and principles.

Humans are capable of collective action when disaster strikes, going beyond self-interests to help others. The uniqueness of our current state is that, in spite of increasing local disasters, we have not fully acknowledged global disaster. If we wait much longer to act, we will go past tipping points announced by scientists. To avoid a global state of anomie, we have to jointly construct a community of life. The key lies in the intergenerational responsibility, where youth start demanding no further destruction of their possibilities to survive on a truly living planet. Involving youth means having them identify their life projects, getting past immediate satisfaction through sumptuous consumption, while investing true efforts to change and being rewarded with quality of life. Life projects today are not about jobs or professions; they are about achieving a higher level of consciousness where individual responsibilities come before individual rights, accompanied by behaviour according to consequences of our actions and inaction and not only individual well-being.

More and more youth, especially those that have more freedom of thought and are not shaped by their parents to follow our current catastrophic patterns of development, are now looking for better livelihoods, based on quality, not quantity, where people are valued for what they are and not for what they have. We must collectively foster this new global society and accelerate the celebration of life on Earth.

– Eduard Müller,
founder and president of the University for International Cooperation, San Jose, Costa Rica,
vice-chair for education and learning at the World Commission on Protected Areas, IUCN

TARA MACLEAN

Instead of continuing to hurt and hide from the devastation I saw in the world, I picked up a guitar and sang what I felt. I sang to others. This one act of choosing not to hide saved my life. It released me and paved the way for a life of connection. I went to protests, blockaded the logging trucks that were clear-cutting the ancient rainforests and spent two weeks in jail. I had never felt so free.

This is a crucial time for real connection. It is time to stop hiding. It is time to forgive. When Buffy Sainte-Marie was asked how she forgives those who have done so much harm to her people, she answered that we are a very young species, and in that understanding, she finds deep compassion for us all. This is an essential key to our survival.

It seems that humanity is in the "toddler" phase of its evolution. We have some words, but mostly we hit, bite and destroy. We are distracted all the time, mostly with our own suffering. We are blinded and trapped by anger, self-pity and righteousness. Mine!

My view, my pain, my reactions! We crash into things, throw tantrums and create chaos.

What if growing up means learning that the pain in life is a necessary part of the experience of being alive? It exists to forge us into stronger, greater beings. We hurt each other, we hurt the Earth and we make mistakes. This is how we learn. Knowing that, we could even be grateful for the suffering and practise *Radical Forgiveness*. So forgiveness and compassion really are the same: seeing clearly that we are not separate.

Forgive yourself and everyone else. Let it go. We are all human and fallible. Stop crashing, start connecting. With this action you help to eliminate the seeds of war. This is a *revolutionary* act because it leads us out of ignorance. With an uncluttered mind, free from anxiety and self-pity, imagine what we could do! We could truly serve one another and the planet, united to face the bigger issues at hand. It is time for a revolution.

Find your words. Sing your song. Save the world.

– Tara MacLean,
singer/songwriter, mother, activist

KIRA SALAK

Do you think this world of ours must be changed? Or must we instead change ourselves?

When we lose our faith in God, in the goodness of the Universe, the world becomes a barren, heartless place, and we, its prisoners.

Hope for this world must start from within.

It must begin with a faith – a knowingness – that all that happens *needs* to happen. *All* of it. The "good," the "bad." Everything is evolving to the next level.

Through our triumphs, we bring grace to the world. Through our pains, our anguishes, we learn how to open our hearts to compassion.

It is compassion that will save this world, and nothing else.

It is compassion that will save all of us.

– Dr. Kira Salak,
writer, journalist, philosopher,
National Geographic Emerging Explorer and extreme adventurer,
author of *The White Mary* and *The Cruelest Journey: 600 Miles to Timbuktu*
www.kirasalak.com

NELSON MANDELA

(Applicable extracts from various public addresses have been arranged below to bring forth Nelson Mandela's representation in Global Chorus.*)*

When I go to the place and area of my birth, so often as I do, the changed geography of the place strikes me with a force that I cannot escape. And that geography is not one of mere landscapes and topography, it is the geography of the people. Where once there were trees and even forests, we now see barrenness …

I try to live by the simple precept of making the world one in which there is a better life for all, particularly the poor, marginalized and vulnerable. A devastated geography makes for a devastated people …

Let us stand together to make of our world a sustainable source for our future as humanity on this planet.[15]

❖ ❖ ❖

The world is becoming ever more interdependent. What each one of us does as an independent nation impacts on others. We therefore have no choice but to build a system of relations which, while it guarantees such independence and seeks to exclude the possibility of one country's imposing its will on another, creates the possibility for each to have a meaningful say in how we should live together in one peaceful, stable, prosperous and free world.[16]

❖ ❖ ❖

The new world that is being born foresees the dawn of the age of peace, in which wars within nations, between countries and among peoples will be a thing of the past.[17]

❖ ❖ ❖

Peace is not just the absence of conflict; peace is the creation of an environment where all can flourish, regardless of race, colour, creed, religion, gender, class, caste or any other social markers of difference. Religion, ethnicity, language, social and cultural practices are elements which enrich human civilization, adding to the wealth of our diversity. Why should they be allowed to become a cause of division and violence? We demean our common humanity by allowing that to happen …

Human beings will always be able to find arguments for confrontation and no compromise. We humans are, however, the beings capable of reason, compassion and change. May this be the century of compassion, peace and non-violence … in all the conflict-ridden parts of the world and on our planet universally.[18]

– Nelson Mandela

BILL MCKIBBEN

I decided some time ago that I was going to spend no more energy trying to figure out if things were going to come out alright or not. We're engaged in a civilization-scale wager with enormously high stakes – my role, I think, is to get up every morning and try to change the odds of that wager a little bit, without any guarantee that it will come out okay.

And there can be no guarantee, I fear, for we've done massive damage to the planet's most important physical systems. The most important of these is the climate – after 10,000 quite stable years, the period that scientists call the Holocene, we've moved on to a new, much tougher period. How tough is still up to us, though the damage done so far (the melted Arctic, for instance) is sobering.

In short, the single thing we must do is get off fossil fuel, and in a matter of years. Physically we could do it, but it would mean a colossal effort, in the face of the power of the coal, oil and gas industries, the richest and most powerful enterprises in human history. It would mean changing some of our rich-world notions about economic growth. And it would mean, most of all, trading in the hyper-individualism of high consumer society for tighter, closer communities. Cultural, technological, political change of large magnitude, in other words. There are days I think it can't be done, and days – looking at the huge swath of organizing 350.org has managed to do in the last three years – when I think we might just figure out a way. But as I say, I'm not going to think any more about it. Back to work, all of us!

– Bill McKibben,
author, educator, environmentalist,
founder of 350.org

XAVIER RUDD

If I think too much about this topic I find myself hitting a brick wall, as the issue is so layered and so vast. If I feel it out in my heart and my dreaming, certain messages arrive: if every human being on the planet began with taking even one minute in their day to simply reflect on the fact that we are *of* this Earth and not just *on* this Earth, would that alone start a swing towards healing the simple energetic connection between human and land? As we know, energy is in everything and its power is often overlooked. And by changing each individual's energetic focus on the importance of our Earth, even without physically doing anything, it would be an important start in reigniting the lost sacred harmony between human and Earth, which has been the platform for so much environmental destruction.

We are seeing more and more little pockets of society taking their own initiatives to educate and implement sustainable living practices and to stand up with force against environmental threat. These ideals need to grow and expand and our children have to be somewhat reprogrammed. The power of the Internet in activism has proven to be amazing and really is all so new in the scheme of things. If we consider victories we've had at this point, it is exciting to imagine the power of our Earth guardians and the spread of imperative environmental education even only ten years from now. It is extremely important that active groups become more united around the planet. There is too much division and that alone is unsustainable. If we are to create conditions necessary for our own survival, we are going to need to build a massive syndicate greater than anything we've ever seen in order to be able to keep things on track.

Yes we have hope – hope is revealed daily in our magical ancient ecosystems still thriving around our Earth. Victories like the recent win at James Price Point in the Kimberley and the many sustainable-living practices growing daily show that we can do it. The big question is time and the balance of the scales between the healing and the destruction. Either way, I feel our great Mother will be okay eventually, whether she hosts humans or not, and that makes me smile.

– Xavier Rudd,
Australian singer, artist and activist

TA'KAIYA BLANEY

We humans have been travelling on a road of consumerism. Ever since the start of the industrial revolution (which brought about corporate colonization and environmental injustice), we've been witnessing signs saying "Stop," "Dead End," "Yield," and "Wrong Way." We continue to drive ahead despite the obvious. Our steering wheel is becoming weaker and weaker, and our brakes are becoming looser and less functional. Our warnings have been given. Someday we'll drive off that cliff and fall, and then there's no turning back. Presently, we're still driving on that road, and our solutions lie right in front of our noses.

Our options for our future under the context of sustainability are vast and wide, yet we make no actions to officially begin using our alternatives. Why? Why do we continue to wait for change in our societies, led by authorities such as our prime ministers and officials? We are denying the fact that if we wait for change it may never come.

We must be the voice, for that is what we were given. Our role is to be the Healer, the Warrior and the Teacher. We must be the change for our many generations to come, and for our Mother Earth.

The decisions made within the last few centuries shaped our society into what it is today. I believe that positive decisions made today to influence sustainability can also shape the society of the next generation and the generations to come. However, we need our actions to flow now, and our change needs to happen before our steering wheel slacks, and we plunge from the cliff. We still have time to turn around.

We have a voice to speak up, and a superpower called change. Let's use it. :)

– Ta'Kaiya Blaney,[19]
singer/songwriter, youth environmental activist

GUUJAAW

what of the Beast
that has no face
no head
no heart within
the motherless Beast
though born of man
became his master

the wily Beast
revels in our selfish desires
while guiding its makers
to their own demise

the Beast feels no guilt
as it spoils the earth
and no regard
for the sentient being

the powerful Beast
it rules the rulers
and rids itself
of those in its way

our fathers sit at its table
do its bidding
then reap its reward
… or be replaced by another

the repulsive Beast
will not be satisfied
and cannot be slain
though the beast be unleashed
it is within …

to the Beast we say
Enough, you loathsome error
you bring no peace
you bring no love
be off with you
We are of life
precious life
it is time for living

— Guujaaw

DAVID W. ORR

No sane gambler would bet on us. Armed and dangerous, we are loading the atmosphere with carbon as fast as we can, thereby changing the climatic and ecological conditions necessary to our own survival. The reasons are said to be economic necessity, but to paraphrase Thoreau, what good is a booming economy if you don't have a decent planet to put it on?

For a species pleased to call itself *Homo sapiens* our situation is ironic. Many scientists saw the peril decades ago, but the powers that be were deaf to warnings and dumb to opportunities.

That too is ironic because the knowledge and capacity to build a sunshine-powered, ecologically resilient civilization has grown in pace with the dangers. It is possible to power civilization by efficiency and sunlight, feed humanity sustainably, eliminate waste and build cities in harmony with Nature. Such things are not just technically possible and economically feasible, they are moral imperatives.

Are there grounds for optimism? Not if you know enough. Are there reasons for despair? Not if you care enough. But in contrast to optimism or despair, hope requires us to act in ways that change the odds. And everywhere on Earth, people are rising to the challenge. They are dreaming, planting, building, tending, caring, healing, organizing and restoring. They are working from the bottom up to lay the foundation for decent and durable communities and societies. And someday, on a farther horizon, our descendants will know that this was, indeed, humankind's "finest hour."

–David W. Orr,
Paul Sears Distinguished Professor, Oberlin College (Ohio, USA)

MAYA ANGELOU

There's a hospital in my town that has the Maya Angelou Women's Health & Wellness Center in it, and in each wing there are statements which say, "I promise to treat every patient as if she's a valued member of my family." "I promise to treat the hospital as my home, and respect it and keep it clean." This is what we should be doing on our planet. Because this is all we have, as far as we can be sure. We may have walked on the moon, but nobody is colonizing another planet. So we should be careful with how we treat this planet, since it *is* not only *our* home now, and *has* been the home of our ancestors, but is *going* to be the home of our children to come. And so we should be careful with it – be careful with the temperature, and we should look after ourselves and our home with respect and gratitude: to have a constant attitude of gratitude.

We really have enough food on this planet to feed everybody alive. We don't need to have somebody starving in order for us to give. We are encouraged by every religious tract, whether the Bible, or the Talmud, or the Torah, or the Bhagavad Gita, to be respectful and care for each other. And that is whether we look alike – whether we are caring for somebody who looks like us and speaks our language or not. Until we evolve into a group which has enough courage to really care about each other, we will continue to be at odds.

When I speak of love, I speak of that condition in the human spirit so profound that it encourages us to develop courage – courage enough to care for somebody else, who may not look like us, who may call God a different name if they call God at all. I don't speak of sentimentality when I'm speaking of love. I speak of that condition which may be that which holds the stars in the firmament. That causes the blood to run orderly through our veins. It's a powerful condition. It crosses ignorance. It spans the mountains and the rivers. It dares us, and allows us, to look after someone else's children. To care about the people who are yet to come. That, to me, is love. And *this* is our way forward.

– Maya Angelou,
poet, memoirist, novelist, educator, dramatist,
producer, actress, historian, filmmaker and civil rights activist

CONTRIBUTOR MAP

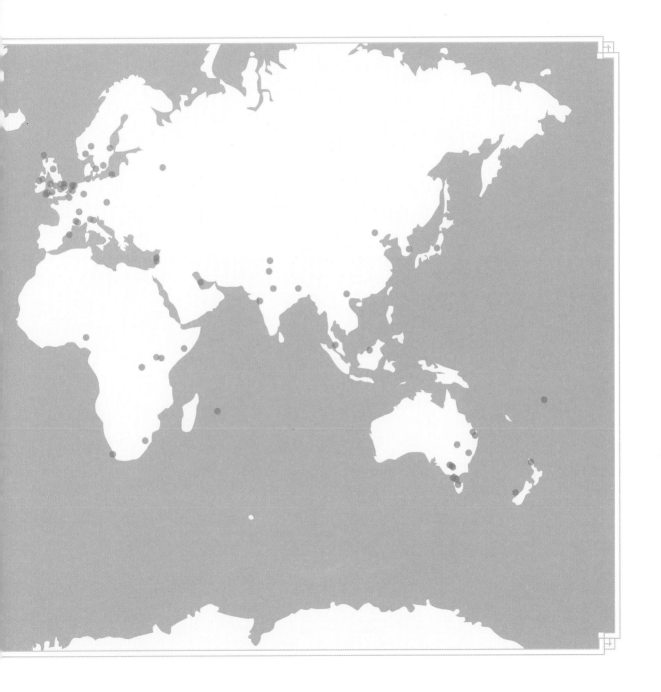

the Jane Goodall Institute of Canada

Founded by renowned primatologist Dr. Jane Goodall, the Jane Goodall Institute is a global non-profit organization that empowers people to make a difference for all living things. The Institute supports wildlife research, education and conservation, with the primary goal of ensuring the survival of great ape populations through community-centred conservation activities in Africa. The Institute also promotes sustainable livelihoods and nurtures new generations of committed, active citizens around the world.

❖ www.janegoodall.ca

The Canadian Red Cross Society is a humanitarian organization which does not take sides in hostilities or engage at any time in controversies of a political, racial, religious or ideological nature. The views expressed herein are those of the authors alone and do not necessarily represent the views of The Canadian Red Cross Society.

❖ www.redcross.ca

The David Suzuki Foundation collaborates with Canadians from all walks of life, including government and business, to conserve our environment and find solutions that will create a sustainable Canada through science-based research, education and policy work. The mission of the Foundation is to protect the diversity of nature and our quality of life, now and for the future. The vision of the Foundation is that within a generation, Canadians will be acting on the understanding that we are all interconnected and interdependent with nature.

❖ www.davidsuzuki.org

1 Assembled with excerpts from Jamie Oliver, "How to Create a Food Revolution," in *Voices on Society: The Art & Science of Delivery*, McKinsey Publishing (April 2013): 38. Accessed Jul. 30, 2014 (pdf) at http://mckinseyonsociety.com/downloads/reports/Voices/ArtofDelivery-web.pdf. Use granted with permission by Peter Berry, head of PR for Jamie Oliver.

2 Drawn from remarks to the 5th World Environmental Education Congress, May 10, 2009, Montreal.

3 Excerpted from an address to the Chemical Society of Washington, DC, May 8, 2008.

4 Paragraph 1 is excerpted from a message delivered on Tibetan Democracy Day, Sep. 2, 1994. Paragraphs 2 and 3 are from a World Environment Day message, Jun. 5, 1986, reprinted from *Tree of Life: Buddhism and Protection of Nature, 1987.* Paragraphs 4 and 5 are from the Dalai Lama's address at the consecration of the statue of Lord Buddha and the International Conference on Ecological Responsibility: A Dialogue with Buddhism, interim report, 1993: Tibet House, New Delhi. Paragraphs 6 and 7 are from a Feb. 4, 1992, address at New Delhi, India.

5 Chris Hedges, *United Church Observer* (Jan. 2013): 13.

6 Assembled with excerpts from Green Cross General Assembly Keynote Address, Geneva, Switzerland, Sep. 2, 2013. Use for *Global Chorus* granted with approval and permission by Paul Garwood, Director of Communications for Green Cross International.

7 Adapted from "What Would Nature Do?," *YES! Magazine (*Winter 2013).

8 Posthumous response is drawn from *The Great Work: Our Way into the Future* (New York: Crown, 1999),

7–8. Special thanks to editor Mary Evelyn Tucker for assistance and direction.

9 Dennis Lee's "Whistledown" appears in *Testament* (Toronto: Anansi, 2012). Used by permission.

10 From excerpts of speech to UN General Assembly, Nov. 2009, obtained by permission.

11 Translated from the original French text submitted for *Global Chorus.*

12 © 2011 by Pema Chödrön. Published by arrangement with Shambhala Publications www.shambhala.com.

13 With permission of the author, text is from an address to the Board of Atomic Scientists, Jan. 2007 [first paragraph], and an interview with The Canadian Press, Jun. 2010 [second and third paragraphs].

14 Assembled with excerpts from "Climate is Culture" by David Buckland, *Nature*, Feb. 12, 2012. Permission granted by the author.

15 From Nelson Mandela's speech accepting the "Planet and Humanity Award" from the International Geographical Union, Aug. 4, 2002.

16 From a statement by Nelson Mandela at the United Nations General Assembly, Dec. 3, 1991.

17 From a statement by Nelson Mandela at the World Economic Forum Annual Conference, Jan. 31, 1991.

18 From a statement by Nelson Mandela at the Global Convention on Peace and Non-violence, Jan. 31, 2004.

19 *Ta'Kaiya* means "Special Water" in the Sliammon First Nation language (Coast Salish, near Powell River, BC).

20 Thomas Berry. *The Dream of the Earth.* San Francisco: Sierra Club Books, 1988.

FEEL FREE TO EXPRESS YOUR *OWN* THOUGHTS ON
THE FUTURE OF THE PLANET IN THIS SPACE...